THE
INESCAPABLE
SELF

THE INESCAPABLE SELF

An introduction to
Western philosophy
since Descartes

Timothy Chappell

First published in Great Britain in 2005
by Weidenfeld & Nicolson

10 9 8 7 6 5 4 3 2 1

A CIP catalogue record for this book is available from the British Library

ISBN 0 297 84735 X

Design by www.carrstudio.co.uk
Printed in Great Britain by Clays Ltd, St Ives plc

Weidenfeld & Nicolson
The Orion Publishing Group Ltd
Orion House
5 Upper Saint Martin's Lane
London, WC2H 9EA
www.orionbooks.co.uk

Contents

Acknowledgements

I began this book in Vancouver in February 2003, during my tenure of a Visiting Professorship at the University of British Columbia, and completed it in Dundee in February 2005. Many people helped me to write it, and to make it a better book than it would otherwise have been. I am especially grateful to Paul Russell, Monte Johnson, Michael Wheeler, Duncan Pritchard, Sarah Sawyer and Michael Brady for helpful discussions. The Spring 2003 Senior Class in Political Philosophy at UBC were a joy to teach, and taught me as much about Aristotle and Hobbes as I taught them. They put up with their professor's late arrivals at class with the same equanimity, whether these were caused by the writing of this book or by benightments on trackless Canadian mountains. Patrick Walsh's enthusiasm and energy helped me to begin the project; Ben Dupré's helped me to complete it. Manjit Kumar, Adrian Bourne and Richard Milbank gave important help as well. My family have been as stable, supportive and loving as ever, and deserve my special thanks.

This book is dedicated to my father, for teaching me to talk back.

TDJC
March 2005

Prelude

Nightmares of Eminent Persons

> **MORPHEUS**
> Have you ever had a dream, Neo, that you were so sure was real?
>
> **NEO**
> This can't be...
>
> **MORPHEUS**
> Be what? Be real?
>
> *The strands thin like rubber cement as he pulls away, until the fragile wisps of mirror thread break.*
>
> **MORPHEUS**
> What if you were unable to wake from that dream, Neo? How would you know the difference between the dream world and the real world?...[1]

0.1 **Nightmare scenarios**

The ultimate nightmare scenario: everything is a nightmare. Reality itself is part of a dream or a hallucination. Nothing is real, and nothing can be trusted.

This is the scenario that Neo faces in *The Matrix*. Morpheus proves to him that the human race has lost all contact with reality.

The computers have taken over and are holding humanity captive to feed off their bodies' natural electricity. But the human race don't know this. The human race don't even know what year it is, because they are living in a computer-simulated virtual reality.

How do we know that *we* are not living in the Matrix? How do we know that *our* 'reality' is real?

In philosophy, this nightmare question – the question of scepticism, as it is usually called – has come back again and again. Plato (427–347 BC) was the first great philosopher who asked it. In the *Theaetetus* he asks how we can tell whether we are dreaming.[2] And in the *Republic* he gives us his famous Myth of the Cave.[3] This portrays ordinary people as prisoners chained up underground. The whole of the 'reality' they imagine they perceive is actually no more than a series of shadows projected, almost cinematically, onto a wall. In its vivid depiction of the possibility that almost everything that ordinary people believe about the world is completely wrong, Plato's Myth of the Cave anticipates the Matrix scenario by a small matter of 25 centuries.

Twenty centuries after Plato and five centuries before us, René Descartes (1596–1650) finds himself gripped by the same sort of sceptical nightmare:

How often, asleep at night, am I convinced of just such familiar events – that I am here in my dressing gown, sitting by the fire – when in fact I am lying undressed in bed!…There are never any sure signs by means of which being awake can be distinguished from being asleep…[What if] there is a deceiver of supreme power and cunning, who is deliberately and constantly deceiving me?[4]

In our own times, Hilary Putnam has restaged the same nightmare in modern dress, in another philosophical tale that is strikingly reminiscent of *The Matrix*:

Imagine that a human being has been subjected to an operation by an evil scientist. The person's brain has been removed from the body and placed in a vat of nutrients which keeps the brain alive. The nerve endings have been connected to a super-scientific computer which causes the person to have the illusion that everything is perfectly normal...but really all the person is experiencing is the result of electronic impulses travelling from the computer to the nerve endings. The computer is so clever that...it can even seem to the victim that he is sitting and reading these very words about the amusing but quite absurd supposition that there is an evil scientist who removes people's brains from their bodies and places them in a vat of nutrients...[5]

The sceptical question is: can we know that these nightmare scenarios are unreal? Can we know that we're not prisoners in Plato's Cave, or deceived by Descartes's demon, or brains in a vat, or victims of the Matrix? In short, can we know that reality is really anything like it seems to be to us?

0.2 The problem of the inescapable self

Actually, the sceptical question cuts even deeper than that. The question can't even be what we can know, or how things seem to us. It has to be what I can know, and how things seem to me. One of the most important things I don't know in the nightmare scenarios is whether other people are real. A major part of the darkness of these nightmares is that in them I am, ultimately, alone. I am a *solus ipse*, a solitary self; that is, I am a solipsist.

This switch from 'What can *we* know?' to 'What can *I* know?' is a crucial one. It makes us see what happens when we (or I) try to get free of the nightmare sceptical questions by finding a rational answer to them. What happens is that I find that I am certain of myself, but uncertain of the world outside myself.

As Descartes famously saw, my own existence seems beyond serious doubt. To doubt anything – even my own existence – I first have to exist. The existence of a world beyond me, however, is not so easily and obviously established. So long as I am still trying to establish the world's existence on the basis of my own existence, I make myself the fulcrum of the world and the judge of the world. My attitude is that if there is to be a world at all, it will have to exist on my terms, in a form that satisfies my standards of proof – standards that are laid down by my certainty that I myself exist. All my other knowledge becomes conditional on my knowledge of my own existence: the only way for me to know anything else is for me to trace it back to my knowledge of myself.

And so an estrangement develops between my *self* and my *world*. The fortress of my certainty about my own existence becomes the prison of my uncertainty about the existence of a world beyond me. The self becomes inescapable, because my self becomes the only thing I can know for sure. I end up in what I am calling 'the problem of the inescapable self' – what philosophers sometimes also call the 'egocentric predicament'. In this form, the problem of the inescapable self is a problem about knowledge. I shall discuss this problem in chapters 1 and 2.

The problem of the inescapable self also takes another form. It can be a problem about ethical value which, with only a little playing on words, we may equally call an egocentric predicament. This problem arises because nightmare-scenario sceptical doubts can hardly be insulated from all my other thoughts. Once raised, these doubts seep into my whole attitude to life. To see the world and other people as a vague mysterious conjecture, myself as a solid and dependable certainty – this is already a deeply loaded way of thinking about how things are, with huge ethical implications.

Before Descartes, it was natural for ethicists to assume that value is objective, 'out there in the world', and that my reasons to act arise as responses to that objective ethical value. When the idea of 'the world out there' becomes problematic, the idea of value 'out there in the world' is bound to become problematic too. Correspondingly, what becomes unproblematic after Descartes is the idea of my own pleasures, desires and preferences. We see the same pattern as before: since my desires and preferences occur inside me, they are things that I can know about with certainty – unlike the world out there.

The *ethical* problem of the inescapable self says that my reasons to act do not arise from objective values out there in the world, but from my own drives and inclinations. Hence a problem about *altruism*. If all my reasons to act are only aimed at satisfying my desires, how can I ever act in a genuinely un-self-interested way – in a way that is not egocentric, in the ethical sense of the word? Hence, also, a problem about *ethical objectivity*. If my reasons to act are only aimed at satisfying my own desires, how can any idea of right and wrong beyond my own desires be justified? The fortress of my certainty about what *I* desire, what *I* value, becomes the prison of my uncertainty about the reality of any values, or even any desires, beyond my own. I will discuss these ethical aspects of the problem of the inescapable self in chapter 3, on altruism, and chapter 4, on objectivity.

Another aspect of the problem of the inescapable self comes into view in chapter 4. Descartes's retreat into the citadel of the certainties of self-consciousness not only puts everything outside the self in doubt. It also divides the whole of reality into two separate compartments: self-consciousness on one side, and every-thing else on the other. This division opens up a deep and problematic rift between the humane and the scientific perspec-tives: a rift between the self's first-person perspective on a world of thought and intelligence, and the scientist's third-person perspective on a world of brute physical forces. We may call this the *mind–world rift*. Since moral value seems to be an integral part of the humane perspective but no part at all of the scientific perspective, the mind–world rift creates further puzzlement about how there can be moral value 'out there in the world'.

In chapter 5, I will show how the mind–world rift and the egocentric predicament work together to create still more problems – this time, for our natural conception of personhood. Descartes's division of the world into self-consciousness on one side and everything else on the other leads him to a particular view about what a person is. He thinks that a person, a self, is no more and no less than a pinpoint of consciousness, a centre of self-awareness. We don't find this view of persons totally unnatural. But we also find it natural to think of persons in completely different ways from Descartes's. For example, we often naturally think of a person as what Martin Heidegger (1889–1976), in his monumental work *Being and Time*, calls 'being in the world': that is, as a human being whose personhood is essentially constituted by his or her body, biography, and context of relationships and roles. All this is put in question both by the mind–world rift and by the egocentric predicament. Your place in the world cannot be *essential* to your personhood, if the existence of the person is certain in a way that the existence of the world, and the bodies and biographies it contains, is not.

The mind–world rift, the split between the scientific and the humane perspectives that results from Descartes's approach, also makes a worrying split in our ideas about consciousness. Despite Descartes's ambition to found all the other sciences on each person's conscious self-knowledge, his all-or-nothing division between the mind and the world tends to make them the subjects of separate and autonomous sciences. The study of the mind, as Descartes conducts it, is governed by the rational laws of logic and inference. But the study of the non-mental world, as Descartes conducts it, is governed by the mechanical laws of physics.

However, the autonomous study of the mind has made relatively little progress since Descartes's time; whereas physics, the autonomous study of matter in motion, has made enormous advances. Each new advance of science has demonstrated once more how much can be explained by the mechanical, reductive approach of Descartes's scientific perspective. It becomes natural to think that the scientific explanatory perspective can be applied to everything. Eventually we think of applying it even to persons and to consciousness. But, of course, to apply the scientific explanatory perspective to persons and consciousness is to treat them as part of the physical world. And how, we might wonder, could there be any space at all in a physical world for something as strange as consciousness? This is the main question I shall pursue in chapter 6.

A third problem created by the rift between the scientific and humane perspectives is the *problem of free will*. How can we understand the intelligent agents that we normally take humans to be as parts of the physical world and as governed by physical laws? If the world is a great machine of physical causes and effects, how can there be room for human action of the kind that we call *free* – the kind that people can be praised or blamed for? I shall raise this problem too in chapter 6.

So chapters 1 to 6 will set up a series of intellectual dilemmas – clashes between different philosophical perspectives, each of which has an almost irresistible appeal but which we cannot see how to hold together. In my last chapter, chapter 7, I will ask what we ought to do about these dilemmas.

I say that the intellectual dilemmas to be discussed in this book are all, in different ways, aspects of the problem of the inescapable self. By this I do not mean to say that they are the very same problem, or even, necessarily, that they are problems with tight logical interrelations. Often, in fact, the connections between the different versions of the problem are more psychological than logical; the problem of the inescapable self is not so much a thesis with corollaries as a theme with different possible variations (or a syndrome, with different possible symptoms). But whether these interrelations are logical or psychological, I do want to insist that they are natural. 'The problem of the inescapable self' is my name for a cluster of more specific problems which naturally go together

– which run into each other at some points, and which tend to reinforce each other. (Sometimes I shall also apply the name to particular problems in this cluster.) My claim is not that, if someone finds one of these dilemmas worrying, then he must logically find all of them worrying. But it is that – as a matter of the history of our culture – people who have found one of these intellectual dilemmas worrying have in fact tended to find all or most of them worrying.

0.3 Why philosophers have to face up to the problem

My brief survey of the different aspects of the problem of the inescapable self stresses its reality and vitality. This is worth stressing, because there is a parody of what philosophers do which makes philosophy no better than a parlour game whose only point is to demonstrate your own cleverness. Philosophers, it is sometimes said, scratch endlessly at non-existent itches; the service they provide is exhaustive answers to questions that no one is asking. Some people think that no one ever seriously doubts whether they are victims of a vast hallucination, or the Matrix, or the Cartesian demon, or Putnam's mad scientist. But these are just the sort of idle questions that philosophers typically spend their time on. So much the worse, they tell us, for philosophy.

I don't deny that philosophers sometimes scratch non-existent itches, and sometimes aim solely at demonstrating their own cleverness. But I do deny that only philosophers ask nightmare-scenario sceptical questions like 'How do I know I'm not dreaming, or a brain in a vat?' Ordinary people most certainly do wonder about these questions. If you don't believe me, go and listen to people who have just seen *The Matrix*.

'But why are these nightmare-scenario questions so central to philosophical thinking?' Because of what philosophy is. Philosophy is the use of reasoned argument to try to develop a view of the whole of reality that makes full rational sense. The reason why sceptical questions arise in philosophy is not because philosophers are idle pedants. It is because philosophers seriously try to understand the world. Reason itself demands that our outlook on the world should be as fully rationally justified as possible. The best philosophers have always taken this demand of reason completely seriously – even when taking it seriously gets them into serious trouble. (Descartes famously got into this sort of trouble; so, even more famously, did that original asker of awkward questions, Socrates himself.)

Anyway, taking a sceptical question seriously certainly doesn't feel like a trivial parlour game. Much of the dramatic impact of *The Matrix* comes from the shattering and terrifying experience that facing up to sceptical questions can be. (The cool martial-arts sequences probably help too.) Seriously confronting the possibility of scepticism means facing dislocation, disorientation, vertigo, metaphysical dizziness. It made Descartes feel like he was drowning:

> It feels as if I have fallen unexpectedly into a deep whirlpool which tumbles me round so that I can neither stand on the bottom nor swim up to the top.[6]

It made David Hume feel something very like despair:

> Where am I, or what?...What beings surround me? And on whom have I any influence, or who have any influence on me? I am confounded with all these questions, and begin to fancy myself in the most deplorable condition imaginable, inviron'd with the deepest darkness, and utterly depriv'd of the use of every member and faculty.[7]

As Robert Fogelin puts it, commenting on this passage: 'When doing philosophy one can become seriously spooked.'[8]

Yet reason itself demands that we should try to find an outlook on the world that is as fully rationally justified as possible. So we'd better face up to that demand, however worrying or spooky we may find it. Facing up to it will involve us in trying to answer the nightmare-scenario sceptical questions that give rise to the problem, or problems, of the inescapable self. It will also involve an exploration of what it feels like to ask these sceptical questions, and of what asking them has done to our culture since the time of Descartes.

This is what this book does. In it, I tell the story of how the subjective self's search for philosophical certainty has led to doubt and scepticism about everything – even the subjective self.

The story begins with a little history, about Descartes himself.

1 From the screenplay of the film *The Matrix* (1997), by Larry and Andy Wachowski.

2 Plato, *Theaetetus* 158b–c.

3 *Republic* 514a–519a.

4 Descartes, Meditation 1, para. 5, and Meditation 2, para. 3; CSM II: 13, 17.

5 Putnam 1981: 5–6.

6 Descartes, Meditation 2, para. 1; CSM II: 16.

7 Hume, *Treatise of Human Nature* 1.4.7; 1969: 316.

8 Fogelin 2003: 164.

1

Descartes's Revolution

1.1 **Descartes upsets the applecart**

Descartes's philosophy begins in dissatisfaction with what we know – or rather, with what we think we know:

> Suppose a man had a basket full of apples and, being worried that some of the apples were rotten, wanted to take out the rotten ones to prevent the rot spreading. How would he proceed? Would he not begin by tipping the whole lot out of the basket? And would not the next step be to cast his eye over each apple in turn, and pick up and put back in the basket only those he saw to be sound, leaving the others?[1]

Most of us, says Descartes, have a vast stock of beliefs, unquestioningly acquired in childhood and never properly examined since. When we begin to philosophize seriously and look at any particular one of these unexamined beliefs, we find that we do not know it with certainty. For all we can tell, that belief could be false. How then are people to separate their false beliefs from their true beliefs, to prevent the false beliefs from 'contaminating the rest and making the whole lot uncertain'?

> The best way they can accomplish this is to reject all their beliefs together in one go, as if they were all uncertain and false. They can then go over each belief in turn and re-adopt only those which they recognize to be true and indubitable.[2]

We are used to the idea that we might be wrong about some things. Descartes proposes a much less familiar, and much more radical, idea: we might be wrong about *everything*. If this apple might be rotten, and this apple might be rotten, and this apple might be rotten...then they might all be rotten. Similarly, if this belief might be false, and this belief might be false, and this belief might be false...then they might all be false.

With the apples, it's no good just to select a few at random off the top, check that they're all right, and hope for the best. Finding *some* sound apples is no guarantee that *all* the apples are sound. We can only find that out by inspecting every apple. And it only takes a single rotten apple in the middle of the cartload to infect all the apples around it, till eventually every apple is rotten.

Similarly with our beliefs. It's no good to say that some of our beliefs seem just fine when we inspect them, so we needn't bother to inspect the rest of our beliefs. Having some true beliefs is no guarantee that *all* our beliefs are true. We can only be sure of that by inspecting every belief.

Moreover, false beliefs, like rotten apples, are a bad influence. As a rule (there are exceptions, but this is usually how things go), false beliefs replicate themselves more easily than true beliefs do:

$$\text{True Belief} + \text{True Belief} = \text{True Belief}$$

and $$\text{False Belief} + \text{False Belief} = \text{False Belief}$$

BUT $$\text{True Belief} + \text{False Belief} = \text{False Belief}$$

Also, it usually only takes one false belief to undo the good work of many true beliefs:

$$\text{True Belief} + \text{True Belief} + \text{True Belief} +$$
$$\text{True Belief} + \textit{False Belief} = \text{False Belief}$$

This is why Descartes encourages us to upset the applecart – us, or at least as many of us as are fit to do his sort of philosophy: 'The simple resolution to abandon all the opinions one has hitherto accepted is not an example that everyone ought to follow.'[3] But anyone who has the necessary intellectual abilities should learn to treat every one of his beliefs with suspicion, as a possible 'rotten apple'. For Descartes, we don't know what we think we know, until we are *sure* that we know it. Socrates (470–399 BC) had thought the same. As Socrates tells us in Plato's *Apology*,[4] most people imagine that they know lots of things, but they can quickly be exposed as ignorant by anyone who stops imagining that *he* knows anything and takes the trouble to question people about what they think. Our world is crowded with naked emperors.

In his first published work, *The Discourse on the Method* (1637), Descartes uses another image. He compares our beliefs to a building that is so rickety, ramshackle, ill-designed and unsafe that the best thing to do is knock it down and start again:

> Sometimes people are forced to pull down their houses when they are in danger of falling down and their foundations are insecure. This example convinced me that…regarding the opinions to which I had hitherto given credence…I could not do better than undertake to get rid of them, all at one go, in order to replace them with better ones, or with the same ones once I had squared them with the standards of reason.[5]

Descartes was convinced that the edifice of knowledge that his own society inhabited was structurally unsound. (And he knew about this edifice from the inside, having been educated himself between 1606 and 1614 at the famous Jesuit college of La Flèche, a stronghold of the old-style scholastic learning that he later came to reject so adamantly.) To Descartes, most of what passed as knowledge in his day was not really knowledge at all. Because that 'knowledge' was not known to the mind with complete assurance, and because it made no attempt to close off every possibility of doubt, it was not secure against the worries raised by scepticism's nightmare scenarios. To kill off these worries permanently, Descartes believed, a revolution in knowledge was needed. And he became convinced that he was the man to start it.

1.2 Sceptics and subjectivists in the age of Descartes

Though Descartes's work is indeed revolutionary, it is also true that his outlook marks him as a man of his time. The climate of thought that Descartes grew up in was already a sceptical and introspective one. 'Descartes must (in April 1625) have heard the reported last words of his former commander, Maurice of Nassau: Asked about his faith, he had replied "I believe that two and two make four."'[6] Maurice's sardonic deathbed joke was entirely in line with the *zeitgeist* of the time, which said that hardly anything can be known for sure, and that what little can be known for sure is so obvious that it is barely worth knowing at all.

An older contemporary of Descartes was Lord Francis Bacon (1561–1626), who wrote in his *Aphorisms* (1620) that 'there is no soundness in our notions', and that 'the subtlety of nature is greater many times over than the subtlety of the senses and understanding'. A little earlier on the time line, Erasmus (1466–1536), the greatest of Renaissance humanists, had combined an ardent enthusiasm for light and elegant pagan authors such as Virgil, Ovid and Cicero with a questioning coolness towards the 'schoolmen' – Aquinas (1225–74), Aristotle (384–322 BC), and the rest of the traditional canon of clerically approved authorities. Descartes's age was the age of Copernicus (1473–1543), Galileo (1564–1642) and Kepler (1571–1630), three men whose combined observational and mathematical discoveries simply blew apart the supposedly certain knowledge found in the 15-centuries-old astronomical system of Ptolemy's *Almagest*.

Descartes's age was also the age of Michel de Montaigne (1533–92), who expressed his cultured and gentlemanly scepticism in a new literary form that he called the 'trial'. Montaigne's 'trials' are short pieces of conversational prose in which he subjects some particular idea or belief to intellectual interrogation. (The French for 'trial' is *essai*: hence the English word 'essay'.)

Montaigne's motto was the Socratic phrase *que sçais-je?*, 'What do I know?' One of his inspirations was the contemporary rediscovery of the work of ancient Greek sceptics such as Sextus Empiricus (2nd century AD). Like Sextus, and indeed like Socrates, Montaigne finds himself suspicious of his own capacities for truth: 'He who remembers having been mistaken so many, many times in his own judgement, is he not a fool if he does not distrust it forever after?'[7] This distrust leaves Montaigne in suspense between alternative beliefs, and certain of nothing:

I can maintain an opinion, but I cannot choose one…whichever school of opinion we first incline to, we will then find lots of evidence to confirm us in that view. The uncertainty of my judgment is so equally balanced in most occurrences, that I could willingly refer it to be decided by the chance of a die.[8]

Even if Montaigne cannot 'choose' opinions, he is at least capable – unlike Sextus – of 'maintaining' some opinions. But how can he know which beliefs are *worth* maintaining? He does it, he tells us, by looking within himself:

I turn my sight inward, and there fix and employ it. I have no other business but myself, I am eternally meditating upon myself, considering and tasting myself. Other men's thoughts are ever wandering abroad, if they will but see it…for my part, I circulate in myself. This capacity of trying the truth, whatever it be, in myself, and this free humour of not over easily subjecting my belief, I owe principally to myself.[9]

Montaigne's method of introspective confirmation can give him an inner assurance of the truth of the beliefs that he thinks are worth 'maintaining'. Indeed, this method can give anyone the same sort of inner assurance – even when their beliefs flatly contradict Montaigne's. This does not bother Montaigne: 'I think my opinions are good and sound, but who does not think the same of his own?'[8] It is not unusual for people today to think that different perspectives can be equally 'valid', i.e. true, even when they contradict each other. (In the words of the Manic Street Preachers: 'This is my truth, tell me yours.') Montaigne thought the same.

1.3 **Descartes and Luther**

Descartes lived in a sceptical and subjectivist age, and Descartes had a use for both scepticism and subjectivism. Yet Descartes himself is no subjectivist. He does think that all philosophy begins with the individual's subjective viewpoint; but he does not think that all philosophy ends there. Unlike Montaigne and many people today, Descartes does not believe that any unexamined subjective belief is as 'valid' as any other.

Nor is Descartes a sceptic. Unlike Montaigne and Sextus Empiricus, Descartes does not think that genuine objective knowledge is impossible. He does not *believe* scepticism, but he does *use* it: Cartesian scepticism is a *via negativa*, a 'negative way' or 'way of purgation'. It is a method of deflating the philosophical overambition and complacency that Descartes finds, above all, in the medieval schoolmen.

The full title of the *Discourse* tells us that Descartes's project is to show us a 'method of rightly conducting the reason and seeking truth in the sciences'. As part of this project, Descartes uses scepticism to show that all methods except his own are not just inadequate but positively misleading. The more comprehensive is Descartes's destruction of all other fraudulent and deceptive routes to knowledge, the more inevitably we will be channelled into the true, Cartesian route to knowledge. Descartes is not a sceptic but a reformer.

Picking up the suggestions of the word 'reformer', we can say this: knowledge in Descartes is like heaven in Luther. To get there, you have to start off in the opposite direction.

For Luther (1483–1546), you do not get to heaven in the way that the Catholic tradition proposed: by starting with the human nature you already have and finding ways of improving and refining, perhaps even perfecting, it.[10] Instead, you start by rejecting and destroying human nature. This happens when you apply the standard of heaven − perfection − to your own human nature. You then realize that by that standard, your nature is utterly corrupt: there is nothing in you that is *perfect*. It is no good trying to meet heaven's standard by upgrading your old human nature. The task is hopeless because the standard is too high. It is better not even to try to meet the heavenly standard. It is better to be a harlot than a Pharisee (Luke 7: 39); at least the harlot, admitting that she has failed, has no false pride in her own virtue. The only thing to do, Luther tells us, is to abandon the old nature entirely. We need to 'put off the old man' (Ephesians 4: 22) and start again from nothing.

Similarly, for Descartes, you do not reach the salvation of true knowledge in the way Aristotle proposes − by starting with the 'customary beliefs' you already have, and finding ways of improving and refining them.[11] Instead, you start by destroying and rejecting your customary beliefs. This happens when you apply the standard of true knowledge − certainty − to your customary beliefs. You then realize that by that standard, your customary beliefs are utterly baseless: there is nothing that you are *certain* of. It is no good trying to meet the standard of true knowledge by refining your customary beliefs. The task is hopeless because the standard is too high. It is better not even to try to meet it. It is better to be a sceptic than a scholastic; at least the sceptic – like Socrates in Plato's *Apology* – knows that he is ignorant and does not falsely imagine that he knows something. The only thing to do, Descartes tells us, is to abandon our former beliefs entirely. We need to 'to rid ourselves of all the opinions we have adopted'[12] and start again from nothing.

The 'nothing' that Luther starts again from is the emptiness of the soul that looks within itself and sees that it can do nothing good. In a miraculous reversal, this helplessness itself becomes the way in for the grace of God which empowers the soul to do good and which would otherwise be rebuffed by the pride of human nature.

The 'nothing' that Descartes starts again from is the emptiness of the soul that looks within itself and sees that it has no knowledge. In an almost miraculous reversal, this ignorance itself becomes the way in for a certainty which empowers the mind to have knowledge and which would otherwise be rebuffed by the pride of human nature. 'I said to my soul, be still, and let the dark come upon you Which shall be the darkness of God.'[13]

1.4 **Cogito, ergo sum**

Descartes's use of sceptical doubt strips me of virtually everything I know. The world vanishes, and I am left with nothing except myself:

> I will suppose, then, that everything I see is spurious. I will believe that my memory tells me lies, and that none of the things that it reports ever happened. I have no senses. Body, shape, extension, movement, and place are chimeras.[14]

Once he has got me into this sceptical nightmare scenario, how is Descartes going to get me out again? The answer – and the 'almost miraculous reversal' – begins with Descartes's celebrated argument *cogito, ergo sum*, 'I think, therefore I am.'

Sceptical doubt has undermined my belief that there is a world outside my own mind or self. Can it do the same to my belief in my own existence? No, because if I am to think that my own mind or self does not exist, there has to be a mind or self to think this. Even if everything that I think happens is only a dream, there is still a me to whom it apparently happens. Even if I am trapped in the Matrix or in Plato's Cave, even if I am the victim of a mad scientist or a deceiving demon, there still has to be a me to be fooled:

> I undoubtedly exist, if he is deceiving me; and let him deceive me as much as he can, he will never bring it about that I am nothing so long as I think that I am something. So after considering everything very thoroughly, I must finally conclude that this proposition, *I am, I exist*, is necessarily true whenever it is put forward by me or conceived in my mind.[15]

Hence, as Descartes triumphantly concludes:

> I noticed that while I was trying to think everything false, it was necessary that I, who was thinking this, was something. And observing that this truth, 'I *am thinking, therefore I exist*' (*cogito, ergo sum*), was so firm and sure that all the most extravagant suppositions of the sceptics were incapable of shaking it, I decided that I could accept it without scruple as the first principle of the philosophy I was seeking.[16]

Two points about the *cogito* argument need discussion at once. One point is that the argument is essentially first-personal; the other is that it is essentially about thought. A little reflection on these two points will bring out what kind of self it is that Descartes leaves us with. In particular, it will show how little there is of this self.

The *cogito* is *essentially first-personal*: it has to be stated as '*I* think, therefore *I* exist'. 'You think, therefore you exist' and 'She thinks, therefore she exists' are both arguments that are valid for the same reason as the *cogito* is valid. (The reason is this: if it is true that any person thinks, then it must also be true that that person exists; in logical notation, $Fa \rightarrow \Box x \; (x = a)$.) All the same, 'You think, therefore you exist' and 'She thinks, therefore she exists' are very different arguments from the *cogito*. Both start from something that cannot be certainly known by me. I can know absolutely for sure that *I* am thinking. I can never know absolutely for sure that anyone else has a mind at all. For all I can tell, everyone else might be a mindless zombie or robot. They might just be automata in cloaks, as Descartes puts it.[17]

The *cogito* is *essentially about thought*: it has to be stated as 'I *think*, therefore I am'. 'I'm pink, therefore I am' and 'I drink, therefore I am' are both valid for the same reason as the *cogito* is valid. (As before, the reason is the logical rule $Fa \rightarrow \Box x \; (x = a)$: if it is true that any thing does anything, it must also be true that that thing exists.) All the same, 'I'm pink, therefore I am' and 'I drink, therefore I am' are very different arguments from the *cogito*. Both start from something that cannot be certainly known by me. I can know absolutely for sure that I am *thinking*. I can never know absolutely for sure that I'm pink or that I drink. For all I can tell, I might be gamboge or vermilion, not pink; for all I can tell, I might be dreaming or drowning, not drinking.

If I ask myself 'Am I drinking?' or 'Is he thinking?', the answer can be 'Yes', 'No' or 'Maybe'. But if I ask myself 'Am *I thinking*?', the answer can only be 'Yes'. For me to ask myself this question is itself for me to do some thinking. It would be self-refuting for me to ask myself 'Am I thinking?' and answer 'No'.

Whatever other beliefs sceptical doubt may strip me of, I cannot coherently doubt that I am thinking when I doubt. Since I cannot be thinking unless I exist, I cannot coherently doubt my own existence either. Descartes's *cogito* proves beyond the slightest doubt that I can't be wrong about whether I am thinking. So it also proves beyond the slightest doubt that I can't be wrong about whether I exist.

But what *is* this 'I' that has been so certainly proved to exist? And what is the thinking that this 'I' has been so certainly proved to be doing?

The argument of the *cogito* depends entirely on the fact that my subjective consciousness is immediately aware of itself. It follows that nothing beyond this self-consciousness is made certain by the *cogito*. When I work through the *cogito*, I certainly prove that 'I exist', if 'I' means 'this self-consciousness that exists right now'. But I do *not* prove that 'I exist', if 'I' means 'Timothy Chappell of Dundee, Scotland, a human being born in Lancashire, England, in 1964'. Still less do I prove that 'I exist', if 'I' means 'the father of Miriam, Caitlin, Imogen, Thalia and Róisín', 'the husband of Claudia', 'the son of William and Gillian', etc.

The *cogito* may prove that 'this self-consciousness that exists right now' is real. But it does not prove that 'this self-consciousness that exists right now' is *connected* to anything else at all. It does not connect this self-consciousness to a living human body or to a place and time in the real world; nor to a context of relationships with other really existing people and institutions; nor to any biography or personal history. It does not even connect this self-consciousness *now* to the same self-consciousness *at previous times*. The *cogito* connects 'this present self-consciousness' to nothing at all except itself. I shall say more about what this fact implies for the problem of personal identity in **5.1** to **5.3**.

Descartes's proof is so irresistible because it proves so little. It proves only the existence of a bare pinpoint of self-consciousness, what Charles Taylor has called a 'punctual self'. But this kind of self could exist as a prisoner of the Matrix or as a brain in a vat! Worse, the *cogito* proves the existence of my punctual self *only to me*. You can't share my performance of the *cogito*, and I can't share yours. Your *cogito* proves nothing to me; mine proves nothing to you. For all the *cogito* shows, not only could we all be prisoners of the Matrix; I could even be the *only* prisoner of the Matrix, and everyone else no more than illusions of mine.

Descartes wanted to find something certain, to provide a sure foundation on which to begin reconstructing the rest of knowledge. In the *cogito*, he may have found something certain. But he has not found something that can be any sort of foundation for a new edifice of knowledge. The *cogito* may be a successful proof, to me, of my own existence. But in the same move whereby it succeeds in proving that, it puts everything else beyond the reach of proof: as I put it in the Prelude (**0.2**), 'The fortress of my certainty about my own existence becomes the prison of my uncertainty about the existence of a world beyond me.' The certainty that the *cogito* gives me of my own existence as a present-tense self-consciousness is perfectly matched by the uncertainty that it creates about everything else. The *cogito* leaves me stranded in the problem of the inescapable self.

Descartes, of course, would not accept this verdict. As I said (**1.3**), he is neither a sceptic nor a subjectivist. So he is not interested only in proving his own existence. He thinks he can go on from there to prove the existence of the external world as well. Even when that is done, his refutation of scepticism is only a preliminary to his main concern. As Descartes's Synopsis of the *Meditations* shows,[18] his project is ultimately *scientific*. 'These six Meditations', he confided to his friend Mersenne, 'contain all the foundations of my physics.'[19] Descartes's project is the establishment of a complete system for all human knowledge, with a fundamental metaphysics, a 'first philosophy', as its basis, and the *cogito* as the foundation of that metaphysics.

Let us look, then, to see if Descartes succeeds in founding a non-sceptical metaphysics on the *cogito*. In **1.5** I'll describe how he tries to do this. In **1.6** I'll explain why his attempt fails.

1.5 **Clear and distinct ideas**

The key to Descartes's reconstructive programme lies in his answer to a question that, in the last section, I left unanswered: what is the thinking that this 'I' has been so certainly proved to be doing?

I've just argued that the *cogito* only proves that I exist as a present-tense self-consciousness. It does not prove that I exist as a human animal with a body and a biography. It's consistent with the truth of the *cogito* that I should exist but be completely wrong about what I am – perhaps because I am trapped in the Matrix, or because I am a victim of a mad scientist or a Cartesian demon. So, I've argued, the *cogito* proves nothing that is the slightest use against scepticism.

Suppose that my criticism is right: I can use the *cogito* to prove with absolute certainty *that* I exist, at the price of complete uncertainty about *what* I am that exists. If so, we should expect something parallel to be true of my thinking. We will expect that I can use the *cogito* to prove with absolute certainty *that* I am thinking, at the price of complete uncertainty about *what* I am thinking.

Crucially, Descartes denies this. He claims that I can know with absolute certainty, not only *that* I am thinking, but also *what* I am thinking. And this claim is pivotal to his response to my accusation that the *cogito* proves nothing useful against scepticism. To understand how his response works, we must look closely at Descartes's notion of a 'clear and distinct idea'.

Descartes derives his notion of a clear and distinct idea directly from reflection on the *cogito*. What is it about the *cogito*, he asks, that makes him so sure that it is a sound argument? Only this, he replies, 'that I see very clearly that in order to think it is necessary to exist'. From this Descartes concludes that he can take it as a general rule 'that the things we conceive very clearly and very distinctly are all true'.[20] If *any* idea that I have is clear and distinct – vivid and definite, without confusion or vagueness – that alone is enough to prove that it is not a deceptive idea. Wherever my ideas are clear and distinct, I can know with absolute certainty, not only that I am thinking, but also what I am thinking. There are no clear and distinct ideas which nonetheless deceive me.

But (we might object), if the deceiving demon can give me delusions about what I am perceiving, it is hard to see why the demon can't give me delusions about what I am thinking. And aren't there obvious exceptions to Descartes's 'general rule'? Aren't there dreams and hallucinations that I 'very clearly and distinctly conceive', but which nonetheless deceive me?

Descartes thinks not. Some dreams are clear and distinct ideas, but don't deceive me: 'If one happened even in sleep to have some very distinct idea (if, say, a geometer discovered some new proof), one's being asleep would not prevent the idea from being true.'[21] Other dreams, hallucinations and other sorts of perceptual illusion do deceive me, but don't involve ideas that are either clear or distinct. The ideas they contain are sense perceptions. And Descartes denies that sense perceptions, in themselves, are ever clear and distinct ideas. For example, 'The ideas which I have of heat and cold contain so little clarity and distinctness that they do not enable me to tell whether cold is merely the absence or vice versa, or whether both of them are real qualities, or neither is.'[22] Or again, stars and other bodies at a great distance appear to us much smaller than they are; and a person with jaundice will see everything as yellow.[23]

Typically, sense perceptions need interpretation. They don't explain things well. They are, literally, superficial – based only on our physical interactions with the surfaces of things. Also, they typically conflict with other sense perceptions: consider the twig that looks bent in a jar of water but not out of it, or the different angles of vision that we might have on a building. Hence we need to use reason to decide what we are *really* perceiving. Only once we have done that will we arrive at genuinely clear and distinct ideas. 'Whereas clear and distinct perception is internally coherent, sense perception is internally incoherent – sense perception on its own generates conflicting beliefs. Clear and distinct perception resolves these conflicts by sustaining one of the beliefs, and correcting the other.'[24]

Where our perceptions conflict or need further interpretations to make sense, we arrive at clear and distinct ideas by resolving the conflicts and finding such interpretations. Once these conflicts are resolved and a fuller interpretation of our experience has been provided, clear and distinct ideas become available to us. And then we can invoke Descartes's 'general rule' – that all our clear and distinct ideas are *true*. Under these conditions, then, we can trust our perceptions of the world.

Our perceptions of the world include our perceptions of our own bodies and of the context that we live in. So in the end, the fact that we can be absolutely certain not only that we are thinking, but also what we are thinking, enables us to reach certainty not only about the fact *that* we exist, but also about *what we are* that exists. When we reflect on our sense perceptions of the world, we can make them into clear and distinct ideas; and we cannot go wrong about the content of our clear and distinct ideas. But we can, with a little effort, attain a clear and distinct idea of our own bodies, histories, biographies and contexts. So we can know with certainty not only that we exist but what we are. Beyond that, we can know the rest of the world as well.

But why *should* our clear and distinct ideas be true ideas? Descartes answers that our clear and distinct ideas are guaranteed true because they do not come from us, or not solely from us. Ultimately they come from God, and 'God is no deceiver':

What I took just now as a rule, namely that everything that we conceive very clearly and very distinctly is true, is assured only for the reasons that God is or exists, that he is a perfect being, and that everything in us comes from him.[25]

How do we know that there exists a God like this? We know, replies Descartes, because we have a clear and distinct idea of him as existing. Indeed, we have an especially clear and distinct idea of this God:

This idea of God...is utterly clear and distinct, and contains in itself more objective reality than any other idea; hence there is no idea which is in itself truer, or less liable to be suspected of falsehood.[26]

If I know anything at all, Descartes concludes, I know that I exist, that the world outside me exists, and that God also exists. I know that I exist, because the *cogito* tells me so. I know that the external world exists, because I have a clear and distinct idea of the world as existing, and clear and distinct ideas are trustworthy. That clear and distinct ideas are trustworthy is illustrated by the *cogito*, which works by combining clear and distinct ideas. The trustworthiness of clear and distinct ideas is also proved by the fact that clear and distinct ideas come from God. And we know that God exists, because our idea of God is the clearest and most distinct idea that we have, and that idea itself implies that God exists.[27]

As Descartes sums up his case, at the end of the sixth and last Meditation:

I should not have any further fears about the falsity of what my senses tell me every day; on the contrary, the exaggerated doubts of the last few days should be dismissed as laughable…And I ought not to have even the slightest doubt of the reality [of the external world] if, after calling upon all the senses as well as my memory and my intellect in order to check them, I receive no conflicting report from any of these sources. For from the fact that God is not a deceiver it follows that in cases like these I am completely free from error.[28]

The world is recovered. The philosophical foundation is laid and ready for science to be built on it. Descartes is ready to move on.

Descartes himself did move on. During his career he did an enormous amount to 'establish the sciences' upon the foundation of the *Meditations*. Descartes was not just a philosopher in the narrow modern sense. He was a philosopher in the much wider 17th-century sense, a sense nowadays preserved only in the titles of those ancient professorships of physics at Oxford and Cambridge which are called 'professorships of natural philosophy'. Descartes was a friend (*philos*) of every sort of wisdom (*sophia*), including and especially the sciences. Besides the *Meditations* and the *Discourse*, he produced writings on the physics of light and refraction, on the colours of the rainbow, on hydraulic compression, on falling bodies, on the physiology and psychology of the emotions, and on the relation of geometry to algebra. (In this last field he made perhaps his most important contribution of all: to put it crudely, he invented the graph.) Nearly all of his published scientific output was important at the time; some of it, especially his mathematical work, is still important today.[29] Descartes does not just lay a foundation for knowledge and stop there. He goes far beyond that foundation.

1.6 **God, error and the Cartesian circle**

Unfortunately, however, he gets called back. Descartes immediately faced – and today still faces – opponents who will not let him move on.

These opponents included the Inquisition, who, elsewhere, hounded the scientist Galileo throughout Descartes's career. In 1632 the Inquisition condemned Galileo for continuing to teach the Copernican view that the Earth goes round the Sun, and placed him under house arrest for the remainder of his life. When Descartes heard of this, he abandoned work on his treatise *The World*, which – as he confided in a letter to his friend Mersenne of November 1633 – was a thoroughly Copernican work.

Other opponents of Descartes's system were more properly philosophical and less inclined to the use of thumbscrews. From the moment of Descartes's first presentation of his new ideas, in *The Discourse on the Method* (1637), other philosophers' reactions were such that he was led to append 'Replies to objections' to the first edition of his *Meditations* (1641).

One objection that was immediately put to Descartes, and is still a standard objection today, concerns Descartes's 'clear and distinct idea of God'. The objection is that some people have no such idea, either because their idea of God is not clear and distinct, or else because they have no idea of God at all: 'the natives of Canada, the Huron and other primitive peoples, have no awareness of any idea of this sort'.[30]

My Canadian friends tell me that in fact the Huron do have an idea of God. Even if they didn't, this objection would still involve a simple misunderstanding. Descartes's clear and distinct ideas are not supposed to be immediately and obviously present in any old mind, just as soon as it tries to locate them in the 'buzzing, blooming confusion' of its own sensations, the frenzy of its own prejudices and conditionings. Like the mathematical ideas that Socrates gets the slave boy to 'recollect' in Plato's *Meno*,[31] clear and distinct ideas are not some random sample of our actual thinking. They are the distillation of our best thinking, and as such are available, in principle, even to 'savages'.

Another standard objection is even more famous – but, I think, no more successful. This is the 'Cartesian circle' objection. Pierre Gassendi (1592–1655) put it like this:

> I note that a circular argument appears to have its beginning at this point, according to which you are certain that there must be a God and that he is not a deceiver because you have a clear and distinct idea of him, and you are certain that a clear and distinct idea must be true because you know that there is a God who cannot be a deceiver.[32]

Descartes's doctrine of clear and distinct ideas depends on his proof of God's existence. Conversely, his proof of God's existence depends on his doctrine of clear and distinct ideas. So – the 'Cartesian circle' objection goes – the doctrine does not really support the proof, and the proof does not really support the doctrine.

In the Second Set of Replies, Descartes responds that he only meant *some* clear and distinct ideas to be supported by appeal to God, namely the ones that we currently do not perceive but only remember. This response is unconvincing and seems to involve Descartes in misinterpreting his own writings. Descartes seems to apply the proposed restriction to *remembered* clear and distinct ideas in only two places.[33] Elsewhere we have, for example, this: 'I must examine whether there is a God, and, if there is, whether he can be a deceiver. For if I do not know this, it seems that I can never be quite certain of *anything* else.'[34] Again, in the Second Set of Replies itself, Descartes says that an atheist 'cannot be certain that he is not being deceived *on matters which seem to him to be very evident*'.[35] This seems like cast-iron evidence *against* Descartes's official response.

Whether or not Descartes himself deals well with it, the Cartesian circle objection is surely overrated. For one thing, there is no good reason why either the proof of God or the doctrine of clear and distinct ideas must come first in the order of support. Nothing but a lack of interpretive charity can stop us saying that the two views can give each other mutual support. (They also bear mutual-support relations to a third doctrine, namely the *cogito*: the Cartesian circle involves three mutually supporting doctrines, not just the two that are usually mentioned.) Modern 'coherentists' routinely criticize Descartes for his 'foundationalism' – that is, for resting all knowledge on a single basic foundation and not allowing that two or more beliefs can corroborate each other by cohering with each other, even though neither of them is a foundation for the other.[36] But maybe, in the case of the Cartesian circle, this is precisely what Descartes does allow.

There is another reason why Descartes should see his proof of God and his doctrine of clear and distinct ideas as mutually supportive. Descartes wants to position himself midway between the two alternatives, rationalism and fideism. Fideism is the view, descended from Luther, that only our trust in God can guarantee our access to the truth. It was defended in Descartes's time by the Jansenists, the 'Catholic Calvinists' of the Port-Royal school. Rationalism – a view held by contemporaries of Descartes such as the English deist Lord Herbert of Cherbury (1583–1648) – is the opposing view that human reason is the only guarantee of truth that we need. Now if Descartes takes the mutual-support view, he finds a middle way between fideism and rationalism. For his appeal to clear and distinct ideas, on its own, might seem like a rationalist move which excludes God from his metaphysics; whereas his appeal to God's undeceptiveness, on its own, might seem like a fideist move which excludes reason from his metaphysics. Descartes's compromise, I suggest, is to make both appeals and claim that they support each other.

Neither of these two objections shows what is really wrong with Descartes's strategy of working outward from the self to the world by way of the self's 'clear and distinct perceptions', and using God as the guarantor of the reliability of these perceptions. What is the real problem?

The real problem with Descartes's appeal to God as the guarantor of the truth of our perceptions is that this appeal either proves too much, if it implies the obvious falsehood that we are never deceived about anything, or else not enough, if it implies anything less.

Does the existence of an undeceiving God preclude all possibility of deception? If the answer is 'Yes', the undeceiving God cannot exist – for after all, as Descartes himself recognizes, at least *some* deception occurs. But if the answer is 'No', at least some deception is possible even though there is an undeceiving God. If this is the case, we can't ever be sure that we are not being deceived right now, and that Descartes's undeceiving God is simply letting deception happen (just as the good God of Christian theology allows Auschwitz and child leukaemia to happen).

In the fourth Meditation, Descartes grasps the second horn of this dilemma. Deception *is* possible, he tells us. This is because 'the scope of the will is wider than that of the intellect'.[37] You can *will* anything at all, but you can only *understand* clear and distinct ideas. Hence you can choose to assent to all sorts of things of which you do not have clear and distinct ideas, and so do not really understand. In such cases, since Descartes's undeceiving God allows you freedom of the will, he will allow you to be deceived (just as the good God of Christian theology allows us the freedom to choose evil).

This explanation of error is quite unconvincing. It presupposes that we believe things because we want to believe them. But surely that's wrong. At least most of the time, we believe things because we think they're true whether or not we want to believe them. (For more on the relation of believing and wanting, see **7.6**.)

Further, Descartes explains all erroneous beliefs as a sort of epistemic rashness (rashness relative to knowledge). He thinks that whenever I form a wrong belief, what happens is that I stubbornly insist on taking a view on a question that I don't really understand. No doubt some wrong beliefs are formed this way. But it isn't the only way of being wrong. Can't I also form a definite belief about a question that I think is completely free from risk and unclarity – and still be wrong?

Descartes would like to answer 'No', because – once more – of his rule of truth: whatever we 'very clearly and distinctly conceive' is true. This rule applies quite well in some areas, such as mathematics. If you're thinking with complete clarity and distinctness, it really does look impossible to think that 37 is not a prime number or that the interior angles of a triangle add up to 365 degrees. But let's think about some of the other mistakes that we make. I can be absolutely clear and sure that the party is tonight, when in fact it's tomorrow night. I can think with complete lucidity that the atomic weight of gold is 80, when in fact it's 79. And I can be completely definite that bats are birds, when in fact bats are mammals.

Mistakes like these suggest that Descartes has only two alternatives:

First alternative: **Some things that we 'very clearly and distinctly conceive' are nonetheless false, and so Descartes's rule of truth is wrong.**

Clearly Descartes can't take this first alternative without giving up completely. So he must take the second alternative:

Second alternative: **Whatever we 'very clearly and distinctly conceive' is true. But we can think that we 'very clearly and distinctly conceive' something when in fact we don't.**

The second alternative raises this question: how am I to *know* that I have a clear and distinct idea? Descartes's rule of truth suggests the following answer: to know that I have a clear and distinct idea, I need a clear and distinct idea of my clear and distinct idea. But this raises another question: how am I to know that I have a clear and distinct idea of my clear and distinct idea? Apparently I will need a clear and distinct idea of my clear and distinct idea of my clear and distinct idea... So this second alternative leads us into a hopeless regress.

Descartes thinks he can block this regress by insisting that our clear and distinct ideas are, to use Timothy Williamson's term, 'luminous'.[38] If I have a clear and distinct idea, then I know *just by having it* that it is clear and distinct. So I don't need a clear and distinct idea of each of my clear and distinct ideas. The idea of luminosity is the idea that our clear and distinct ideas come to us *marked* as clear and distinct ideas – and so as true ideas.

This gambit doesn't work either. Imagine you receive these two postcards:

Hi!

Weather fine here.
We spent yesterday
at the beach. Today
we're at the casino.
We're having a great
time, but missing you.

Love from - Bill

Hi!
Weather fine here. (NB THE
LAST STATEMENT IS TRUE.)
We spent yesterday at the
beach. (NB THE LAST STATEMENT
IS TRUE.) Today we're at the
casino. (NB THE LAST
STATEMENT IS TRUE.) We're
having a great time, but missing
you. (NB THE LAST STATEMENT
IS TRUE.)
　　　　　Love from Jill

Jill's postcard assures us, repeatedly, of its own reliability. Does Jill's assurance that she is telling us the truth make her postcard a more reliable message than Bill's? No, because Jill's assurance is itself part of Jill's message. We only have reason to trust Jill's assurance if we already have reason to trust the message containing that assurance. But if we already trust Jill's message, we don't need any further assurance. And if we already *dis*trust Jill's message, we won't heed any further assurance. Jill's postcard is only a long-winded way of telling us exactly what Bill's postcard tells us. (Unless it also tells us that Jill is protesting too much, or is mildly deranged, or has done too much philosophy.)

For the same reason, nothing is gained by suggesting that our clear and distinct ideas come clearly and distinctly marked as true. If we already trust our clear and distinct ideas, we won't need them to bear the mark of truth. If we already *dis*trust our clear and distinct ideas, we won't heed the fact that they bear the mark of truth. The claim that our clear and distinct ideas luminously contain assurance of their own truth adds precisely nothing to our reason to trust them. To think that it could add anything is like thinking that you can make a newspaper more reliable by naming it *Pravda* (Russian for 'truth'). Or it is like thinking that there's a special tone of voice, such that anything you say in that tone is bound to be true.[39]

So in the end, Descartes's rescue mission fails. Having got us into the problem of the inescapable self – the sceptical predicament where nothing is certain to each of us except our own existence – Descartes is, ultimately, unable to get us out again. His project to reconstruct knowledge cannot even begin without his appeal to our clear and distinct ideas, and to God as their guarantor. This appeal fails; and with it, Descartes's whole project.

Where does this leave us, Descartes's co-meditators? Like investors in a bubble company, we find ourselves philosophically bankrupted. We consented to be reduced to scepticism about everything, because Descartes promised us that this consent would win us a complete vindication of knowledge. But his promises have turned out empty. We find ourselves abandoned in the jaws of the sceptical trap. The problem of the inescapable self remains untouched.

1.7 **Locke and Reid in the sceptical trap**

What else could have got us out of the sceptical trap, except the failed appeal to God and our clear and distinct ideas? The shortage of attractive alternatives here is uncannily well illustrated by comparing the cases of two other philosophers: Thomas Reid (1710–96)[40] and John Locke (1632–1704). On Reid – 'the philosopher of common sense', as he is often called – Christopher Hookway writes as follows:

Simply pointing out [, as Reid does,] that a variety of standards are natural or 'self-evident' does not establish that we are not victims of a systematic illusion. Why does Reid think that holding this common sense view of the world is legitimate? I suspect that Reid's own response to this challenge invokes the goodness of God...Since God is known to be the benevolent creator of a world which displays intelligence and design, He [will] ensure that our instinctive standards for rationality [are] adequate for our developing intellectual aspirations.[41]

As an empiricist, Locke is a completely different style of philosopher both from Reid and from the rationalist Descartes. Nonetheless, when Locke's great project in the *Essay concerning Human Understanding* (1690) is already almost complete, he succumbs to a sudden attack of Cartesian vertigo:

I doubt not but my reader, by this time, may be apt to think that I have been all this while only building a castle in the air; and be ready to say to me...'How shall the mind, when it perceives nothing but its own ideas, know that they agree with things themselves?'[42]

Like Descartes's, Locke's account of knowledge faces the danger that the thinker might be trapped inside his own mind. Like a dreamer or a victim of the Matrix, the thinker can manipulate his own ideas; but for all he can tell, he makes no real contact at all with the world (if there is one) outside his own mind.

In the case of what he calls our 'complex ideas', Locke simply admits this problem. Where our complex ideas are supposed to reflect the way the world is, we can't ever be totally sure that they do reflect it.[43] However, our complex ideas are always compounded out of our simple ideas. And in the case of our simple ideas, Locke's account of knowledge meets this Cartesian danger with a thoroughly Cartesian response:

Since the mind can by no means make [simple ideas] to itself, [they] must necessarily be the product of things operating on the mind, in a natural way, and producing therein those perceptions which by the Wisdom and Will of our Maker they are ordained and adapted to. From whence it follows, that simple ideas are not fictions of our fancies, but the natural and regular productions of things without us, really operating upon us…this conformity between our simple ideas and the existence of things, is sufficient for real knowledge.[42]

Here Locke gives two reasons why I should trust that my simple ideas really do give me knowledge of a world outside my own mind. Locke's first reason is that I could not make these ideas up, so they *must* come from outside me. Descartes reaches the same conclusion in the *Meditations*: 'These ideas [of perception] are produced without my co-operation and often even against my will.'[44] Locke's second reason is that God is wise and (implicitly) good: in Descartes's words, 'God is no deceiver.' The parallel between Locke's argument and Descartes's could hardly be more obvious. The problems for their arguments are parallel, too. Above all, both face the objection that the appeal to God either proves nothing at all or far too much.

1.8 **Malebranche and Berkeley:** 'We see all things in God'

I said above that the parallel between Locke and Descartes shows how difficult it is to find responses to scepticism other than the appeal to a trustworthy God. All the same, there are other responses. One neat response to scepticism is to finesse it by agreement in spades. Instead of refuting the sceptic, you tell him that he is absolutely right to raise his worry. However, he hasn't taken the worry far enough. The surprise is that, if he did take it as far as he should, he wouldn't be a sceptic after all.

Descartes's own philosophy itself uses scepticism to create this sort of finesse: that is one way of describing what's going on *en route* to the *cogito*. As for Nicolas Malebranche (1638–1715), he finesses Descartes's finesse. Malebranche takes up Descartes's worry that perhaps we have no real access to the world outside us. Instead of refuting this worry, Malebranche takes it even further than Descartes. In his immense and ingenious book *The Search after Truth* (1675), Malebranche makes a list of all the apparently possible ways in which we might have contact with the external world. He finds four; and he dismisses them all. The only possibility left standing is that 'the soul is joined to a completely perfect being that contains all intelligible perfections, or all the ideas of created beings'.[45] In other words, I have *no* contact with the external world. But I do have direct contact with God, and the ideas of all things are in God.[46] So 'we see all things in God': without ever actually being in touch with the external world, I can know all about it indirectly, by inspecting God.[47] Thus Malebranche's profoundly sceptical route brings us to what he thinks is an anti-sceptical conclusion, a sort of mystical Platonic inward certainty.

Here, as David Hume (1711–76) caustically commented, 'we are got into fairyland'.[48] Or in Descartes's words, 'Nothing can be imagined which is too strange or incredible to have been said by some philosopher.'[49] Malebranche's metaphysics is a genial fantasy, extravagant and incredible. Moreover, Malebranche's arguments for it are often unconvincing. For example, he dismisses the possibility of direct perception of the external world by arguing that 'material objects do not transmit species resembling them' – i.e. by arguing against the Aristotelian account of this possibility.[50] Other and better accounts of perception are possible – as Malebranche knew from reading Descartes's account. Before reasonable people will concede that the truth really is the strange thing that Malebranche makes it, they will want better arguments than Malebranche provides.

Malebranche himself insisted that the best argument for his own system was that the only alternative to it was scepticism. But is his system really an alternative to scepticism, rather than a form of scepticism? Even if it is, it is not a much more attractive option than scepticism. The choice between these options is more finely balanced than Malebranche admits.

As the Catholic priest Malebranche is to Descartes, so the Anglican bishop George Berkeley (1685–1753) is to Locke.[51] As we saw in **1.7**, Locke says that all our thought about the external world is no more and no less than simple ideas and their conjunction to form complex ideas. He then faces an apparently insuperable problem about how we can ever know that these ideas *inside* our minds correspond to anything *outside* our minds.

Berkeley shares this worry with Locke; except that Berkeley finesses Locke by arguing that the worry is unanswerable. Berkeley accuses Locke of proposing a system that cuts us off entirely from the existence of the external world and leaves us, without knowledge, in a mire of scepticism and atheism. Locke assumes that if we don't have knowledge of an external world of material objects, we don't have knowledge at all. But, says Berkeley, Locke's own arguments show that 'if there were external bodies, it is impossible we should ever come to know it'.[52] Therefore Locke's own principles imply scepticism.

According to Berkeley, the only answer to this scepticism is to drop the assumption that we can't have any knowledge at all unless we have knowledge of an external and material world. After all, we certainly have knowledge of our own ideas. But there is no reason to see these ideas as evidence of an external and material world. Seeing them that way does not explain anything: 'The production of ideas or sensations in our minds can be no reason why we should suppose Matter or corporeal substances, since that is acknowledged to remain equally inexplicable with or without this supposition.'[53] Nor is there any practical need to see our ideas as a reason to believe in an external and material world. We can carry on our lives exactly as we always have, *without* that belief:

> Suppose – what no one can deny possible – an intelligence without the help of external bodies, to be affected with the same train of sensations or ideas that you are, imprinted in the same order and with like vividness in his mind. I ask whether that intelligence hath not all the reason to believe the existence of corporeal substances, represented by his ideas, and exciting them in his mind, that you can possibly have for believing the same thing?[52]

In short, our belief in a material world, existing in its own right outside us, is both groundless and pointless. Not only that, it is incoherent:

> It is indeed an opinion strangely prevailing amongst men, that houses, mountains, rivers, and in a word all sensible objects, have an existence, natural or real, distinct from their being perceived by the understanding...yet [this opinion involves] a manifest contradiction. For, what are the forementioned objects but the things we perceive by sense? And what do we perceive besides our own ideas or sensations? And is it not plainly repugnant that any one of these, or any combination of them, should exist unperceived?[54]

Locke begins by saying that our minds never know anything but their own ideas: 'that which a man's mind is applied about whilst thinking' is 'the ideas that are there' in the man's mind.[55] But he ends up saying that our minds can know a world that is *not* just our own ideas. Locke's ending contradicts his beginning.

Berkeley concludes that our ideas are not and cannot be what Locke thought they were – evidence of the existence of a physical world outside us which they represent. Rather, our ideas are evidence that there is a God who gives to each of us a series of perceptions. There is no more to my physical world than my series of perceptions, no more to your physical world than your series of perceptions, and no more to the 'shared' physical world than God's series of perceptions:

> We perceive a continual succession of ideas, some are anew excited, others are changed or totally disappear. There is therefore some cause of these ideas, whereon they depend, and which produces and changes them. This cause cannot be any quality or idea or combination of ideas...It must therefore be a substance; but it has been shewn that there is no corporeal or material substance: it remains therefore that the cause of ideas is an incorporeal active substance or Spirit.[56]

Berkeley cheerfully concedes that our experience is *just as if* there were a material world outside us. But, he tells us, the reason for this is not that there is such a world. It's because God makes it *look as if* there is such a world. This means that Berkeley's God *is* a deceiver. Berkeley's view is that Descartes was right to worry about the 'evil demon' – and failed mainly in not taking his worries far enough. If he had, suggests Berkeley, then Descartes would have seen that God is a demon all right, but a *good* demon. Berkeley's God creates, for our benefit, a systematic illusion: the illusion that the physical world exists. For Berkeley too, we see all things in God.

Since Berkeley's God is a benign deceiver, Berkeley faces the same objection as Malebranche. Berkeley's system is not an alternative to scepticism; it *is* scepticism. Hume's caustic comment on Malebranche applies equally well to Berkeley: this too is a fairyland theory of knowledge. We should not adopt Berkeley's theory either, until we are quite sure that no less fantastical alternative is available.

Surely, then, soberer routes to knowledge have been found, so that today we need not echo Descartes's and Locke's appeals to God's goodness, or Malebranche's and Berkeley's finesses of the sceptic? In chapter 2 we will move on from the history of philosophy and take our first look at some contemporary philosophy, to see what new ways of defeating scepticism and solving the problem of the inescapable self it has discovered. Especially since the beginning of the 20th century, philosophy has grown exponentially, both in quantity and in quality. A huge amount of energy has been devoted to what Immanuel Kant (1724–1804) called 'the scandal of philosophy' – the unsolved problem of scepticism. After so much attention, surely a better solution to the problem of the inescapable self, as a problem about knowledge, must be available by now?

1 Descartes, Replies to Objections 7, CSM II: 324; compare II: 349.

2 CSM II: 324.

3 *Discourse* 2, CSM I: 118.

4 Plato, *Apology* 19a–23b.

5 Descartes, *Discourse* 2, CSM I: 117.

6 Rodis-Lewis 1992: 35.

7 Montaigne 1957: 454.

8 Montaigne, Essay X, 'On Presumption'.

9 Montaigne, Essay X. Montaigne's advocacy of the 'inward turn' echoes St Augustine's (*de Vera Religione*, section 39): *Noli foras exire, in te ipsum redi; in interiore homine habitat veritas* ('Do not go outside, go back within yourself: truth dwells in the inward man').

10 For the Catholic idea that grace supplements nature rather than replacing it, see Aquinas, *Summa Theologiae* 1a2ae.109.2c: 'Human nature is not altogether corrupted by sin, so as to be shorn of every natural good. Even in the state of corrupted nature it can, by virtue of its natural endowments, work some particular good.'

11 Aristotle, *Nicomachean Ethics* 1145b2. For the Catholic idea that revealed knowledge supplements natural knowledge rather than replacing it, see Aquinas, *Summa Theologiae* 1a2ae.109.1c: 'Man does not need a new light added to his natural light, in order to know the truth in all things, but only in some that surpass his natural knowledge.'

12 Descartes, Meditation 1.

13 T. S. Eliot, *Four Quartets*, 'East Coker'. Here Eliot has in mind what St John of the Cross (1542–91) calls 'the dark night of the soul': the medieval mystics' idea that God is most richly present in the deserts of his apparent absence. Descartes and Luther knew about this idea too.

14 Descartes, Meditation 2, CSM II: 16.

15 Meditation 2, CSM II: 17. St Augustine proposes a very similar answer to the sceptic in *de Libero Arbitrio* II.3: *Si fallor, sum*, 'If I am deceived, then I exist.' See also *de Trinitate* X.x.14–16; XV.xii.21; *de Civitate Dei*, XI.26. Arnauld points out the parallel in the Fourth Set of Objections to the *Meditations*, CSM II: 139.

16 *Discourse* 4, CSM I: 127.

17 Meditation 2, CSM II: 21.

18 CSM II: 9.

19 Letter of 28 January 1641; CSMK 172.

20 *Discourse* 4, CSM I: 127.

21 CSM I: 130. Compare the dream in which the scientist Kekule discovered the shape of the benzene molecule, described in Asimov 1962.

22 Meditation 3, CSM II: 30.

23 *Discourse* 4.

24 Loeb 1992: 223.

25 Descartes, *Discourse* 4, CSM I: 130.

26 Meditation 3, CSM II: 31.

27 Strictly, Descartes offers *two* arguments to prove that God's existence follows from the content of my clear and distinct idea of God. First, I could only have got an idea with *that* content from God himself (the 'trademark argument', Meditation 3). Second, my idea of God is an idea of an absolutely perfect being. But no being could be *absolutely* perfect without existing. So the content of my idea of God guarantees God's actual existence (Descartes's ontological argument, Meditation 5).

28 Meditation 6, CSM II: 61–2.

29 See Gaukroger 1995.

30 Descartes, Second Set of Objections, CSM II. 89.

31 Plato, *Meno* 82b–86b.

32 Gassendi 204.

33 Descartes, Meditation 5, para.15, and *Rules for the Direction of the Mind*, Rule 3.

34 CSM II: 25, emphasis added.

35 CSM II: 101, emphasis added.

36 For more about foundationalism and coherentism, see Greco and Sosa 1999.

37 Descartes, CSM II: 40.

38 Williamson 2000, ch. 4, 'Anti-Luminosity'. Compare Ayer's metaphor of the 'inner searchlight': Ayer 1956: 20.

39 See Wittgenstein, *On Certainty* #30: 'Certainty is *as it were* a tone of voice in which one declares how things are, but one does not infer from the tone of voice that one is justified.'

40 Reid's main works are his *Inquiry into the Human Mind on the Principles of Common Sense* (1764) and his *Essays on the Intellectual Powers of Man* (1785). One of Reid's main targets is his contemporary and compatriot Hume.

41 Hookway 1990: 116.

42 Locke, *Essay* IV.4.

43 For Locke's distinction between simple and complex ideas, see *Essay* II.12.1. With Locke's view that we can err in our complex but not in our simple ideas, compare Aquinas, *Summa Theologiae* 1a.85.6, who agrees. In the case of perception, Locke further distinguishes between simple ideas of *primary* qualities (which exist whether or not we perceive them) and of *secondary* qualities (which exist only when we perceive them).

44 Descartes, Meditation 6, CSM II: 55.

45 Malebranche, *The Search after Truth*, 219.

46 Much else in Malebranche is wildly unorthodox, but his thesis that the ideas of all things are in God is mainline scholasticism (Aquinas, *Summa Theologiae* 1a.14.6): 'God sees Himself in Himself, because He sees Himself through His essence; and He sees other things not in themselves, but in Himself, since His essence contains the similitude of things other than Himself.' Perhaps this means that Aquinas' God is in a Matrix too.

47 Malebranche, *The Search after Truth*, 230. To the objection that things in the world seem to engage in causal interactions with each other quite independently of us (and of God), Malebranche ingeniously replies that God acts on them to make them *look* as if they interact. This bizarre view, occasionalism, is also found in Leibniz.

48 Hume, *Enquiry concerning Human Understanding* VII.I.

49 Descartes, *Discourse* 2, CSM I: 118.

50 Malebranche, *The Search after Truth*, 220.

51 Berkeley rejects the comparison with Malebranche. In the third edition of the *Second Dialogue between Hylas and Philonous*, Berkeley inserted a passage noting three differences between his own views and Malebranche's. (1) Malebranche 'builds on the most abstract general ideas, which I disclaim.' (2) 'He asserts an absolute external world, which I deny.' (3) 'He maintains that we are deceived by our senses, and know not the real natures of…extended beings…I hold the direct contrary.' As I argue, Berkeley misrepresents his own views here at least with respect to point (3).

52 Berkeley, *Principles* 1.20.

53 *Principles* 1.19.

54 *Principles* 4. Berkeley's thesis that 'our ideas can only exist when they are perceived' means that there can be no thought without a thinker, and no perception without a perceiver. This is the claim that leads to the famous question whether the tree in the forest makes a sound when it falls with no one to hear it. (The question is not quite put this way by Berkeley himself, but see Berkeley 1954: 42.)

55 Locke, *Essay* II.1.

56 Berkeley, *Principles* 1.25–6.

2

The Scandal of Philosophy

2.1 **The scandal continues**

So is such a solution available? Actually, no. Despite all the attention and energy that modern philosophers have devoted to refuting Cartesian scepticism, the problem of scepticism remains unsolved. Kant's 'scandal of philosophy' is still a scandal today. So the problem of the inescapable self remains unsolved as well, insofar as solving the problem of the inescapable self depends upon refuting Cartesian scepticism.

My project in this chapter is almost entirely negative. It is simply to demonstrate that the commonest responses to Cartesian scepticism – most of which are represented on the contemporary philosophical scene – come nowhere near refuting it. Once I have argued this, I will have completed my picture of the problem of the inescapable self as a problem about knowledge. I will then be ready to explore the versions of the problem of the inescapable self in which it shows up as a problem about ethics (chapters 3 and 4), and as a problem about the place of persons and/or minds in the world (chapters 5 and 6). It will only be time to think about how, if at all, we might solve the problem of the inescapable self once we can see all the different parts of the problem (chapter 7).

2.2 **Scepticism today:** the basic sceptical argument

To get us into the contemporary debate about the problem of scepticism, we first need a contemporary way of stating the problem. I shall follow Barry Stroud by laying out the basic sceptical argument as four steps (the premises) leading to a fifth step (the conclusion), like this:[1]

1. We seem to know about the external world by experiencing it.
2. But our experience could be exactly the same even if there were no external world.
3. So we don't know that our experience has been produced directly by an external world, rather than by a dream or an evil demon, or by the Matrix, or by Putnam's nefarious neurosurgeons manipulating brains in vats.
4. If we don't know that crazy sceptical hypotheses like the ones in step 3 are false, then we don't know anything much about the external world.
5. So scepticism is justified.

This statement of the basic sceptical argument is going to be fundamental to the rest of this chapter.

Any decent argument, the basic sceptical argument included, has a number of different 'working parts'. You can disable a clock or a fridge if you remove just one vital component, while leaving everything else exactly as it is. Similarly, you can disable an argument by proving the falsity of just one of the premises that get you to the conclusion, or by showing that the conclusion does not follow from the premisses, while leaving everything else exactly as it is. (You might be justified in attacking at more than one point, of course; but you won't need to do so to refute the argument.)

The basic sceptical argument fails if any of steps 1 to 4 makes a false statement, or if any of steps 2 to 5 does not follow from earlier steps in the argument. So, in most contemporary attacks on the basic sceptical argument, philosophers try to put their finger on where the argument goes wrong by trying to identify a false premiss, or a step that does not follow from previous steps.

This chapter is structured by this search for a hole in the argument. I shall take each of the steps in turn, and describe at least some of the arguments that contemporary philosophers have put up, to show that this is the step where the basic sceptical argument fails. I shall conclude that all of these attacks on the basic sceptical argument are unsuccessful; hence, the basic sceptical argument remains unrefuted. Descartes's sceptical problems about the existence of the external world and other minds, and with them the problem of the inescapable self, are still unsolved today.

I hope my discussion will give the reader some sense of the dizzying intricacy and subtlety of modern philosophical argument. This is impressive even when, as here, the arguments are ultimately unsuccessful.

And so to work. Readers may find that bookmarking the first page of this chapter, where the basic sceptical argument has just been laid out, helps them to keep a grip on the shape of the argument as it develops. It is only fair to warn the reader that the argument will not be simple!

We begin with:

Step 1 We seem to know about the external world by experiencing it

This premiss is common ground between sceptics and non-sceptics. No one has thought this premiss worth denying, or thought that the basic sceptical argument might go wrong as early as this.

The second step needs more discussion:

2.3 **Step 2** But our experience could be exactly the same even if there were no external world

Many philosophers have attacked this premiss. Some of their attacks miss the point completely. For example, Daniel Dennett contends that we can't be brains in vats because it would be too technically difficult to make a brain in a vat seem to experience an environment as complex as ours.[2] The obvious problem with this response is that, if we are brains in vats, then the technical problems that Dennett describes are part of our illusion.

Not every attack on step 2 can be so swiftly dealt with. I shall consider five more impressive attacks, each of which will need fairly detailed treatment. The five attacks I'll consider, and reject, are these: the campaign against 'the way of ideas' (**2.3.1**); Wittgenstein's Private Language Argument (**2.3.2**); disjunctivism (**2.3.3**); Putnam's disquotation argument (**2.3.4**); and two versions of the idea that it just doesn't make sense to suppose that we could be in massive error of the sort that the sceptic imagines – Aristotle's (**2.3.5**) and Wittgenstein's (**2.3.6**).

2.3.1 The campaign against 'the way of ideas' 'What do we perceive besides our own ideas or sensations?' asks Berkeley.[3] His question is rhetorical: Berkeley means that we perceive *nothing* except our own ideas or sensations. This is an assumption that Berkeley inherits from Locke:

> Every man being conscious to himself that he thinks; and that which his mind is applied about whilst thinking being the ideas that are there [in his mind]...[4]

And Descartes:

> What was it about [my sense perceptions of the earth, sky and stars] that I perceived clearly? Just that the ideas, or thoughts, of such things appeared before my mind...But there was something else which I used to assert...This was that there were things outside me which were the sources of my ideas and which resembled them in all respects.[5]

Descartes, Locke and Berkeley, like many other philosophers since, take 'the way of ideas'. They take it for granted that all our experience is experience of our own ideas, and all our knowledge is knowledge of our own ideas. As a result, there is always a question about the correspondence of these ideas to what they are ideas of, out in the world. As it is sometimes picturesquely put, 'the veil of perception' always hangs between us and the world.

For Locke and Descartes, the sceptical problem is how to tell whether our 'knowledge of our own ideas' is *only* knowledge of our own ideas, or is also knowledge of the world as represented by those ideas. Now if there are no ideas, then it can't be true that any of our experience is experience of our own ideas. And if that isn't true, then maybe our experience couldn't be exactly the same if there were no external world. So maybe we can defeat the basic sceptical argument by attacking step 2, and do that by denying the assumption that all our experience is experience of our own ideas.

As critics have been pointing out at least since the time of Thomas Reid (1710–96), that assumption looks rather problematic anyway. It suggests the model of experience that Gilbert Ryle calls 'the inner Cartesian theatre'.[6] On this model, the mind provides a space or stage upon which there appears an object of inner perception, an idea. And I, the inner observer of this inner perception, sit in the audience and watch the performance.

You only need to state this model of experience to see its difficulties. The model commits itself to the existence not only of the ideas that appear on the stage of the inner theatre, but also of the inner theatre itself, not to mention the inner observer who occupies that theatre. These all look like weird entities. As the well-known principle called Ockham's Razor tells us, the best explanation is the one that does the most work with the fewest and most unsurprising assumptions. It would be much better to do without these weird entities if we can.

The model faces other problems besides its commitment to weird entities. If I experience the public world because an 'inner observer' in my head experiences a private world, that just raises the question of how my inner observer experiences his private world. Does the inner observer in my head have an 'inner inner observer' in *his* head? If he does, we're off on a vicious regress. If he doesn't, we still have no explanation of how his experience does happen. In any case, we can't even understand the proposal that there is an inner observer of inner objects unless we already understand the idea that there are normal, 'outer' observers of normal, 'outer' objects, and treat the inner case as an analogy to the outer case. But then it is reasonable to ask how exactly the analogy is supposed to work. And that is a hard question too.

How might we develop a different picture of experience? Roderick Chisholm proposes an *adverbial* account.[7] On this account, experience of (say) trees or dogs does not have weird objects called ideas or sense-data, because such experience does not have any objects, apart from the trees or dogs. To say that I have a perception of a tree does not commit us to the existence both of the tree and also of something called my perception of the tree. Perceptions are not themselves objects; they are ways of being affected by objects. My perceptions and experiences are not *things* that somehow appear to me, as ideas or sense-data would presumably be. Instead, my perceptions and experiences are ways I can be affected.

Another alternative to the way of ideas is the *dispositional* model of perception. As David Armstrong puts it, the dispositional view says that perception is simply a disposition to acquire information: perception is 'nothing but the acquiring of true or false beliefs concerning the current state of the organism's body and environment'.[8] So perceiving trees, for instance, is just being disposed to acquire beliefs about trees.

By one or other of these routes, the first proposal about how to attack step 2 of the basic sceptical argument denies that there are any such things as ideas. The first proposal replaces this model with an adverbial model, in which perception is a way of being affected, or by an informational model, in which perception is all about dispositions to acquire beliefs; or by some other alternative model of what perception involves.

All very interesting. But does it really help us against scepticism? Well, it may help us against Descartes's, Locke's and Berkeley's forms of scepticism, all of which depend on the claim that what we experience is always ideas or sense-data. But this is a red herring, because scepticism does not have to make that claim. Step 2 of the basic sceptical argument says that 'our experience could be exactly the same even if there were no external world'. 'Our experience being exactly the same' does not have to involve our having exactly the same ideas, whether or not those ideas correspond to anything in reality. It might equally involve our being affected exactly the same way, whether or not that way corresponds to anything in reality. Or it might involve our being disposed to acquire exactly the same beliefs, whether or not those beliefs correspond to anything in reality. Scepticism is not dependent on Descartes's and Locke's ideas-based model of perception. It can be stated equally well using an adverbial model of perception, or a dispositional model of perception.[9]

It looks like it is no use to attack step 2 – the claim that experience could be exactly the same even if there were no external world – by attacking the ideas-based model of perception. However, we should not leave the topic without mentioning what may well be the most powerful way of running this attack. This is the famous Private Language Argument of Ludwig Wittgenstein (1889–1951). There has been enormous controversy about the correct interpretation of this argument, which I cannot enter into here.[10] I will simply present and criticize my own interpretation of the argument, which is not quite the orthodox one.

2.3.2 The Private Language Argument is designed to refute the basic sceptical argument by refuting step 2.[11] It begins by asking: what would it be like to be in the solipsist's predicament? If solipsism were true, how would I, the solipsist, have succeeded in making the apparent sense that I have made of my experience? Wittgenstein replies that I could only have made the apparent sense that I have made, by learning to classify my own experiences inside my own head:

> Let us imagine the following case. I want to keep a diary about the recurrence of a certain sensation. To this end I associate it with the sign 'S' and write this sign in a calendar for every day on which I have the sensation.[12]

You might do something like this, of course. People do keep diaries of their aches and twinges, for instance if they have an arthritis check-up coming and want to supply the doctor with some data. However, when they keep such diaries, they use *public* names for their twinges, names that are words of a common language which they learned to use from other people, and their use of which other people can and do criticize and correct: for example, the words 'ache' and 'twinge'.

It is crucial to Wittgenstein's argument that the sign S is not a word of a common language, but a *private* sign, which is supposed to get its meaning only from my decision that it has a particular meaning: the decision I express by saying to myself 'S means *this sensation here*'. The point of the Private Language Argument is that no word could possibly get its meaning in this way.

To see why not, consider any occasion, after my initial decision that 'S means *this sensation here*', on which I try to use S. Is my new use of S correct or incorrect? I could call it either, and the trouble is that it seems to be entirely up to me which I say. By that I don't just mean that I can fool myself into thinking that I am using S correctly when really I am not. Rather, I mean this: nothing determined what S was to mean the first time I used it, except for my decision at that time. So likewise nothing determines what S is to mean the second or the third time I use it, except for my decision at *these* times.

But 'the use of [a] word stands in need of a justification which everybody understands':[13] one person's decisions, all on their own, cannot give any sign a meaning. Why not? Because my decision, too, is a private object. So not only is it true that nothing determines the meaning of S except my decision that 'The meaning of S is X.' It's also true that nothing determines the meaning of *this* decision that 'The meaning of S is to be X' – except, presumably, a further decision that 'The meaning of "The meaning of S is to be X" is Y.' And now we have an obviously hopeless regress.

No sign, Wittgenstein concludes, has a meaning without a 'criterion of correctness' – a way of telling whether the sign has been used rightly or wrongly, such as we appeal to in our public language when we say, for example, 'The traffic light is green, not red.' In contrast to the public case, I can decide anything I like about whether I have used S rightly or wrongly. So it would be vacuous to appeal to my decisions to supply a criterion of correctness for the use of S:

> One would like to say: whatever is going to seem right to me is right. And that only means that here we can't talk about 'right'.[14]

No term can have a meaning unless you can make a non-arbitrary distinction between using that term correctly and using it incorrectly. But private decisions about the meanings of private terms like S cannot establish a non-arbitrary distinction between using S correctly and using it incorrectly. So private terms like S cannot have a meaning. So there cannot be a language consisting of such private terms. This is the sense in which there cannot be a private language.

This is the Private Language Argument. How is it relevant to step 2 of the basic sceptical argument – the claim that experience could be exactly the same even if there were no external world?

According to Wittgenstein, what the Private Language Argument shows about solipsism is that the solipsist cannot possibly succeed in the task that we set him – of making sense of his own experience. To do that, Wittgenstein claims, the solipsist would have to learn to classify his own experiences inside his own head. But he could only do this by establishing a private language. And this would mean starting with a series of decisions such as 'S means *this sensation here*.' The Private Language Argument shows that no language whatever can be established by such decisions. Therefore, anyone in the solipsist's predicament can have no language. (The argument shows that he cannot have a private one; the assumption that he is a solipsist shows that he cannot have a public one.) By contrast, *we* obviously do have a language – a public one. Therefore we are not in the solipsist's predicament. And, contrary to step 2, things would be utterly different if we were.

The Private Language Argument is one of philosophy's most famous and most fascinating arguments. Does it work as a proof that there can't be a private language? Maybe – and maybe not: for my own part, I don't *seem* to find any difficulty in devising and applying private code-names for my sensations.[15]

Does the Private Language Argument work against scepticism? No, for a simple reason. This is that it misdescribes the solipsist's predicament. The solipsist is not trying to *set up* a language, private or public. He already has a language, and it is an apparently public one. The solipsist is not wrestling with the problem of how, if at all, he can contrive to give names to his own sensations or sense-data. Like the non-solipsist, he is using language in what Wittgenstein would call a public way: there seem to be other people around him, who seem to be capable of criticizing or questioning his use of this public language. The solipsist's problem is not the sensations, but the 'seem to be'. His problem is whether the *apparent* other people who act as external regulators of his language are *real* external regulators. If they are not, maybe the solipsist only seems to be using a language: he is deceived even in his idea that what he says makes sense. But this is a perfectly real sceptical possibility. We will meet it again in **2.3.4**.

2.3.3 Disjunctivism   The adverbial and disposition theories of perception try to block the sceptical argument by denying the existence of ideas or sense-data (**2.3.1**). Another possibility is that perception *sometimes* involves sense-data – but only when things go wrong. In a case of successful perception, you don't perceive an idea of a tree; you perceive a *tree*. It's only in cases of *mis*perception that what you perceive is merely an idea of a tree.

John McDowell is a prominent advocate of this way of blocking step 2 of the basic sceptical argument, which we may call *disjunctivism*. As its name suggests, disjunctivism is an either/or thesis. It is the thesis that 'an appearance that such-and-such is the case can be *either* a mere appearance *or* the fact that such-and-such is the case making itself perceptually manifest to someone'. The proposal is that our experience is not 'exactly the same' when we are deceived in our perceptions as when we are not deceived:

> the object of the experience in the deceptive cases is a mere appearance. But in the non-deceptive cases the object of the experience is [not] a mere appearance…On the contrary, the appearance that is presented to one in such cases is a matter of the fact itself being disclosed to the experiencer. So appearances are no longer conceived as in general intervening between the experiencing subject and the world.[16]

Maybe you don't perceive the very same thing in deceptive and non-deceptive cases. (Maybe; though so far as I can see, McDowell never actually argues this thesis rather than simply proposing it.) But can you tell whether you are perceiving the thing itself, or the mere appearance? McDowell finds it obvious that you can't:

> Of course we are fallible in our judgements as to the shape of…the world as we find it. That is to say that we are vulnerable to the world playing us false; and when the world does not play us false we are indebted to it. But that is something we must simply learn to live with, rather than recoiling into the fantasy of a sphere in which our control is total.[17]

If McDowell is right, step 2 is false. Our experience isn't exactly the same, no matter whether scepticism is true or false: we have one sort of experience where scepticism is true, and another sort of experience where scepticism is false. Unfortunately, however, we can't tell which sort of experience we are having. So step 2 is true *for all we can tell* – even if it is in fact false. Our experience does not put us in a position to rule out sceptical hypotheses.

McDowell's proposal does not refute the basic sceptical argument. (In the last sentence of the quotation just given, he himself seems to admit as much.) It just prompts a restatement of step 2. Instead of saying that 'Our experience could *be* exactly the same even if there were no external world', step 2 will now say 'Our experience could *feel* exactly the same even if there were no external world.' With this adjustment made, the basic sceptical argument can carry on as before.

2.3.4 The disquotation argument The fourth attack on step 2 that I'll review comes from Hilary Putnam – the originator of **0.1**'s nightmare scenario where we are all just brains in a vat of nutrient fluid, having our cerebral cortices automatically stimulated to create the illusion of our familiar external world.[18] (In this section I shall stick with this 'we' version of Putnam's nightmare. Obviously we could run an 'I' version too, about a single envatted brain.)

Putnam's own response to his nightmare scenario is to argue that the envatment hypothesis only seems possible; it isn't really possible. To prove his case, Putnam asks this question: if we *were* in this bizarre predicament, what kind of thoughts would we be able to have?

> The brains in the vat are *functioning brains*, and they function by the same rules as brains do in the actual world...But the fact that they are conscious and intelligent does not mean that their words refer to what our words refer to...Do their verbalisations containing the word 'tree' actually refer to *trees*?...Can they refer to *external* objects at all? (As opposed to, for example, objects in the image produced by the automatic machinery.)[19]

Putnam's answer is 'No'. The brains in the vat can't refer to, or talk about, the external world. Why not? Because 'there is no connection between the *word* "tree" as used by these brains and actual trees':

> Their images, words, etc. are qualitatively identical with images, words, etc. which do represent trees in *our* world...But qualitative similarity to something which represents does not make something a representation...The brains in a vat are not thinking about real trees when they think 'There is a tree in front of me' because there is nothing by virtue of which their thought 'tree' represents actual trees.[20]

Here Putnam is presupposing the view that you can't refer to things that you are not connected with in the right way. (The Sunday-best name for this view is the 'causal theory of reference'.) The envatted brains can't refer to (real live) trees, because their experience has never brought them into causal contact with such trees. Consequently, they may have images in their consciousness that look to them just like trees, and words to refer to these images. But they do not have images *of* trees, and they do not have words to refer to trees. So when an envatted brain thinks 'There is a tree in front of me', it cannot mean the same by 'tree' as I do. As philosophers say, the language used by the envatted brains does not 'disquote': '*tree*', as the brains use it, does not mean *tree*.

For this reason, the brains use almost no referring terms in the same way as we use them. One exception is this: the brains can use the word 'I' in just the same sense as we use it, to refer to a present-tense self-consciousness.[21] But as we saw in **1.4**, this doesn't help the conscious mind present in the envatted brain to know anything else *beyond* itself and its own existence − for instance, that it is a brain in a vat. In particular, it doesn't help the brains to use 'vat', 'nutrient fluid' or 'brain' as we use these terms. When they use the word 'vats', they do not refer to real vats. Perhaps they do not refer to anything. If they do refer to something, presumably they refer to the illusions of vats that can be created by the automatic machinery. Likewise, when the brains use the word 'brains', if they refer to anything, they refer to illusions of brains, not to real brains. And so on.

From this it follows that, if we *are* brains in a vat, we cannot have the thought that we are brains in a vat. Nor, indeed, can we have the thought that we are *not* brains in a vat:

If we are really the brains in a vat, then what we now mean by 'we are brains in a vat' is that *we are brains in a vat in the image*…But part of the hypothesis that we are brains in a vat is that we aren't brains in a vat in the image...So if we are brains in a vat, then the sentence 'we are brains in a vat' says something false.[22]

But obviously, the sentence 'We are brains in a vat' also says something false if we are not brains in a vat. So what it says is false, whether or not we are brains in a vat. Either way, then, we are not brains in a vat. And a parallel treatment will deal with other crazy sceptical hypotheses, such as the Matrix hypothesis.

So, contrary to step 2 of the basic sceptical argument, our experience would not be exactly as it is, if some crazy sceptical hypothesis like envatment were true. On the contrary, the way our experience is entails that no such sceptical hypothesis can possibly be true.

Putnam's argument seems to develop a suggestion of Wittgenstein's: 'I cannot seriously suppose that I am at this moment dreaming. Someone who, dreaming, says "I am dreaming", even if he speaks audibly in doing so, is no more right than if he said in his dream "It is raining", while it was in fact raining.'[23] The argument is ingenious. However, as I shall now show, it fails to exclude scepticism.

Putnam's argument depends upon the claim that there is not just one sentence consisting of the sounds 'We are brains in a vat'. There are two different sentences in two different languages which consist of those same sounds:

What the sentence sounds like	Language	Translation into normal English
1 'We are brains in a vat'	Normal English (i.e. the language we speak if we are not brains in a vat)	'We are brains in a vat'
2 'We are brains in a vat'	Vat-English (i.e. the language spoken by the brains in the vat)	'In the image generated by the machinery, we are brains in a vat'

Putnam is right that sentence (1) is false whenever uttered. Indeed, (1) is false by definition: it is a sentence of Normal English, and Normal English is the language we speak if we're *not* brains in a vat.

Likewise, Putnam is right that sentence (2) is false whenever uttered. (2) is a sentence of Vat-English which, translated into Normal English, says that *the image we have of ourselves* is that we are brains in a vat. But if we are brains in a vat, then our image of ourselves is precisely not that we are brains in a vat, because the envatment machinery is designed to deceive us. So in Vat-English too, the sentence consisting of the sounds 'We are brains in a vat' is bound to be false.

Does this show that there is no case in which it could be true that we are brains in a vat? No, it doesn't. It only shows that if we are brains in a vat, then we can't say so in our own language (because Vat-English has no words for 'brains', 'vat' and so on). Putnam has not closed off the sceptical possibility that the Normal English sentence 'We are brains in a vat' *would* be true as spoken by the brains, *if* the brains could speak Normal English. But in Putnam's scenario this is the only sceptical possibility worth excluding.

The question is: are *we* speaking Normal English or Vat-English? If we are speaking Normal English, everything's fine, because by definition we are not envatted.

But if we are speaking Vat-English, everything is *not* fine, even though, as Putnam's argument shows, the Vat-English sentence 'We are brains in a vat' is false whenever we utter it. The guaranteed falsity of the Vat-English sentence 'We are brains in a vat' is only the guaranteed falsity of its Normal English translation: 'In the image generated by the machinery, we are brains in a vat.' And obviously, the guaranteed falsity of *that* sentence is no guarantee at all that we are not brains in a vat. On the contrary: since Vat-English is by definition the language of the envatted brains, the supposition that we are speaking Vat-English entails that we *are* brains in a vat – even though we can't say so.

So can we tell whether we are speaking Normal English or Vat-English? If we could, the sceptic really would be refuted. But we can't. As Putnam's own argument proves, the brains in the vat can't have the Normal English thought that they are brains in vats. By the same token, then, they cannot have the thought that they are speaking Vat-English, the language of envatted brains. But none of this shows that they *aren't* speaking Vat-English (or aren't brains in a vat). It only shows that they can't think the Normal-English thought that they are speaking Vat-English (and are brains in a vat).

Conclusion: if you are a brain in a vat, speaking Vat-English, you won't be able to tell that you are a brain in a vat, speaking Vat-English. Like the difference that disjunctivism emphasized, between deceptive and non-deceptive experience, the difference between Normal English and Vat-English, between being humans and being brains in a vat, is 'invisible from the inside'. Putnam's argument does not answer the sceptical question 'How can I tell whether or not I am a brain in a vat?' It simply replaces it with another sceptical question: 'How can I tell whether I am speaking Vat-English or Normal English?' So Putnam's argument fails to disprove step 2 of the basic sceptical argument – the claim that our experience could be exactly the same even if there were no external world.

Here is one moral we should draw from this discussion of Putnam's disquotation argument: semantic externalism is not enough. Let me pause to develop this moral.

You can if you like devise a theory of the meanings of words (a semantics) that makes those meanings depend on the existence of an *external* world (thus, a semantic *externalism*). This move is supposed to show that, since we know how to talk about e.g. trees and brains, we must already be in touch with an external world just to talk about them. But the move has no such effect. It proves only this: either we are in touch with the external world, or else we are mistaken to think that we really know how to talk about it. (Compare my response to the Private Language Argument in **2.3.2**.) The sceptic can simply take the second alternative. There is no more to disturb him in Putnam's argument than there was in McDowell's disjunctivism (which, of course, is also a version of externalism: externalism about perceptual content, as we might call it).

Externalism, usually but not always semantic, is all the rage these days. As a research programme for understanding the workings of our awareness of meanings, contents, experiences or whatever, it has much to recommend it in many ways. But externalism is not enough, on its own, to refute scepticism about the external world. Against serious scepticism, externalism simply begs the question.

As further evidence of this, consider **Sartrean externalism**, a position expounded by Mark Rowlands in his discussion of Sartre's externalist claim that 'All consciousness is consciousness *of* something.'[24] As Rowlands puts it, 'Consciousness is pure emptiness: it exists only as directedness towards things that are other than itself [which are] not part of consciousness.'[25] It is not clear how cogent Rowlands thinks a Sartrean argument against scepticism can be.[26] At any rate, the Sartrean argument is not cogent. The very most it shows is that there is a distinction between consciousness and its objects. Since – as we know from Freud – there is such a thing as the *sub*conscious, this is not even enough to prove that those objects are outside the mind.

Consider another externalism, the **Wittgensteinian externalism** found in writers such as Anthony Grayling. Developing ideas similar (but not identical) to those found in Wittgenstein's Private Language Argument, Grayling suggests, in an online paper, that 'talk of an egocentric predicament' (such as the inescapable self presents) 'fails to make sense':

> This is because it turns on the idea of a wholly subjective perspective, in which the subject is supposed to recognise his perspective as his own without having any way of locating it in a setting of other perspectives, since these *ex hypothesi* do not exist.

And what is wrong with this supposition, we might ask? Grayling replies:

> it would seem that the notion of a sense of self, or at least of a sustained centre of experience which in some sense recognises that experience as its own, cannot be rendered intelligible independently of systematic relations to other such perspectives – other selves – and this implies that to be a self is necessarily to be a member of a community of such things.

So you wouldn't think of yourself as a self, unless you had learned to relate yourself to *other* selves. And so, 'the notion of an egocentric predicament is incoherent'.

I call Grayling's argument Wittgensteinian because of its obvious affinities to the Private Language Argument.[27] There are traces of a similar argument in Kant before Wittgenstein, and in Jürgen Habermas and Peter Strawson after him.[28] I call Grayling's argument *externalism*, because its point is that the very meaning of the word 'self' is constituted by external factors, and constrained by external rules, including the rules of language itself. Whatever we call it, its failure to refute scepticism can be quickly shown. Grayling's position rests on the premiss that we can make no sense of the notion of a self 'independently of systematic relations to other selves'. But even if this is true, it's as hard as it was with the Private Language Argument to see why these other selves would have to be *real* to play their constituting role. And if they do have to be real to play this role, then as before the sceptical question is simply relocated. The question becomes, not whether there are any other selves, but whether *I* am really a self (since I can't be if there are no other selves).

2.3.5 The unintelligibility of massive error (I): *Aristotle* Aristotle makes a fifth sort of attempt to block step 2's claim that our experience could be exactly the same even if there were no external world. Aristotle knows all about scepticism from his teacher Plato, whose views I mentioned in the Prelude (**0.1**). Aristotle also knows about the earlier Greek thinkers who took scepticism even further than Plato. For instance, there was Zeno (490–425 BC), best known for his celebrated paradoxes of motion, such as Achilles and the tortoise,[29] all of which were designed to show that motion (and the rest of the physical world) could not possibly exist. There was also Gorgias (483–378 BC), who famously argued (1) that nothing exists; (2) that if anything did exist, it would be unknowable; and (3) that if anything did exist and could be known, this knowledge would be incommunicable.

Despite his familiarity with scepticism, Aristotle, unlike Descartes, never wrings his hands over the possibility that everything everyone has ever believed might turn out to be false. On the contrary, Aristotle takes it for granted that true belief is the norm, false belief a deviation from that norm. Aristotle thinks that it could not be the other way round, with true belief the deviation and false belief the norm. For Aristotle, it's a matter of scientific necessity that the percentage of our beliefs that are true must be higher than the percentage that are false. (At any rate, this is certainly true if 'we' are competent observers of the world. Aristotle is an elitist, and so is sometimes inclined to deny that most observers are competent.)

How do we manage to be so successful in acquiring knowledge? Aristotle's answer is that humans are creatures equipped with a natural capacity to have knowledge of the world:

in the opening words of his *Metaphysics*, 'All human beings by nature seek to know.' It is an axiom of Aristotelian science that, in general and in the long run, natural capacities get realized. So in general and in the long run, we do have knowledge of the world (or we will). Aristotle's solution to the problem of scepticism is as simple as that.

It's not that Aristotle thinks that false belief cannot occur at all. As he had learned from Plato's *Theaetetus*, it is just as paradoxical to say that *no* beliefs are false as to say that *all* beliefs are false.[30] Of course *some* beliefs are false. But any false belief is the result of a malfunction in the natural system whereby we gain knowledge. Since, necessarily, natural systems don't *normally* malfunction, we can be confident that most of our beliefs are true.

The sceptic will ask why Aristotle feels so sure that natural systems don't normally malfunction. Maybe the way things are in our world is precisely the result of massive natural malfunctioning! More specifically, the sceptic may ask why Aristotle feels sure that our natural system points us towards believing what is true and not, perhaps, towards what is false, or what has survival value. Aristotle's bluff, dogmatic confidence will hardly satisfy the sceptic.

Not that Aristotle cares; he doesn't think it's his job to satisfy the sceptic. We saw one reason why he thinks this in **1.3**. Aristotle has an anti-Cartesian method in inquiry. His method is to refine pre-existing beliefs: 'All teaching and all intellectual learning come about from already existing knowledge.'[31] If we can make good enough sense of the beliefs we already have by ironing out the contradictions and obvious mistakes in them, we have no reason to look any further for the truth. 'What *appears* true to everyone, we say that this *is* true,' Aristotle concludes, and sees no better alternative assumption: 'Anyone who undermines this conviction will replace it with nothing *more* convincing.'[32]

A second reason why Aristotle is not interested in satisfying the sceptic is that, for him, the sceptic asks the wrong questions. 'Not every philosophical problem', he remarks drily, 'should be examined. We only need to look at the ones that can be resolved by argument, rather than by perception – or by a beating.'[33] If the sceptic cannot just *see* that knowledge is possible, there is no point trying to argue with him (though you might try knocking the truth into him). When the sceptic starts asking his questions, Aristotle thinks, he simply shows himself up as a poor inquirer, by starting in the wrong place. Aristotle thinks that this is an important mistake; but he does not think that it is a philosophically interesting mistake.

In short, Aristotle is just not interested in scepticism. Like a fair number of contemporary philosophers, he simply wants to change the subject and talk about something else. At times we may be forgiven for feeling the same way. All the same, to change the subject is not to solve the problem. In the end, Aristotle's response to scepticism is too perfunctory – and too dogmatic – to be intellectually satisfying.

This word 'dogmatic' is an interesting one, by the way. Aristotle's sort of response (perhaps that should be sort-of response) to scepticism was first called *dogmatism* by the Greek sceptics – Pyrrho (360–270 BC), Carneades (213–129 BC) and others – who lived in the two centuries after Aristotle. When these sceptics accused Aristotle and his followers of being dogmatic, what they meant was the specific charge that he was affirming a judgement (Greek *dogma*) that he could not know for certain was true. In our modern sense, the word 'dogmatic' is less philosophically precise and more pejorative than this: it has overtones of obstinacy, dismissiveness and high-handedness. When we look closely at what Aristotle says about scepticism, it is easy to see how this modern pejorative sense of 'dogmatic' arose from the original technical sense.

2.3.6 The unintelligibility of massive error (II): *Wittgenstein* Our sixth position is another Wittgensteinian one. In his posthumous notebook *On Certainty*, Wittgenstein writes as follows:

> The *questions* that we raise and our *doubts* depend on the fact that some propositions are exempt from doubt, are as it were like hinges on which those [doubts] turn.
> That is to say, it belongs to the logic of our scientific investigations that certain things are *in deed* not doubted...
> My *life* consists in my being content to accept many things.[34]

The anti-sceptical strategy hinted at in the last quotation suggests that sceptical doubts are always raised against a background, or within a context, which cannot itself be put in doubt. Without that context, the doubt itself makes no sense: 'The game of doubting itself presupposes certainty'; 'A doubt without an end is not even a doubt.'[35] This implies the denial of step 2. If we could not so much as raise a doubt if some crazy sceptical hypothesis were true, then clearly, under scepticism, our experience would not be exactly as it is.

Wittgenstein's point is not that there is some special class of privileged propositions that we simply can't doubt. That would be a rather Cartesian point, and Wittgenstein's philosophy is anything but Cartesian. His point is that, whenever we choose to doubt some particular proposition, we only succeed in doubting that proposition because there are lots of other propositions that – at that time and in that context – we just don't doubt.

Sometimes, for example, doubt is reasonable in the context of chess: you might doubt whether you should castle or get your pawns out. Or in the context of geography: you might doubt whether Lusaka is in Zambia or in Kenya. Or in the context of arithmetic: did you add up your shopping bill correctly? In each of these contexts, doubts make sense. But that is only because, in each context, there is a very great deal that is *not* in doubt: the existence of the chessboard, the reliability of the atlas, the possibility of *generally* getting shopping sums right. This background makes it possible to have doubts, and possible (in principle) to resolve them. Where there is no such background, says Wittgenstein, the doubt itself makes no sense. That is what is wrong with sceptical doubt.

One way of putting the point is this: Descartes went wrong right at the beginning. Descartes – you could say – begins his philosophy by arguing that since *any* of our beliefs might be false, therefore *all* of our beliefs might be false (**1.1**). But this is a fallacious argument. (Compare: 'Any of these strangers might be the Scarlet Pimpernel; therefore every one of these strangers might be the Scarlet Pimpernel.') What is true of *any* belief is not necessarily true of *every* belief. So – the claim would be – Descartes's system rests on a fallacy (the 'any/all fallacy', as it is sometimes called). However, this line of thought is not convincing. Descartes does not need to commit this fallacy to make his basic point that, for all we can tell, there is a great deal more error around than we think – and that there can be error in our background beliefs, too.

A closely related argument which looks more plausible is developed by Donald Davidson, who claims that the unintelligibility of massive error follows from the 'principle of charity' – the principle that we should interpret other people's utterances so as to make as many of them as possible come out as true and reasonable.[36] A rather similar case is made by Crispin Wright's argument that Cartesian scepticism refutes itself because it presupposes the reliability of our methods of reasoning and perceiving. I cannot go into the intricacies of Davidson's and Wright's arguments here. But I can make some simpler points about the Wittgensteinian prototype of their arguments.

Wittgenstein's idea is that doubts only make sense in some contexts, and not in others. Each of these contexts is what

Wittgenstein famously calls a 'language game'. The term is perhaps an unfortunate one, as it may well have reinforced the popular perception that philosophy is 'just playing with words' (**0.3**). But there is nothing frivolous about Wittgensteinian language games. They are called games, not because they are frivolous, but because they are particular and autonomous forms of human linguistic activity with their own rules. The trouble with crazy sceptical hypotheses, according to Wittgenstein, is that they don't crop up in any of the various language games that make up the texture of ordinary life in the world. That is why it doesn't make sense to discuss them.

The more you think about this claim, the less plausible it looks. When I ask the question 'Am I now dreaming?', it certainly seems to make sense for me to raise this question, and for me or others to offer answers to it. So how do we explain this appearance of sense, if it is actually a mirage? Wittgenstein offers no satisfactory answer to this question.

If, on the other hand, the sceptic's discourse does make sense, then there seem to be two swift ways of disposing of Wittgenstein's objection that the sceptic isn't playing any legitimate language game in his discourse, and so is talking nonsense. The first is to say that, since the sceptic is not in fact talking nonsense, it can't be a test for the meaningfulness of any discourse that it should form part of a Wittgensteinian language game. The second is to say that, since the sceptic's discourse makes sense, it must form part of a Wittgensteinian language game – a particular form of human linguistic activity with its own rules – called the 'scepticism game'. Either way, Wittgenstein has to be wrong to think that his notion of a language game can be deployed to show the unintelligibility of scepticism. So this manoeuvre does not block step 2 of the sceptical argument.

This concludes my discussion of step 2 of the basic sceptical argument, the claim that our experience could be exactly the same even if there were no external world. I have examined six ways of attacking step 2, and argued that none of them succeeds. It's time to move on to step 3.

2.4 **Step 3** So we don't know that our experience has been produced directly by an external world, rather than in some crazy sceptical way

The great English philosopher Bertrand Russell (1872–1970) puts one simple way of rejecting step 3 like this:

> No logical absurdity results from the hypothesis that the world consists of nothing but myself...and that everything else is mere fancy. But although this is not logically impossible, there is no reason whatever to suppose that it is true; and it is, in fact, a less simple hypothesis, viewed as a means of accounting for the facts of our own life, than the commonsense hypothesis that there really are objects independent of us, whose action on us causes our sensations.[37]

If the sceptic and the non-sceptic accept steps 1 and 2, then they agree with each other that we have experiences that are *just as if* there were an external world. We can then ask: what is the *best explanation* of these experiences? Russell answers that the simplest explanation is the best; and the simplest explanation is the commonsense explanation. So we know that there is an external world because we seem to experience an external world; and the best explanation of our seeming to experience it, is that we really do experience it.

Russell's argument is an instance of the form of argument known as *abduction*, or *inference to the best explanation*. One problem with his argument is simply the question whether it really yields *knowledge* of an external world, or merely the conjecture that there *probably is* such a world. (Notice Russell's words elsewhere: 'For the present, let us assume *as a working hypothesis* the existence of other people, and of unperceived physical things.'[38])

A second problem for Russell is one that faces any argument that appeals to inference to the best explanation. The problem is the move from 'X is the best (or simplest) explanation of Y' to 'X is the true explanation of Y'. Unless Y is the *complete* set of *all* the relevant facts (and how can we tell that?), this move is obviously invalid. Suppose sixteen very similar murders occur in one city in one month. On the facts we have, the best (and simplest) explanation of the murders might well be that the murders were all committed by the same criminal. It obviously doesn't follow that this explanation is *true*: there will be many facts that we are not explaining by this hypothesis, because we don't know them. Inference to the best or simplest explanation is obviously a useful intellectual strategy, perhaps an indispensable one. All the same, the best explanation won't always be the true explanation. Likewise with the simplest explanation.

There is another problem about 'simplest', too. It isn't obviously simpler to explain our experience Russell's way rather than Malebranche's or Berkeley's ways (**1.8**). Which is the simpler hypothesis: to suppose with the sceptic that there is nothing outside me except an evil demon? Or to suppose with Russell that there is an external world outside me, containing New York, dromedaries, Beethoven's 'Emperor' piano concerto, Andromeda, penicillin, *art trouvé*, *War and Peace*, tax returns, castanets, Australian Rules football, the grebes in Auckland harbour, and a pig named St Francis Xavier? As Berkeley liked to point out, to suppose that the external world exists is to suppose the existence of something enormously more complex than any experience we might ever need to explain. The hypothesis that there is an external material world is not a *simple* explanation at all.

As for calling it the *best* explanation of our experience, this looks dangerously close to saying merely that we accept this explanation because we want to accept it. But to say that we only believe in the external world because we want to, is to admit, as David Hume for example admits, that we have no good *reason* to believe in it. In other words, it is to admit the truth of scepticism.

2.5 **Step 4** If we don't know that crazy sceptical hypotheses like the ones in step 3 are false, then we don't know anything much about the external world

Step 4 of the basic sceptical argument is the step most often attacked by its opponents today. Here is an explanation of the idea behind step 4.

Suppose you are a no-nonsense, commonsensical, unsceptical person who claims to possess all the usual knowledge of the external world. So, to take G. E. Moore's favourite example of everyday knowledge of the external world,[39] you claim that:

A I can see my hand in front of my face.

Now **A** entails **B**:

B I am not a victim of a crazy sceptical hypothesis.

If **A** is true, then **B** must be true. If I really can see my hand in front of my face (and have all the other usual knowledge of the external world), then I can't be a victim of a crazy sceptical hypothesis.

So what does it take for me to *know* that I can see my hand in front of my face? Many philosophers think that what it takes is captured by the Closure Principle:

The Closure Principle Knowledge is closed under known entailment: if you know *p*, and know that *p* entails *q*, then you also know *q*.

So if I am to know **A**, that 'I can see my hand in front of my face', I must know everything that I know is entailed by **A**. For example, I must know **B**, that 'I am not a victim of a crazy sceptical hypothesis.' But as Descartes showed, I *don't* know **B**, and neither does anybody else. Unless someone already has a disproof of scepticism, no one can prove that she is not a brain in a vat, or the victim of an evil demon or the Matrix. So I don't know **B**; and I am not entitled to claim to know **A** unless I do know **B**; so I can't say that I have the kind of knowledge of the external world of which **B** is an example. The Closure Principle gives us a very quick argument indeed for scepticism.

2.5.1 A quick and dirty argument against scepticism Of course, you could also use the Closure Principle to argue *against* scepticism. You could insist that you do know **A**, that you can see your hand in front of your face, and use your assurance of **A**, and other homely evidences of the external world, as a basis for insisting on **B** – that you are not a victim of a crazy sceptical hypothesis. You can't be, because you know **A**, and know that **A** entails **B**! On this view, the Closure Principle *itself* guarantees the falsity of scepticism. We don't need any other reason for denying crazy sceptical hypotheses. As Moore argues, the brute fact of our knowledge of the external world is itself sufficient reason to deny them.

This is a pretty quick argument against scepticism. But perhaps it is also a rather dirty one. What justifies this brusque confidence that we do have knowledge of the external world? Philosophers who *begin* the discussion of knowledge and scepticism by affirming that they know the external world are helping themselves, right at the start of the inquiry, to what's meant to be its main goal. This response to scepticism is another example of dogmatism (**2.3.5**). As with Aristotelian dogmatism, there is something unsatisfactorily perfunctory about it.

Most philosophers are not prepared to use the quick and dirty argument against scepticism. Instead, they attack step 4 of the basic sceptical argument by questioning the Closure Principle – the principle that if you know *p*, and know that *p* entails *q*, then you must also know *q*. Here are three ways of questioning it. I'll label them *over-demandingness*, *relevant alternatives* and *reliablism*, and argue that all three fail. This will leave the Closure Principle, and step 4 of the basic sceptical argument, intact.

2.5.2 Demandingness Perhaps the most obvious problem with the Closure Principle is that it looks as if it may be *over-demanding*. This is because, for each thing we know, it requires us to know indefinitely many other things as well.

The Closure Principle tells us that if we know *p*, and know that *p* entails *q*, then we must know *q* as well. But any truth entails, and obviously entails, indefinitely many other truths. For example, 'I am sitting at my desk' obviously entails the denial of all the sceptical hypotheses: 'I am not dreaming', 'I am not a victim of the Matrix', 'I am not being deceived by an evil demon', 'I am not a brain in a vat', and so on. It also entails – and again, obviously entails – the denial of all sorts of more-or-less humdrum non-sceptical alternatives to sitting at my desk: 'I am not running in the Sydney marathon', 'I am not buying blackcurrants at the greengrocer's', and so on.

So according to the Closure Principle, I can't know that 'I am sitting at my desk' is true, unless I know not only that all the sceptical alternatives are false – I am not a brain in a vat, not in the Matrix, etc.; but also that all the humdrum alternatives are false as well – I am not running in any marathon, I am not at the greengrocer's, etc. But, says the demandingness objection, there's just too much of this stuff that I have to know is false before I can count as knowing that I'm sitting at my desk. It's psychologically impossible that, before you adopt any belief, you should first close off all these alternatives, both sceptical and non-sceptical. There simply isn't time. And anyway (the objection continues), it isn't important to close them all off. In practice, if I am trying to decide whether I am sitting at my desk, I will do it simply by taking a look at my own position. I will make no effort whatever to exclude the possibility that I might be a brain in a vat, or running in some marathon. I will simply ignore these possibilities. And I have the right to ignore them, because the Closure Principle's requirement that I take them seriously is an over-demanding requirement.

There are at least two ways of answering the demandingness objection to the Closure Principle. First, the defender of Closure can point out that there's a difference between *knowing* something and *thinking* about it. Since thinking is an event, whereas knowing is a disposition, it takes time to think about something, but no time at all to know it. For example, I know that I weigh 175 pounds. Knowing that entails knowing that I don't weigh 275 pounds, or 375 pounds, or 475 pounds, and so on. But it doesn't entail *thinking* about these facts. Which is just as well, because if it did, I could never know my own weight. Once we see this difference, we will see that the demandingness of the Closure Principle is exaggerated by its critics.

The defender of Closure has a second line of response too. This is to ask: what is so unreasonable about the demand that you should not claim to know things, unless you know that nothing inconsistent with them is true? How could you possibly count as a rational inquirer if you were prepared to tolerate possible inconsistencies between your beliefs? On this view, accepting the Closure Principle is a basic requirement of epistemic rationality. To reject it just because it is epistemically demanding is like rejecting the principle that you should give food to the hungry just because that is ethically demanding.[40] The rejection of the Closure Principle on grounds of convenience alone looks suspiciously like philosophical laziness. It would be nice to have a justification for rejecting it.

2.5.3 Relevant alternatives

The opponent of the basic sceptical argument might find this justification, if he could find a plausible way to tone down the demands of the Closure Principle. One popular suggestion about how to do this appeals to relevance. To know something, I don't need to be able to do what the Closure Principle requires me to do, and exclude every alternative possibility, no matter how bizarre. Instead, I only need to be able to exclude every *relevant* alternative possibility.

The contemporary American philosopher Fred Dretske has a little story that makes this point. Suppose you take your son to the zoo and see several zebras. Do you know they are zebras, Dretske asks?

> Well, most of us would have little hesitation in saying that we did know this. We know what zebras look like, and besides, this is the city zoo and the animals are in a pen clearly marked 'zebras'.[41]

As before, the Closure Principle apparently undermines our claim to know that these are zebras. For 'something's being a zebra implies that it is not a mule cleverly disguised by the zoo authorities to look like a zebra.' How can we exclude the possibility of disguise? Dretske's response is that we don't try to exclude it: 'Have you checked with the zoo authorities? Did you examine the animals closely enough to detect such a fraud? You might do this, of course, but in most cases you do nothing of the kind.'

Not only do we not try to exclude the crazy hypothesis that these apparent zebras are really mules in mufti. According to Dretske, we don't need to exclude it. We can count as knowing that these are zebras even if we don't know that they are not disguised mules. The hypothesis that they are disguised mules is an *irrelevant* alternative.

By contrast, a relevant alternative is the kind of hypothesis suggested at the beginning of Dretske's story: 'I have confused zebras with okapis', 'I have misread the sign', 'I have got lost and am not in the zoo after all'. It is only these sorts of alternatives – exactly which they are will depend on the context – that we need to be able to exclude before we can claim to know that 'These are zebras'. But it is not so hard to exclude these alternatives. So Dretske's revision of the Closure Principle, limiting it to excluding the relevant alternatives, gives us a principled way of avoiding the objection that the Closure Principle is over-demanding. It also gives us a principled basis for rejecting step 4 of the basic sceptical argument.

Why does Dretske say that the disguised-mules hypothesis is irrelevant, whereas the sign-misreading hypothesis is relevant? Apparently, just because the disguised-mules hypothesis is so much less *likely*. As Dretske puts it, 'You have some general uniformities on which you rely, regularities to which you give expression by such remarks as "That isn't very likely" or "Why should the zoo authorities do that?"' This appeal to likelihood begs the question. Everyone knows that scepticism is unlikely, and that the natural assumption is the anti-sceptical one that we can see familiar uniformities and regularities in nature. The point is that, even though scepticism is unlikely, *it could still be true*. So it's hard to see how Dretske could be justified in distinguishing relevant from irrelevant alternatives in the way that he does, unless he already knew that scepticism was false. In which case, as has been pointed out by Edward Craig,[42] the problem about the precise scope of the Closure Principle would never have arisen in the first place.

2.5.4 Reliablism The same sorts of problem look relevant to our third and last strategy for opposing the Closure Principle. This strategy, which is in fact often combined with the relevant-alternatives view, is known as reliablism. As Alvin Goldman states the view:

> What kinds of causal processes or mechanisms must be responsible for a belief if that belief is to count as knowledge? They must be mechanisms that are, in an appropriate sense, 'reliable'. Roughly, a cognitive mechanism or process is reliable if it not only produces true beliefs in actual situations, but would produce true beliefs, or at least inhibit false beliefs, in counterfactual situations.[43]

For the reliablist, knowledge is *true belief produced by a reliable method*. I believe truly that I'm looking at zebras because I've gone to the zoo to see zebras, and here I am in front of the pen marked 'Zebras'; why, I can *see* the beasts, and they certainly look like zebras to me. And that, says the reliablist, is all I need for knowledge. My belief that 'These are zebras' is (let's suppose) true; the mechanisms or methods by which I got that belief – commonsense inference and the use of perception – are reliable ones. *That's it*; I need nothing more to be able to claim to know 'These are zebras'. In particular, says the reliablist, I don't need to eliminate every conceivable alternative hypothesis, no matter how crazy, before I can make this claim. So we can reject the Closure Principle.

Reliablism interestingly implies that I can know things without knowing that I know them. Indeed, according to reliablism I can know things without knowing very much else at all. In the zoo case, for instance, I might have no idea that commonsense inference and the use of perception are reliable methods of acquiring knowledge, and I might have grave doubts about whether these beasts are in fact zebras at all. Provided I still manage to form the true belief that 'These are zebras' on the basis of those reliable methods, I still count as knowing 'These are zebras'.

In fact the reliablist will say that I can be even more ignorant than that and still know things. Suppose I find myself a guest on the bridge of the Starship *Enterprise*. To keep me amused, Captain Kirk points out the warp-drive monitor, and asks me to tell him what our warp-drive is right now. I have no idea what warp-drive is, and hence no idea what a warp-drive monitor measures, or whether it measures it reliably; I have no idea whether the number that I read on the dial is good news, bad news, or no news at all. All the same, I read the dial and tell Captain Kirk, 'The warp-drive right now is 6.' Because what I say is in fact true, and because I came to say it by what is in fact a reliable process, I count as *knowing* that 'The warp-drive right now is 6.' This in spite of the fact that I understand almost nothing about what I mean when I say it. As John McDowell points out, 'In the purest form of this approach, it is at most a matter of superficial idiom that we do not attribute knowledge to thermometers.'[44]

Another case of knowing without knowing that (or how) you know is a real-life one. Apparently, as Linda Zagzebski reports, there are professional chicken-sexers 'who can determine the sex of baby chicks without knowing how they do it or even if they do it correctly…Philosophers with strong externalist intuitions about knowledge have no hesitation in saying that such people *know* the sex of the chick.'[45]

Alongside this distinction between *knowing* and *knowing that you know*, there is another interesting distinction that reliablism draws. This is the distinction between *knowing* and *being certain*. Reliablism insists that you can know without being certain, because it insists that you don't need to be able to exclude every wacky alternative to your belief before you can count as knowing that belief. In drawing these two distinctions, reliablism reveals itself as another example of an externalist epistemology (**2.3.4**): an epistemology that starts, in anti-Cartesian fashion, from the outside.

Despite these two advantages (if that is what they are), reliablism clearly faces some difficult questions. The first and most obvious question is: which methods of acquiring beliefs are reliable?

The problem here for reliablism is not simply that, unless we know which methods of belief-acquisition are reliable, we will never be able to know that we know anything. Since the reliablist is an externalist, he isn't trying to put us in a position where we can know that we know; he's only after a position where we can *know*. Rather, the problem is that the question 'Which methods of acquiring beliefs are reliable?' is like the question 'Which alternatives are relevant?' The answer depends on what sort of world we are living in.

Suppose we are living in a world where some crazy sceptical hypothesis is true, so that we are in fact dreaming, mad or brains in a vat. In cases like these, if anything at all counts as a reliable method for us to acquire true beliefs, it will almost certainly not be any of the methods that are reliable for the inhabitants of a world where no crazy sceptical hypothesis is true. So reliablism cannot steer us in the direction of reliable methods of acquiring beliefs, and away from unreliable methods, unless we already know that scepticism is not true. Which means that reliablism, if it is to help us at all to choose between alternative ways of acquiring beliefs, must beg the question against scepticism.

It seems to be a corollary of this that it is important not only to know, but also to know that you know. The reason is that you need *epistemic feedback*. If you know something but don't know that you know it, you can't use the fact that you know it to help you to modify your epistemic behaviour in the direction of greater accuracy than before.[46]

Another question: when reliablists say that knowledge is true belief acquired by a reliable method, what do they mean by 'reliable'? The broad idea of reliability is obvious enough. Looking a word up in a dictionary is reliable, guessing its meaning isn't. Doing a chemical pregnancy test is reliable, asking yourself if you *feel* pregnant isn't. Consulting a professional gambler about who'll win the 2.30 at Chepstow is reliable, consulting an astrologer isn't. Examples like these give us good reason to contrast reliable and accidental true belief.

Still, to restate a dilemma posed by Jonathan Dancy,[47] how reliable is reliable? Suppose the reliablist will only allow true belief to count as knowledge where the method involved is *perfectly* reliable. In that case, it looks like the reliablist will count almost nothing as knowledge. After all, there aren't very many perfectly reliable methods of finding anything out. (Dictionaries, pregnancy tests and professional gamblers are all notoriously fallible; especially pregnancy tests.)

Suppose, on the other hand, that the reliablist says that you can have knowledge when you acquire a true belief by a generally but not perfectly reliable method – such as performing a pregnancy test. Your method for gaining true beliefs might have worked *this* time. But another time, since the test is only (say) 95 per cent accurate, it might not have done. Moreover, it looks like we don't have, and can't have, a good account of why your method worked this time but failed the other time. After all, your method is only generally reliable, which means there is no general explanation of why it sometimes fails. (If there were a general explanation of this, we could refine the method to exclude these failures.)

So if you do acquire a true belief by your imperfectly reliable method, the question is: why shouldn't we say that you just got lucky? On *this* occasion, your method for gaining true beliefs worked out right: it did give you a true belief. But on another occasion, you would have obediently followed the same method, and it would have given you a *false* belief. How different are you from someone who tries to decide whether she is pregnant by tossing a coin? After all, the coin-tossing method of acquiring true beliefs about whether you're pregnant sometimes works too: in the long run, it will work 50 per cent of the time. The only difference between the methods is that the chemical pregnancy test has a higher success rate – 95 per cent as opposed to 50 per cent. But surely, a 45 per cent difference in accuracy is not enough to ground a difference between accidentally true belief and knowledge!

We can also imagine a more comprehensive form of 'getting lucky', where a cosmic fluke brings it about that some accidental way of making predictions, say astrology or guessing or tossing a coin, *is* in fact reliable in our experience. In such cases, apparently, the reliablist will have to count astrology-based, guess-based, or coin-toss-based true beliefs as knowledge. This is a problem for reliablism. It isn't all that easy to see how to formulate reliablism to avoid it.

Again, if reliablism were the right analysis of knowledge, then it always ought to be true for anyone who buys a National Lottery ticket to say 'I know I won't win the Lottery.' After all, your chance of winning the National Lottery is one in 6 million, or something equally negligible. So your belief, each time the Lottery draw is made, that you won't win is based upon a method of belief-acquisition which statistically has a much better success rate than 95 per cent, and so counts as very reliable indeed. All the same, you *don't* know that you won't win. So it looks like knowledge is not 'true belief acquired by a reliable method'. If so, reliablism is not the right analysis of knowledge.

2.6 **Step 5** …So scepticism is justified

Suppose then that steps 1 and 2 are right, and our apparent experience of the external world would be exactly the same whether or not some crazy sceptical hypothesis is true. Hence (step 3) we can't tell whether or not we are victims of the various scenarios painted by the sceptical hypothesis. And suppose step 4 is right, and we can't know anything about the external world unless we know that all crazy sceptical hypotheses are false. Suppose, in fact, that the whole of the basic sceptical argument is an unqualified success up to step 4. Does this force us to concede (step 5) that scepticism is justified?

It does not. It is still possible to claim that step 5 does not follow from steps 1 to 4: all four of those steps could be true, while step 5 was nonetheless false. In this section I will consider three strategies for refuting the basic sceptical argument by denying the inference from steps 1–4 to step 5. These strategies are semantic contextualism (**2.6.1**), logical positivism (**2.6.2**) and Kantianism (**2.6.3**); finally I shall consider naturalized epistemology (**2.6.4**). As before, I shall argue that all these strategies fail. This will mean that no objections to the basic sceptical argument are left standing. And so we will reach the simple negative conclusion at which this chapter aims: the basic sceptical argument is sound, and the epistemological form of the problem of the inescapable self looks insoluble.

2.6.1 Semantic contextualism Consider the word 'flat'. You can use it to say all sorts of true things: for example, that Cambridge is flat, that a cricket field is flat, that a snooker table is flat, and that the reflective mirror on the Hubble Space Telescope is flat. So would the surface contours of Cambridge form a suitable surface for the Hubble's mirror? Of course they wouldn't. And will snooker players happily agree to play their game on a typical cricket field? They certainly won't. Or has a cricket groundsman failed to do his job, if he has failed to produce a field that is as flat as the Hubble's mirror? Obviously he hasn't.

What counts as flat depends on your *context*. (Your *semantic* context – hence the theory's name.) Cambridge is flat as towns go: the relevant contrast here is with other towns or regions of the

Earth's surface, such as Edinburgh, La Paz or Dunedin. A snooker table is flat as tables go: being a table that is built for playing snooker on, it's a lot flatter than most tables. Similarly, a cricket field is flat as fields go. As for the Hubble's reflective mirror, this is flat by the standards of astronomical telescopes, and those standards are extremely high. (Imagine a technician on the Hubble Space Telescope who accidentally knocks the mirror with a spanner and makes a nanometre-sized indentation in it: 'Oh no,' he exclaims, 'the mirror isn't flat any more.') In general, the truth of 'X is flat' depends on the context, and on the standards that apply in that context.

Lots of other words besides 'flat' behave like this: for instance, 'straight' and 'proved'. A legal throw-in to a rugby lineout, and the shortest distance between two points in Euclidean space, are both lines that we can truly say are straight. But the standards for straightness involved are very different. Likewise a legal verdict of 'guilty' and a mathematical theorem are both things that we can truly say need to be proved. All the same, mathematical and legal proof are very different sorts of proof.

So maybe the truth of 'X is known' depends on context too. Maybe there are different standards for 'X is known' in geography, in history, in a lawcourt and in mathematics. If so, then there are plenty of contexts in which scepticism is defeated, because in each of those contexts, it is known (in the sense relevant to that context) that we are not dreaming, not brains in vats, not deceived by an evil demon, and so on. This, according to the semantic contextualist, is the point that shows the falsity of scepticism. To put it another way, the semantic contextualist wants to build a theory on this almost commonplace exchange:

'I know that John's in Paris.'
'Do you really *know* that?'
'Well, I don't *know* it in your italicized sense; but I do know it in the ordinary sense.'

The contextualist wants to reinstate the humbler uses of the verb 'to know', and to resist the pressure towards its more high-faluting uses.

Wittgenstein seems to be arguing for something like semantic contextualism when he imagines a pupil who will not let his teacher explain anything to him, and continually interrupts with doubts, for instance as to the existence of things or the meaning of words. What should the teacher say? Should he start his class on history or geography with a proof of the reality of the past, or of the existence of the world? No, says Wittgenstein. He should tell the pupil that 'So far your doubts don't make sense at all':[48]

> Perhaps the teacher will get a bit impatient, but think that the boy will grow out of asking such questions…The teacher will feel that this is not really a legitimate question, that this was only holding them up, that this way the pupil would only get stuck and make no progress. And he would be right.[49]

Why don't the pupil's doubts 'make any sense'? Because they are not live doubts in the context in which the pupil raises them. The existence of the world is not in doubt in the context of geography; the reality of the past is not in doubt in the context of history. By the standards for knowledge that count in geography, the geographer knows that the world exists; by the standards for knowledge that count in history, the historian knows that the past really happened. This is how semantic contextualism shows that scepticism has no impact on claims to knowledge made within the contexts of geography and history. And likewise for other contexts.

If this is all that semantic contextualism shows, then it does not show enough to refute scepticism – any more than scepticism is refuted by the rather similar points that I made above (**2.3.6**) about Wittgensteinian language games. It's hardly news to say that, when we are doing geography, we assume that we know that the world exists. But the sceptic is not doing geography; he is doing philosophy. So the sceptic can happily concede to the semantic contextualist that, by geographical standards of knowledge, we count as knowing that the world exists. For it's perfectly consistent for the sceptic to concede this while insisting that, by philosophical standards of knowledge, we do not count as knowing that the world exists.

How should the semantic contextualist respond to this? I can only see two responses that he might make. One is to reject the whole idea that there is any such thing as a philosophical standard for knowledge, and say that the only standards that count are standards like geography's, history's and so on. But this seems a desperately high-handed manoeuvre. As an argument, it is no better than Wittgenstein's rather dogmatic refusal, which it closely parallels, to entertain the idea that philosophy might form a legitimate language game.

The second response is to say that both philosophical and non-philosophical standards for knowledge are admissible, but in different contexts; so we needn't think that scepticism is justified except when we are doing philosophy. This response has a grave drawback: it concedes everything to the sceptic. For it admits that, provided we are using 'know' according to the standards appropriate in the context of philosophy, the basic sceptical argument is completely correct – which is all that the sceptic was ever trying to prove. The contextualist might shrug this off by saying that the philosophical standard for knowledge isn't a very important one, or perhaps doesn't count at all. But to say this is to do what Wittgenstein does: to give up on philosophy altogether (on which see **7.3** below).

2.6.2 Logical positivism The most famous exposition of logical positivism is given by A. J. Ayer.[50] The logical positivists were the 'angry young men' of the 1930s – a group of innovative young philosophers who based their philosophy upon a theory of meaning. As their slogan put it, 'The meaning of a statement is its method of verification.' For the logical positivists, if you want to know what 'Salt is soluble in water' really means, or what '2 + 2 = 4' really means, then you should ask *what anyone could do to prove* that salt is soluble in water, or that 2 + 2 = 4. And similarly for all statements. For the logical positivists, the cash value of any statement comes down to what evidence, if any, could in principle be produced to prove it or disprove it.

What if there is nothing anyone could do, even in principle, to prove or disprove a particular statement? In that case, says logical positivism, even if the statement seems to make sense, it is really nonsense. This surprising conclusion follows directly from the logical positivists' slogan. If the meaning of a statement is its method of verification, then it must follow that a statement without any method of verification is a statement without any meaning.

The logical positivists thought that their slogan had drastic implications for large areas of traditional philosophical discourse, including theology, ethics and epistemology. Take the theological claim that 'God is love'. The logical positivists complained that theologians refused to allow any evil event, however dreadful, to count as evidence against the claim that 'God is love'. ('God is still love,' the theologian will say; 'he's just testing our faith.') The logical positivists added that nothing in our experience really counts as evidence *for* the claim that God is love either. There is no way of proving or disproving the claim. Therefore, the logical positivists concluded, that claim is meaningless.

The logical positivists saw a similar problem about the meaningfulness of ethical claims. You can say if you like that 'Murder is wrong'. But what kind of evidence can you ever produce for or against that claim? To show that people generally agree that murder is wrong does not show that it *is* wrong. To show that murder has bad consequences does not show that it is wrong, either. The logical positivists thought that there was no evidence for or against the truth of any ethical claims. They therefore concluded that ethical claims were literally meaningless.

The logical positivists took the same brisk approach to epistemology. Consider the sceptical hypothesis that worries Descartes: 'I am being perfectly and undetectably deceived by an evil demon.' Descartes is worried that he might not be able to show that this hypothesis is false, and goes to great lengths to find a disproof of it. The logical positivist says that Descartes needn't have bothered, because there can never be any evidence either way.

Why not? Because the evil demon's deception is undetectable. If anything ever did count as evidence for the deception, it wouldn't be undetectable. So it's guaranteed that nothing will ever count as evidence *for* the deception.

But it's also guaranteed that nothing will ever count as evidence *against* the deception. For what could such evidence be? Writing 'You are not being deceived by an evil demon', in letters of fire across the sky, certainly won't do it. The evil demon can easily produce this effect, and many other spectaculars too. To take the writing in the sky as evidence against the evil demon hypothesis, you have to assume that your *perception* of the writing in the sky is trustworthy – which is precisely what the evil demon hypothesis puts in question (compare the two postcards in **1.6**). Only a watertight logical proof that 'You are not being deceived by an evil demon' would be sufficient evidence to disprove the deception. But, of course, you can never be sure that the logical proof that you think disproves the deception really does disprove it. Maybe you have made a mistake somewhere in your reasoning; maybe the whole 'proof' is just another hallucination that the evil demon has inflicted on you. Consequently, nothing can count as evidence that disproves the deception.

So there can be no good evidence either for or against the sceptical hypothesis that 'I am being perfectly and undetectably deceived by an evil demon.' Therefore, this sceptical hypothesis is a statement without any means of verification. Therefore, the logical positivist concludes, this sceptical hypothesis is a *meaningless* statement. And likewise for other sceptical hypotheses. Since, in the nature of the case, no evidence counts either for them or against them, these hypotheses are nonsensical. So step 5 of the basic sceptical argument is false, even if the rest of the basic sceptical argument is true. Scepticism is not justified, because scepticism does not even make sense.

There is an obvious flaw in this argument that scepticism does not make sense. The flaw is that an exactly parallel argument shows that *anti*-scepticism does not make sense, either. The logical positivist argues that the sceptical hypothesis is nonsense, because it is unverifiable. But if that's right, then the anti-sceptical hypothesis must be unverifiable too; and therefore must be nonsense too. It follows that logical positivists cannot claim to have refuted scepticism and vindicated anti-scepticism. If successful, they have refuted both.

But is logical positivism successful anyway? Can it really be right to say that the meaning of any statement is its method of verification? Most philosophers nowadays regard logical positivism as thoroughly refuted. One simple reason for rejecting it can be seen when you apply it to itself. What method of verification could possibly prove that 'The meaning of any statement is its method of verification'? It seems entirely probable that *no* method of verification can prove it. If so, the logical positivist slogan is self-refuting. Among the statements that it condemns as meaningless is – itself.

2.6.3 Kantianism Historically speaking, logical positivism is a kind of descendant of the theory of knowledge developed by Immanuel Kant (1724–1804), most famously in his *Critique of Pure Reason* (1781). Kant's theory of knowledge is enormously subtle, complex and ingenious; I can here offer only the most lightning summary of it.

Kant's most basic and famous idea is 'the Copernican turn'. All previous philosophy, he thinks, has been done the wrong way round. Without any false modesty, he sees it as his mission in life to show the world how philosophy can be done the right way round:

> Hitherto it has been assumed that all our knowledge must conform to objects. But all attempts to extend our knowledge of objects...have, on this assumption, ended in failure. We must therefore make trial whether we may not have more success in the tasks of metaphysics, if we suppose that objects must conform to our knowledge...We should then be proceeding [like] Copernicus. Failing of satisfactory progress in explaining the movements of the heavenly bodies on the assumption that they all revolved round the spectator, he tried [supposing] the spectator to revolve and the stars to remain at rest.[51]

Kant wants philosophers to give up the assumption that 'All our knowledge must conform to objects', and replace it with the assumption that all 'objects must conform to our knowledge'. (So there is a disanalogy between Kant's revolution and Copernicus's: Copernicus removes us from the centre of the universe, Kant reinstalls us there.) What does it mean for philosophy to undergo this revolution?

Descartes and Locke had asked, 'What can be known about things in the world?' Kant believes that their question is fruitless because it leads us straight into scepticism; and scepticism successfully shows that nothing can be known about the world, in itself and apart from our perceptions of it. But Kant does not conclude from this that (in the words of step 5) scepticism is justified.

Instead, he proposes that philosophers should ward off the sceptical conclusion by asking a different question. His question is, roughly, something like this: 'What kind of knowers are we? And what does the answer to *that* question show about the question of what can be known about things in the world?'

Kant's Copernican revolution involves giving up our vain attempts to tear through the veil of perception (**2.3.1**), so as to discover which of the many possible pictures of the world behind it is the true one. Instead, we should try thinking about all the possible pictures that we might have of what the world is like. What kind of order and structure is implicit in *any* picture of the world that we might adopt? What kind of conditions of coherence and consistency must be satisfied by *any* account of reality that we can find credible, if it is to count as a possible account of reality?

Our awareness of the world around us begins as 'one great blooming, buzzing confusion' of perceptions.[52] We are bombarded by what Kant calls 'intuitions': sensations, feelings, flashes of colour, twinges of pain – perceptual inputs of all kinds. Animal experience of the world, as Kant sees it, never gets any further than this disordered mayhem of sensations. By contrast, the characteristically human experience of the world is shaped by our ability to find ways of making sense of this confusion.

Our ability to give shape to the confusion of our 'intuitions' is our ability to reason: it is our rationality. According to Kant, rationality is a matter of finding 'rules for the understanding', and applying them to our experience to give it some sort of shape. Without this rational activity on our part, Kant thinks that there is a sense in which 'nature' or 'the world' would not even exist:

> The understanding is something more than a power of formulating rules through the comparison of appearances; it is itself the lawgiver of nature. Save through it, nature, that

is, synthetic unity of the manifold of appearances according to rules, would not exist at all.[53]

We can know about the world – indeed, there can *be* a world for us – only insofar as we can bring our experience under rules for the understanding that we can apply with complete generality. Kant also calls such rules for the understanding *concepts*. So his view is that, if (for example) the concept of space, or of possibility, or of bananas is to be of use in making sense of the world, then that concept must be applicable the same way every time. An inconsistent concept is not a concept at all.

So what, on Kant's view, can human beings know? In one way his answer to this is very ambitious; in another way it is very limited indeed.

Here is the sense in which Kant's view of what we can know is very ambitious. Kant believes that he can prove the existence of a rich, complex and coherent set of concepts, each of them applicable the same way every time, which are the very concepts that all humans are bound to use to make sense of any and every experience that they could possibly have. This unique set of coherent concepts that order our experience is what Kant calls the 'synthetic *a priori*'. Another name for it, the one I shall use here, is a 'conceptual scheme'.

An obvious question arises about the conceptual scheme. If his argument works, Kant has shown that all human experience necessarily has a certain structure, namely the structure that his account of the conceptual scheme imposes on it. To say this is to say that humans inevitably see the world in a certain way, in line with the conceptual scheme that Kant believes he has proved to be the necessary and inevitable structure of our thought. But what if our conceptual scheme is deceptive, or incomplete? What if our way of seeing the world makes us see some things wrong, and other things not at all?

This is the sense in which Kant's view of what we can know is very limited. For Kant's answer is simply that this question is unanswerable and meaningless. Like his philosophical descendants the logical positivists, Kant is not afraid to rule certain questions as simply beyond the human capacity to ask, let alone answer. We can, he tells us, have no proof that the world is not, in itself, radically different from the way in which we conceive it. The only thing we can be sure of is that a world radically different from our conception of it is inconceivable.

But that, of course, just means that 'Our conception of the world can't differ from how the world is on our conception of it.' And this is simply a truism: a truism which, moreover, does not dispel the doubt that Kant has not really dealt with scepticism at all. Kant's talk about what is 'conceivable' can equally be expressed as talk about what is 'conceivable *by us*'. (Kant himself often talks this way.) For all we can tell, then, our picture of the world may be radically misleading, although, of course, we cannot picture *how* it misleads us – any more than brains in a vat can shape the thought that they are brains in a vat (**2.3.4**). In which case, Kant has not resolved what he called 'the scandal of philosophy', the scandal that sceptical doubt remains unanswered. His own theory of knowledge does not rule out scepticism, or show that it is unjustified. Instead, his theory of knowledge just engenders a new and improved form of scepticism. It leads to a scepticism which does not just put our senses or our reason in doubt, but opens up the sceptical danger that our entire conceptual scheme, our whole way of looking at the world, might be radically misleading.

2.6.4 Naturalized epistemology So much for responses to scepticism that accept all the premises of the basic sceptical argument, while nonetheless rejecting its conclusion that scepticism is justified. This, at last, completes my survey of attempts to refute the basic sceptical argument. However, before I draw a conclusion to this chapter, I should perhaps mention one other response to scepticism. This is naturalized epistemology, which is not, so far as I can tell, an attempt to refute the basic sceptical argument, so much as to ignore it.

Naturalized epistemology presupposes *naturalism*, the view that the subject-matter of science is the whole of reality. In the words of W. V. Quine, a prominent proponent of the view, 'Naturalism consigns the question of reality to science.' For the naturalist, the only world there is is the natural or scientific world; the only facts there are are the natural or scientific facts. Science will be complete when it has explained everything; and there is nothing real that it can't explain.

The idea of naturalized epistemology, then, is that there are no serious questions for epistemology to ask that cannot equally well, or better, be asked by the various special sciences. 'Epistemology in its new setting', Quine tells us, 'is contained in natural science, as a chapter of psychology.'[54]

Another form of naturalized epistemology, appealing not to science so much as to 'the social context of justification', is offered by Richard Rorty:

I want to urge that [there is no role left for traditional epistemology]. To understand the matters which Descartes wanted to understand – the superiority of the new science to Aristotle, the relations between this science and mathematics, common sense, theology and morality – we need to turn outward rather than inward, towards the social context of justification rather than to the relations between inner representations...[55]

The standard objection to naturalized epistemology (in either Quine's or Rorty's form) is that it is merely descriptive, and not normative, as a proper epistemology ought to be. It describes how we do *in fact* form beliefs about the world, but it has nothing to say about what beliefs about the world we are *entitled* to form. Thus naturalized epistemology does not refute, replace or defuse in any way the force of the basic sceptical argument. It would be perfectly consistent to accept both the basic sceptical argument and naturalized epistemology. Quine and Rorty, therefore, have not solved the problem of external-world scepticism; they have simply proposed that we should stop thinking about it. By dropping the normative side of epistemology, they have also – in the view of many observers, Jaegwon Kim, for example – undermined epistemology itself: 'For epistemology to go out of the business of justification is for it to go out of business.'[56]

Since I think that this standard objection to naturalized epistemology is simply correct, I have nothing to add to it.

2.7 **Conclusion**

There have been many attempts to refute scepticism about the external world. And there has been a change in philosophical fashion that has made 'Cartesian' a dirty word among philosophers. As the case of naturalized epistemology conspicuously shows, the trend of much recent philosophy has been towards what we might tease Heideggerians by calling 'a forgetfulness of reasoning'. It has become fashionable to turn away from the problems of scepticism as if they didn't matter, or had already been solved – or were simply too hard for us to be bothered addressing them.

Whatever the reasons for this fashion, the evidence of this chapter is that the basic sceptical argument has not been refuted. Apparently, there really is no good answer to scepticism about the external world. For all we have seen so far, the sceptic is right to say that the self really can have no knowledge of the existence of anything beyond itself. As a problem about knowledge, the problem of the inescapable self remains unsolved.

In the next two chapters, I'll consider the ethical forms of the problem of the inescapable self.

1 Stroud 1984.

2 Dennett 1991: 3–7.

3 Berkeley, *Principles* 1.4.

4 Locke, *Essay* II.1.

5 Descartes, CSM II: 24–5.

6 Ryle 1949, ch. 1.

7 Chisholm 1989: 95–6.

8 Armstrong 1968: 209.

9 Assuming, at least, that these are plausible models of perception in other respects: which the adverbial model may be, but the dispositional model is not. There are lots of ways of being disposed to acquire beliefs. A decent theory of perception needs to say something about the very special way in which *perception* disposes us to acquire beliefs. At least in the bald form in which I've stated it here, the dispositional model conspicuously fails to do this.

10 A good starting-point is Candlish 1998.

11 This isn't the *only* purpose of the Private Language Argument, which (for example) has important implications for the theory of meaning too. But it is *one* purpose.

12 Wittgenstein, *Philosophical Investigations* I, 258; compare I, 243.

13 *PI* I, 261.

14 *PI* I, 258.

15 Compare Blackburn 1993: 227, who argues that the problems that the Private Language Argument raises for a private language apply with equal force to a *public* language.

16 McDowell 2001: 387.

17 McDowell 2001: 407.

18 At least, Putnam originated the nightmare scenario in philosophy, though Adam Morton has suggested to me that Putnam may have got the idea from the science fiction of Philip K. Dick.

19 Putnam 1981: 12.

20 Putnam 1981: 12–13.

21 If this *is* how we use 'I', which many writers, e.g. Anscombe 1974, dispute.

22 Putnam 1981: 15.

23 Wittgenstein, *On Certainty* #676; contrast Kekule's benzene dream (ch.1, endnote 21).

24 Rowlands 2003, ch. 4 on Sartre 1958: xxxvi.

25 Rowlands 2003: 65.

26 It is much clearer that McCulloch 2003 thinks that some such argument actually refutes scepticism.

27 Compare Scruton 1982: 35 expounding Wittgenstein: 'there can be no knowledge of experience that does not presuppose reference to a public world.'

28 Kant 1929: 244–7 (B275–9); Habermas 1981; Strawson 1959: 106.

29 See Kirk, Raven and Schofield 1983: 272.

30 Plato, *Theaetetus* 188c–200c.

31 Aristotle, *Posterior Analytics* 71a1.

32 Aristotle, *Nicomachean Ethics* 1172b36–a2.

33 Aristotle, *Topics* 105a4.

34 Wittgenstein, *On Certainty* ##341–4.

35 *On Certainty* #115; #625.

36 Davidson 1984, Essay 14.

37 Russell 1912: 22.

38 Russell 1956: 138.

39 Moore 1939.

40 The analogy between epistemic and ethical demandingness is interesting, but I can't pursue it here. I'll say more about the general analogy between the epistemic and ethical forms of normativity in **7.5**.

41 Dretske 1970.

42 Craig 1989.

43 Goldman 1976.

44 McDowell 2001: 401.

45 Zagzebski 1996: 265.

46 Too much of the debate about knowing that you know has focused on the question whether knowing *entails* knowing that you know. (The classic work in the area is Hintikka 1962.) In the normal sense of 'know', it surely doesn't. But that doesn't make knowing that you know unimportant.

47 Dancy 1985: 32.

48 Wittgenstein, *On Certainty* #310.

49 *On Certainty* ##314–15.

50 Ayer 1936.

51 Kant 1929: 22.

52 James 1890: 462.

53 Kant 1929: 148.

54 Quine 1969: 83.

55 Rorty 1980: 210.

56 Kim 1988: 43.

3

Reluctant Egoists

3.1 **The invisible man and the experience machine**

Sceptical nightmares owe much of their darkness to their loneliness. When I first made this point (**0.2**), I was talking about the sceptical nightmares that go with the problem of the inescapable self understood as a problem about knowledge. The same loneliness is apparent when we consider how the problem of the inescapable self manifests itself as a problem about ethics. To show this, and to introduce my discussion of the ethical forms of the problem of the inescapable self, here are two more philosophical fables. (At least one of them could also be called a nightmare scenario.)

The first fable is an old one, at least as old as Herodotus (485–426 BC). In Book 2 of the *Republic* (*c.*380 BC), it is retold by Plato's character Glaucon.

> *The Invisible Man.* Gyges the Lydian was a shepherd who found a ring of invisibility. So he got himself appointed as a messenger to the king, and used his ring to seduce the queen, murder the king, and take over his kingdom.
>
> Suppose there were two rings of invisibility like this, and the just man put on one of them and the unjust man put on the other. No one, it seems, would prove so adamant in virtue that he would abide in justice, and have the self-discipline to restrain himself from laying even a finger on what

belongs to others. After all, he could, with impunity, take whatever he liked from the marketplace itself. He could go into men's houses and have sex with whichever of their wives he fancied. He could kill anyone he liked, or spring them from prison; he could do anything he liked among mortals, just as if he were a god. But in acting like this, the just man would do nothing that the unjust man would not also do: both of them would have the same objective.[1]

The second fable is modern and comes from Robert Nozick:

> **The Experience Machine.** Suppose there were an experience machine that could give you any experience you desired. Superduper neuropsychologists could stimulate your brain so that you would think and feel you were writing a great novel, or making a friend, or reading an interesting book. All the time you would be floating in a tank, with electrodes attached to your brain…Would you plug in? *What else can matter to us, other than how our lives feel from the inside?*[2]

What is it like to be the Invisible Man? What is it like to be in the Experience Machine? The simple answer, I think, is this: it's lonely.

The loneliness of the man on Nozick's Experience Machine is obvious. It is really no different from the loneliness of Putnam's brain in a vat (**0.1**, **2.3.4**). (In effect, the man on Nozick's Experience Machine *is* a brain in a vat.) The loneliness of the Experience Machine is the loneliness of solipsism, the loneliness of total isolation. While you're on it, nothing exists except yourself and your experiences; or if anything does exist, it is completely inaccessible.

Of course, once someone has plugged in, he won't know about his own loneliness, and about the unreality of everything he experiences. (If he did know, his experiences would not be exact simulations of real experiences – and the whole point of the Experience Machine is to give you exact simulations.) But this only means that the Experience Machine involves *two* kinds of loneliness. One is the loneliness of being on it, which is real enough, even if – to reuse a phrase from **2.3.4** – it is 'invisible from the inside'. The other, perhaps more subtle, loneliness is the loneliness of choosing to go on it. This is what you might call an *existential* loneliness. It is the loneliness of freely choosing to isolate yourself from reality.

The Invisible Man Gyges shares this existential loneliness. His is the loneliness of a freely chosen isolation from society: not the solipsist's loneliness, but the criminal's or the solitary's. (Compare Albert Camus's 'outsider', in his novel *L'Étranger*.) As we might also say, Gyges's loneliness is the loneliness of the egoist: the loneliness of the person whose motivations are all directed towards himself, and his own benefit.

Compare the other story, from the *Republic*. Glaucon suggests that the just person and the unjust person, if both are put into Gyges's shoes, will have 'the same objective'. The objective Glaucon means is the person's own interest. The moral of the story of Gyges is that people who appear to be just are really no less exclusively self-interested than anyone else. They may be more prudent about cloaking their self-interest in an impressive show of concern for other people, or for moral standards, or for religion, or whatever. But, says Glaucon, the just man's show of justice is merely a part of his overall plan for advancing his own interest. Indeed, part of the point of the story of Gyges is that it is hard to see how anything else could motivate anyone except self-interest.

What characterizes an egoist like Gyges is his inability to appreciate other people as other people: his inability to conceive that other human beings might matter (at least to themselves) just as much as he matters (at least to himself). Compare what is going on in the thinking of someone who agrees to plug into the Experience Machine. Presumably the person who is happy to plug into the Experience Machine has no interest in the difference between the way things really are and the way things seem to him. So, for instance, he does not think it matters whether he really makes friends with other people, or just has a series of experiences exactly like making friends with other people. Why doesn't he think this difference matters? The answer is likely to be: because he does not think that other people matter, in and of themselves. This suggests that the loneliness of the Invisible Man and the loneliness of the Experience Machine have much in common.

3.2 **The ethical problem of the inescapable self**

In chapters 1 and 2 we have seen how the problem of the inescapable self develops as a problem about knowledge. Descartes wants to find a basis for science that will be as certain as mathematics. So he suspends every belief that he finds it possible to doubt. The only beliefs that he finds it is not possible to doubt are his beliefs that he is thinking, that he exists, that God exists, and that his own clear and distinct ideas are true. On this basis of certainty he tries to re-establish everything that he has put in doubt. But as I've argued, his certain and indubitable beliefs can prove nothing beyond themselves. This leaves Descartes stuck in the problem of scepticism. Looking beyond Descartes, none of the attempts to get out of that problem that I reviewed in chapter 2 has succeeded either. The problem of the inescapable self, as a problem for knowledge, seems insoluble.

In the next two chapters, we'll see that the ethical forms of the problem of the inescapable self are no less intractable. The ethical forms of the problem develop fairly directly out of the epistemological form of the problem about knowledge. How and why do they develop, though? What is the line of thought that gets us from the epistemological problem to the ethical problems? It is, I suggest, something like this.

If I am a Cartesian thinker, caught in the problem of scepticism, my assurance of my own reality is balanced by my uncertainty about the existence of other people, and indeed of the rest of the world outside me. This combination of certainty and uncertainty is likely to make it impossible for me to take fully seriously the idea of ethical values 'out there in the world', as opposed to the idea that my own pleasures, desires and preferences – known to me, with certainty, 'from the inside' – might be the source of these values. Hence I am likely to come to think that the only sort of value that really matters is the kind of value that *I* see in having *my* pleasures, desires and preferences catered for. From my perspective, other kinds of value will simply vanish.

Like the man on Nozick's Experience Machine, I will think that value is *subjective*: it attaches directly to me as a subject, and to nothing else. I am also likely to think that value is *relative*: any subject in my position would see his own pleasures, desires and preferences just as I see mine – as the source of the only sort of value that *he* can have reason to care about. I will also conclude that value is *reducible*: my values are completely explicable in terms of my pleasures, desires and preferences, without any mysterious leftovers. Hence, finally, I will draw the moral that value is *non-realistic*: since each subject has different pleasures, desires and preferences, there is no sense in trying to work out a theory of value that makes the realist assumption that value is some one thing, over and above the particular pleasures, desires and preferences of particular subjects.

A second line of thought that gets us from the epistemological problem of the inescapable self to an ethical variant of the problem is this. Someone in the 'egocentric predicament' just described will naturally see the distinction between himself and the world around him as a fundamental one. This *mind–world rift*, as I called it in **0.2**, will make natural a fundamental distinction between the scientific and personal perspectives, so it is no surprise to see that this distinction is also fundamental for Descartes. But this divorce of the scientific and personal perspectives is likely to create a problem about the existence of ethical value beyond myself. The problem is simply that ethical value, for all its personal importance, is no part of the scientific picture. Within a physical and mechanical framework of explanation, the existence of ethical value becomes as hard to make sense of as something else that also seems obvious from the personal perspective – the existence of consciousness.

In these various ways, the problem of the inescapable self appears as an ethical problem because it leads to *vanishing values*. It makes it hard – perhaps downright impossible – to be a moral realist. I'll say a little more about this problem about moral realism, and the mind–world rift, in **3.7–3.9**, where my focus will be on how scientific or otherwise 'impersonal' thinking tends to undermine our belief in the possibility of altruism; the issue of moral realism will also be the main focus of chapter 4.

What I want to focus on first, however, is a more direct way in which the ethical form of the problem of the inescapable self makes it very hard to be an altruist. We can see this if we carry on the same train of thought a little further. An altruist is someone who is genuinely and directly concerned about the well-being of other people. But how could anyone in the Cartesian predicament really have *that* concern? If you are genuinely caught in the sceptical trap, you will not even know that other people exist, never mind that they matter. Your general scepticism about the existence of values 'out there in the world' will cover other people, too. Your motivations will be just like the Invisible Man's in Plato's story: the only thing that will motivate you will be your own benefit. You will be convinced that the only values that can possibly matter to you are those that attach to the satisfaction of your own desires, pleasures and preferences. This conviction will force you to think that direct altruistic concern for other people is simply impossible for you, even if you would like to be capable of it. And if there are any other people, altruism will be impossible for them too, for just the same sort of reasons. It will be hard to see how they can reasonably be anything but egoists – even if they are reluctant egoists.[3] When we develop this version of the problem of the inescapable self, it becomes clear that it makes altruism deeply philosophically problematic. This problem about altruism is the main focus of this chapter.

It is worth noting, however, that Descartes does not develop any such line of thought. Although he takes scepticism about knowledge about as far as anyone has taken it, he imagines that he can simply close off the danger that scepticism about knowledge will lead to scepticism about ethics. He tries to head off this danger by laying out for himself a list of 'provisional moral maxims' which tell him, among other things, 'to be as firm and decisive in my actions as I could, and to follow even the most doubtful opinions, once I had adopted them, with no less constancy than if they had been quite certain'.[4]

This combination of scepticism about knowledge and dogmatism about ethics does not look at all philosophically stable. Certainly the rationale for it that Descartes offers in Part 3 of the *Discourse* is unconvincing. He compares the Cartesian sceptic seeking ethical guidance to a man lost in a wood. The best strategy for both of them, he suggests, is to keep on going in the direction they've already taken.

This is a weak response to the ethical problem. If Descartes's blank cheque in favour of our present prejudices was a legitimate way to avoid *ethical* scepticism, it would equally be a legitimate way to avoid epistemological scepticism. As an answer to the doubts he raises at the beginning of the *Meditations*, Descartes could just have offered the picture of the man lost in the wood, and had done with it. Conversely, if we really do need the Cartesian method to deal adequately with epistemological scepticism, then presumably we need a parallel method to deal adequately with ethical scepticism. This explains why Descartes's combination of scepticism about knowledge and dogmatism about ethics looks unstable.

Whether or not it is unstable, the fact that Descartes generally refuses to entertain ethical scepticism means that we can't use his writings to show how the ethical version of the egocentric predicament – egoism – emerges from the epistemological version – solipsism. But it would be nice to study the detail of how that happened. This detail would also provide a historical foundation for our consideration of the ethical forms of the problem of the inescapable self, to parallel the historical foundation that chapter 1 provided for our consideration of the epistemological form of that problem. The materials for this are not found in Descartes, but in one of Descartes's keenest contemporary readers and critics: the English philosopher Thomas Hobbes (1588–1679).

3.3 **Hobbes's epistemology**

Someone who read only Hobbes's best-known work, his political treatise *Leviathan* (1651), could be forgiven for thinking that Hobbes was the mirror-image of Descartes. Whereas Descartes takes seriously the epistemological problem of the inescapable self, but not the ethical one, Hobbes seems to be interested in the ethical problem, but not in the epistemological one.

In fact, Hobbes's other works disprove this impression. The first chapter of his earlier and lesser-known work *The Elements of Law* (1640) shows that it is not just Hobbes's ethics, but his whole philosophy, that begins in a scepticism like Descartes's:

> There be in our minds continually certain images or conceptions of the things without us, insomuch that if a man could

be alive, and all the rest of the world annihilated, he should nevertheless retain the image thereof, and of all those things that he had before seen and perceived in it; every man by his own experience knowing that the absence or destruction of things once imagined, doth not cause the absence or destruction of the imagination itself.

What does this passage say? In the words of the 'basic sceptical argument' of **2.2**, it says that an individual's experience could be exactly the same even if there were no external world. So how do we know there is an external world? How does Hobbes think anyone can tell that his or her experience is caused by the familiar external world, rather than being produced by a dream or an evil demon, or by the Matrix, or by nefarious neurosurgeons? Hobbes's response to this is fairly clearly that we can't tell: 'I know no criterion or mark,' he repeatedly insists, 'by which anyone can discern' waking from sleeping.[5] Hobbes does point out that our waking experience is generally more coherent, and less absurd, than our sleeping experience.[6] But obviously, if the world changed enough, it might be the other way around; a sceptical point which Hobbes accepts, but Descartes denies.

According to Hobbes, all any individual knows about the real nature of the outside world is merely that *something* is out there.[7] The individual can know this much, because his own thoughts and perceptions change and move, and nothing, according to Hobbes, can change or move itself. (As Richard Tuck explains, Hobbes believes this on the grounds of the principle of sufficient reason, 'the principle that there has to be some new feature in a situation to explain some new alteration in it. A body which displayed no other alteration in its condition could not therefore start to move.'[8])

So there must be something changing, outside the individual's thoughts and perceptions, to make those thoughts and perceptions change within the individual. Moreover, Hobbes adds, this something must be physical. For unlike Descartes, Hobbes is a materialist, and holds that nothing exists except physical objects:

substance and body signify the same thing; and therefore, *substance incorporeal* are words which, when they are joined together, destroy each other...the proper signification of *spirit* in common speech is either a subtle, fluid, and invisible body, or a ghost, or other idol or phantasm of the imagination.[9]

Scandalously to his contemporaries, Hobbes even held that God was material:

By the name of spirit we understand a body natural, but of such subtilty that it worketh not on the senses...therefore when we attribute the name of spirit unto God, we attribute it...as a signification of our reverence, who desire to abstract from him all corporeal grossness.[10]

The external world is something we know very little about, which is physical and 'in motion' or changing, and which presses in on us to give us perceptions and thoughts. So much, and no more, is all the Hobbesian individual can know about the external world. It follows that he has no guarantee at all that his perceptions and thoughts in any way resemble the external world:

Whatsoever accidents or qualities our senses make us think there be in the world, they are not there, but are seemings and apparitions only. The things that really are in the world without us, are those motions by which these seemings are caused. And this is the great deception of sense...Apparition of light without, is really nothing but motion within.[11]

If this is all the Hobbesian individual can know, how can he possibly have any knowledge of the existence of other individuals like himself?

Hobbes's answer to this is never made explicit. Implicitly, I think his answer is like his answer to Descartes's dreaming-scepticism. The answer is that the individual can't know that there are others like himself around – any more than he can know that he is not dreaming. He can only know that it *looks* as if there are others like himself around – just as it looks as if he isn't dreaming – and work pragmatically on the basis of that appearance. But Hobbes never follows Descartes in trying to close off the sceptical possibility that this appearance that others exist might be a deceptive one. In fact, it looks as if he himself accepts the sceptical view that it *is* deceptive. After all, the only way I can know anything about the existence of other people is via my senses. And as Hobbes has just told us, he thinks our senses are comprehensively misleading.

3.4 **Hobbesian individuals**

Result: in Hobbes's epistemology as in Descartes's, we begin with the isolated individual. Contact with others comes, if it comes at all, at a secondary stage. For Hobbes as for many other philosophers since, the first use of language is not to communicate with others, but to be more accurate in one's own thinking. The fact that language enables peaceful interaction between humans is a real, but secondary, benefit:

> The most notable and profitable invention of all other was that of SPEECH, consisting of *names* and *appelations* and their connexion, whereby men register their thoughts, recall them when they are past, and also declare them one to another for mutual utility and conversation, without which there had been amongst men, neither commonwealth, nor society, nor contract, nor peace, no more than amongst lions, bears, and wolves.[12]

Thus the original state of isolation that is the foundation of Hobbes's epistemology is the foundation of Hobbes's ethics as well. His conception of individuals is, in a fairly precise sense, *atomistic*. He sees individuals as separate and competing units of force, as discrete particles whose energies act and impact percussively upon one another:

> Nature hath made men so equal in the faculties of mind and body that, though there be found one man sometimes manifestly stronger in body or of quicker mind than another, yet when all is reckoned together, the difference between man and man is not so considerable as that one man can thereupon claim to himself any benefit to which another may not pretend as well as he. For as to the strength of body, the weakest has strength enough to kill the strongest...and as to the faculties of the mind...I find yet a greater equality amongst men than of strength.[13]

Hobbes's measure of the equality of individuals is characteristically pessimistic: it is that every individual is capable of killing every other. All persons are equal, because all persons are an equal *threat* to one another. Like an atomic particle acting on the other particles around it, each human individual exerts at least roughly the same forces on all the other human individuals around him, constraining each of those other human individuals to react in self-defence.

So what will happen when two different people both want the same thing?

> From this equality of ability ariseth equality of hope in the attaining our ends. And therefore, if any two men desire the same thing, which nevertheless they cannot both enjoy, they become enemies; and in the way to their end, which is

principally their own conservation, and sometimes their delectation only, endeavour to destroy or subdue each other.[13]

Whenever any individual realizes that this is how things are, he will naturally attempt to forestall others' likely attempts to attack him:

From this diffidence of one another, there is no way for any man to secure himself so reasonable as anticipation, that is, by force or wiles to master the persons of all men he can, so long till he see no other power great enough to endanger him. And this is no more than his conservation requireth, and is generally allowed.[13]

By very obvious steps, Hobbes shows how the natural forces of his atomistic individuals will inevitably tend to collide. Even where they don't actually collide, there will rapidly emerge a battery of such hostile expectations about others' intentions that collision might as well have occurred. The simple and natural process whereby each Hobbesian individual pushes his forces outwards into the world quickly leads all Hobbesian individuals into a world where everyone seeks to 'get his retaliation in first'. It is a world of incessant pre-emptive lethal aggression, where no co-operation is possible because no trust in others is possible, and where self-interest is the root of all motivation.

Hobbes's description of this world of mutually assured destruction is the most famous passage he ever wrote:

During the time that men live without a common power to keep them all in awe, they are in that condition which is called war, and such a war as is of every man against every man...Whatsoever therefore is consequent to a time of war...the same is consequent to the time wherein men live without other security than what their own strength and their own invention shall furnish them withal. In such condition there is no place for industry, because the fruit thereof is uncertain; and consequently, no culture of the earth; no navigation, nor use of the commodities that may be imported by sea; no commodious building; no instruments of moving and removing such things as require much force; no knowledge of the face of the earth; no account of time; no arts; no letters; no society; and which is worst of all, continual fear and danger of violent death; and the life of man, solitary, poor, nasty, brutish, and short.[13]

Hobbes does not summon up this vision of dystopia to celebrate it, but to replace it. Hobbes's central project in ethics is to show how individuals in the condition of war, who are interested only in their own 'conservation' and 'delectation' (their own safety and pleasure), can nonetheless learn to co-operate enough to get out of their deadly and horrible condition of war.

In other words, Hobbes's ethical project is to show how altruism can emerge from egoism. Compare Descartes's epistemological project, which is to show how knowledge of an external world can emerge out of an isolated mind that, to begin with, is aware only of itself. The projects are clearly analogous; for they are responses to different sides of the same problem, the problem of the inescapable self. It seems very likely that Hobbes would have been far less inclined to set up his ethical project as he did, had Descartes not set up his epistemological project as *he* did. As Richard Tuck writes, 'Hobbes's philosophy gives the impression of having been developed as the next move in a game where Descartes was the previous player.'[14]

It is a vivid testimony to the ethical power of the problem of the inescapable self that Hobbes's project is still often seen today as pretty well *the* issue for normative ethical theory. In **3.6**, I shall present Hobbes's solution to the problem of egoism. After that, I shall first describe the nature of modern egoism a little more closely, and then compare some other solutions. I shall argue that none of the solutions is convincing – and that there is something wrong with the problem anyway.

But first a question of Hobbes scholarship needs a brief airing: is Hobbes an egoist at all?

3.5 **Is Hobbes an egoist?**

In the present state of Hobbes scholarship, this question is controversial. My interpretation of him will be disputed by many scholars. Gregory Kavka has argued that Hobbes is a rule egoist – he believes that the right thing for me to do is always to act in accordance with whatever rule(s) it will most promote my interests to follow.[15] Against this, I would argue first that Hobbes is a psychological egoist, not an ethical egoist:[3] he is not *advising* men to act in their own interests, but taking it as read that they can and will do nothing else. Second, Kavka's interpretation falls into a class of readings of Hobbes, all of which go wrong in supposing that Hobbes thinks that our main reason to keep rules or contracts is the bare fact that we have made those rules or contracts.[16] On the contrary, Hobbes holds that our main reason to keep rules or contracts is that they work in our interest.

Others deny that Hobbes is an egoist at all. One example is David Boonin-Vail, who interestingly reads him as a virtue ethicist, essentially on the ground that (to put it crudely) Hobbes's virtuous man *enjoys* being virtuous.[17] (He does indeed; but the point is that his enjoyment of being virtuous is his motivation for being virtuous – which is clear evidence that he's an egoist.) Similarly, Tom Sorell rejects the psychological-egoist reading of Hobbes,[18] and criticizes Bishop Butler, for example, for reading egoism into Hobbes's remark that 'there can be no greater argument to a man of his own power, than to find himself able not only to accomplish his own desires, but also to assist other men in theirs; and this is that conception wherein consisteth *charity*.'[19] Sorell claims that this passage 'identifies charity with finding oneself able to assist others in accomplishing their desires'. But surely charity is not the *ability* to help others, it is the *desire* to help others. Sorell adds that this passage 'does *not* identify charity with the love of power'. But Butler need not say that it does. He need only say that Hobbes explains the attraction of charity via the love of power. This is what the passage seems to be doing; which makes it, *pace* Sorell, evidence of egoism.

Sorell himself quotes the clinching evidence for an egoist reading of Hobbes: 'Of the voluntary acts of every man, the object is some *good to himself*.'[20] As Sorell interprets this, Hobbes's view is that 'all reasons for action are traceable ultimately to a desire or interest one is merely subject to…namely the desire to preserve one's life'. This seems more than enough to show that Hobbes *is* a fairly strict sort of egoist.[21] Indeed, if anything, Sorell takes Hobbes to be an egoist in too strict a sense. The real spirit of Hobbes's egoism is better captured by his famous remark, 'In the first place, I put for a general inclination of all mankind, a perpetual and restless desire of power after power, that ceaseth only in death.'[22] Hobbes recognizes other basic motivations besides self-preservation, for example 'delectation' or pleasure, and the desire to be esteemed by others;[23] Hobbes's own grouping of our motivations under 'a perpetual and restless desire of power after power' is as neat a way of categorizing them as any. But if these are not – all of them – egoistic motivations, I don't know what would be.

3.6 **Hobbes's solution**

If 3.5 is right, then Hobbes is a psychological egoist: he holds that individuals are only motivated to secure their own safety and procure their own pleasure. So how do moral and altruistic behaviour emerge when individuals come together in society?

Hobbes's answer is implicit in the 'nasty, brutish and short' quotation given in **3.4**. First, Hobbes notes that failure to co-operate is costly. By failing to co-operate, humans in the state of war miss out on all sorts of good and useful things: industry, agriculture, navigation, 'commodious building', arts, letters, society, and so on. So even though each individual is an egoist, it's still in each individual's interest to co-operate with others. If your basic motivations are to secure your own safety and procure your own pleasure, then you should be a co-operator. For by co-operating with others, you can secure your own safety and procure your own pleasure far more effectively than you ever could by not co-operating. So the route from egoism to morality will go via the notion of co-operation. The idea will be that morality is a system of rules about how to co-operate so that everyone's best interests are secured.

The trouble is, of course, that co-operation between egoists is risky. To see this, consider this chapter's third philosophical fable – the story of the deer hunters, Strong and Swift, which Rousseau tells in his *Discourse on the Origin of Inequality*. For a reason that will emerge, I am going to tell this story in 10 numbered paragraphs:

(1) Swift has the speed to chase the deer towards Strong; and Strong has the strength to catch and kill the deer. But Strong is not swift, and Swift is not strong. Strong and Swift both know these things. So they know that they will do better if they hunt together and divide their catch than if each of them hunts on his own. So they agree to hunt together for 10 days.

(2) On days 1 to 6 they catch four deer a day – a total of 12 deer each – and all is well. But then at the beginning of day

7 Strong asks himself a question about day 10: 'When we've finished hunting at the end of day 10, what's to stop me knocking Swift over the head and taking his two deer as well as my own? That way, I get 22 deer out of our agreement, instead of 20. And I lose nothing on day 11, because we're not hunting together on day 11 anyway.'

(3) Meanwhile Swift is doing some thinking too. Swift knows that he's fast enough to escape Strong, but not strong enough to carry four deer. So he can't run off with Strong's deer on day 10. But Swift realizes that Strong will reason as in paragraph 2 and break their agreement on day 10. Swift calculates that if he doesn't show up for hunting on day 10, he will get no deer, whereas if he does show up for hunting on day 10, he will get no deer and a blow over the head. He therefore decides not to show up on day 10.

(4) Because Strong and Swift are both rational, Strong realizes that Swift will reason as in paragraph 3 and won't show up on day 10. Strong therefore decides that he'd better hit Swift over the head on day 9.

(5) Because Strong and Swift are both rational, Swift realizes that Strong will reason as in paragraph 4 and will now be planning to hit him over the head on day 9. Swift therefore decides not to show up on day 9 either.

(6) Strong now realizes that Swift will reason as in paragraph 5 and won't show up on day 9. Strong therefore decides that he'd better hit Swift over the head on day 8.

(7) Swift realizes that Strong will reason as in paragraph 6; so he decides not to show up on day 8.

(8) By the same reasoning as before, Strong now decides to hit Swift over the head on day 7...

(9) So Swift does not show up on day 7 either.

(10) So their agreement is over already, as soon as they start thinking about the logic of their agreement!

Strong and Swift's problem is that their self-interested rationality seems self-defeating. Each of them is motivated by his own self-interested desires to catch deer and avoid injury. This egoistic motivation leads them to make an agreement to co-operate. The trouble is that the very same egoistic motivation, when combined with a little rational thinking, makes that agreement unworkable. In the story as I've just told it, the agreement becomes unworkable on day 7. But, of course, that is only because day 7 is the day when Strong and Swift first think clearly about the logic of their situation. If Strong and Swift had been intelligent enough, they would have realized that their agreement was already unworkable on day 1. And then there would have been no co-operation between them whatever – which would have meant that neither of them would have caught any deer at all.

That, of course, would be bad news for Strong and Swift. If they can't co-operate, they can't get out of the state of war. Yet if they are both egoistically motivated and clear-headed, it is hard to see how they can avoid the logic that unravels their agreement backwards from its last day, and so prevents them from co-operating at any point.

One simple way out, apparently, would be for Strong and Swift not to be egoists. Perhaps it just isn't true that Swift and Strong only have egoistic motivations. Presumably Strong and Swift are supposed to be realistic models of actual humans. And maybe, as David Hume (1711–76) and Joseph Butler (1692–1752) suggest, actual human beings in fact have all sorts of different motivations, only some of them selfish, and many of them directly opposed to the individual's self-interest. What, to take Joseph Butler's example, about charity and revenge?

> If it were [the language of mankind to call every action self-love that involves doing something because it pleases you to do it], we should want words to express the difference between the principle of an action proceeding from cool consideration that it will be to my own advantage, and an action, suppose of revenge, or of friendship, by which a man runs upon certain ruin, to do evil or good to another.[24]

Or as David Hume puts it, in a discussion that is clearly indebted to Butler's: 'The voice of nature and experience seems plainly to oppose the selfish theory [i.e. psychological egoism].'[25]

Even if Butler and Hume are right about this, they haven't disproved egoism. Remember that ethical egoism (the thesis that all agents *ought* to be motivated solely by self-interest) is quite distinct from psychological egoism (the thesis that all agents are *in fact* motivated solely by self-interest). Butler's and Hume's appeal to the evidence of ordinary life does not disprove ethical egoism, because the ethical egoist can still ask whether it makes sense to be motivated by charity, friendship, or revenge; he can deny that motivations like charity or revenge *justify* actions as well as motivating them. Arguably, their appeal to the evidence doesn't disprove psychological egoism, either – not at least if psychological egoism is stated with a little caution, as the thesis that all agents are as a matter of fact motivated solely by self-interest *wherever they think clearly about what they are doing*. If this is psychological egoism, it can be defended against the evidence of cases of charity or revenge simply by denying that charitable or vengeful agents are clear-headed.

This possibility that Strong and Swift are not clear-headed might seem to offer another way out of their problem. Suppose they just avoid thinking too clearly! If they are intelligent enough to see the need for co-operation, but not intelligent enough to see the possibility of breaking their agreement, then they will never get clear about how the logic of their agreement undermines that agreement. And then they will avoid their problem about how to co-operate.

This may be how moral codes have sometimes worked in primitive societies, where morality is presented as a mysterious taboo or a source of ill-thought-out guilt. However, it is obviously not a very good solution to the problem. For one thing, it leaves Swift and Strong at the mercy of anyone who comes along who *is* intelligent enough to see the possibility of breaking agreements. For another, it is untrue to real life, where ordinary human beings are constantly aware of that possibility.

How about this, though: couldn't Swift and Strong make an agreement *with no time-limit*? If they do not agree a last day on which they will co-operate, there will be no moment at which Strong suddenly has nothing to lose by breaking his agreement with Swift. And so, the logic that unravels their agreement backwards from day 10 all the way to day 1 will cease to apply.

This is a much better solution, and probably does give the explanation of why many agreements between more or less purely self-interested parties (nations and multinational companies, for example) do not in practice get broken. However, first, this solution does not apply to every co-operative agreement, because some co-operative agreements *are* time-limited, and so subject to the unravelling logic that I've described. And second, this solution is inadequate to explain distinctively moral co-operation. Morality tells us to co-operate even when we *are* in a time-limited agreement which we have nothing to lose by breaking. Morality tells Strong not to break his agreement with Swift, even though

Strong has nothing to lose by breaking it; and morality tells me to honour my promise to Mrs Figg on her death-bed that I will give all her money to the cats' home, even though nobody heard me make this promise except myself and Mrs Figg. So this solution does not go far enough.

Hobbes's own solution, in the opening words of the *Leviathan* passage quoted above, is 'a common power to keep them all in awe'. Hobbes thinks that the only thing that will effectively stop Strong from breaking his agreement with Swift is *fear*. What Swift and Strong need to enable them to co-operate is a police force with sufficient clout to make them afraid of the consequences if they don't co-operate:

> The only way to erect such a common power as may be able to defend them from the invasion of foreigners and the injuries of one another, and thereby to secure them…is to confer all their power and strength upon one man, or upon one assembly of men, that may reduce all their wills…unto one will…as if every man should say to every man *I authorise and give up my right of governing myself to this man, or to this assembly of men, on this condition, that thou give up thy right to him, and authorise all his actions in like manner.*[26]

The name of this power is, of course, Leviathan:

> This done, the multitude so united in one person is called a COMMONWEALTH, in Latin *civitas*. This is the generation of that great LEVIATHAN, or rather (to speak more reverently) of that *Mortal God* to which we owe, under the *Immortal God*, our peace and defence. For by this authority, given him by every particular man in the commonwealth, he hath the use of so much power and strength conferred on him that by terror thereof he is enabled to conform the wills

of all of them to peace at home and mutual aid against their enemies abroad.

Hobbes's solution is that Swift and Strong should freely choose to create a sovereign that causes them such 'terror' that they will keep their co-operative agreements. This conclusion looks paradoxical, but the reasoning that gets Hobbes there is clear enough. It is in Swift's and Strong's interest to co-operate, and to know that the other party to any agreement will co-operate too. They do much better if they can co-operate than if their agreements break down all the time because neither of them is trustworthy.

To help them achieve their own long-term advantage, Swift and Strong need a way of preventing themselves from going for short-term advantages, like the one that Strong seeks in the story when he decides to knock Swift over the head on day 10. The point of the power called Leviathan is to *cancel* such short-term advantages. If Strong sees that the price of breaking his agreement and walking off with Swift's share of the deer hunt is a really heavy punishment from Leviathan, then he will see that it's not worth it – and so won't do it. It is therefore nothing but long-term rational self-interest that tells Swift and Strong, and us as well, to submit to a common power which can frighten us enough to ensure that we keep our agreements even when it looks to be in our short-term interest to break them.

This is why Hobbes concludes that it is in Swift's and Strong's long-term interests to set up Leviathan, even though that power (so long as it is functioning properly) will always stop them from pursuing their own short-term interests by breaking agreements, and punish them for trying to break those agreements. Perhaps even by executing them: Hobbes himself notes a sense in which, in the state he proposes, the condemned criminal has actually agreed to his own execution: 'Because every subject is by this institution author of all the actions and judgements of the sovereign instituted, it follows that, whatsoever he doth, it can be no injury to any of his subjects, nor ought he to be by any of them accused of injustice.'[27]

So this is Hobbes's solution to the problem of egoism, the problem of how the self-interested motivations of isolated, atomistic individuals can be transformed into the altruistic motivations of genuinely moral individuals. All sorts of subtle technical criticisms of this solution have been offered. But for our purposes, a very simple objection will do.

The objection is that Hobbes's solution does not get us *out* of egoism at all. As we have just seen, when Hobbes's agents set up Leviathan, they do so for purely egoistic reasons – to further their own long-term self-interest. Once Leviathan is established, their reason for keeping the moral code that Leviathan enforces is also purely egoistic. Their reason is that it's not worthwhile to break the moral code, because the punishments for breaking it are (as the agents themselves have made sure!) prohibitively severe. At no point do Hobbes's agents transcend self-interest; at no point are any motivations transformed from egoism to altruism.

Not at least by any rational route. Of course people in a Hobbesian state might come to *feel* like being altruistic. But the point is that Hobbes gives them no justification for being altruistic. The ethical problem of the inescapable self is the problem how an individual agent can *rationally* go beyond his own self-interest and arrive at genuinely ethical motivations. And Hobbes does nothing whatever to solve this problem.

This objection should bother anyone who wants to solve the problem of how we might rationally move beyond self-interest. It evidently did not bother Hobbes, who seems to have been as cheerfully cynical about the project of giving a rational justification of 'genuinely ethical motivation' as he was about the project of giving a rational justification of most of our knowledge of the external world. We've already encountered Hobbes's view that 'sense' is a 'great deception', and that perception only appears to tell us anything real about the external world (**3.3**). Hobbes's view that altruism too is a deception, and only appears to be based upon genuinely unselfish motivations, stands in strict parallel:

> One time, I remember, going in the Strand, a poor and infirm old man craved [Hobbes's] alms. He gave him 6 pence [in those days' monetary values, a generous but not enormous donation]. Said a divine (Dr Jaspar Mayne) that stood by: 'Would you have done this, if it had not been Christ's command?' 'Yea,' said he. 'Why?' quoth the other. 'Because', said he, 'I was in pain to consider the miserable condition of the old man; and now my alms, giving him some relief, doth also ease me.'[28]

It is obtuse of John Aubrey, the source of this story, to conclude (as he does) that this anecdote shows that Hobbes 'was very charitable', and had 'eyes of pity and compassion' for the poor. What the story actually shows is Hobbes's response to an interesting criticism of *Leviathan*. The point of Mayne's question is that the system of *Leviathan* suggests that there is no motive for alms-giving except to avoid punishment for failing to observe the divine command to give alms. The point of Hobbes's reply is that, if there is any other motive, it will have to be just as self-serving as the motive of avoiding punishment. Though the dialectic of the exchange seems to have gone over Aubrey's head, what happens here is that Mayne offers Hobbes a bullet – 'Aren't you saying that all motivations are merely selfish?' – and Hobbes simply bites it – 'Yes, I am.'

In the end, then, Hobbes no more offers us a way out of egoism in ethics than he offers us a way out of scepticism in epistemology. Hobbes takes over Descartes's predicament, but generalizes it so that it applies both to ethics and to knowledge, and adds his own pessimistic twist. His position is that we have no prospect of escape from either of these forms of the problem of the inescapable self.

3.7 **Egoism and evolution**

Hobbes's sort of egoism is common enough today. Egoistic assumptions, and a corresponding scepticism about altruism, are both a familiar part of our own intellectual and cultural landscape. This is obvious enough to anyone who teaches philosophy. Every time I run an ethics seminar on altruism, I hear my students echoing Hobbes's scepticism about the idea that anyone could ever act in a genuinely altruistic way: 'Mustn't Mother Teresa really be working for her own self-satisfaction?', 'OK, so the sergeant dives on the hand-grenade, and sacrifices his life to save his platoon. But isn't the real reason why he does this that he couldn't live with his guilt if he didn't do it?' Philosophy students in 21st-century Britain are just as naturally attracted by egoism as Hobbes was in 1651. In this they reflect a society that very commonly assumes that people's basic motivations are self-interested, and that if someone appears to act in an unselfish way, the real explanation of their action will have to show how what they did was not really as unselfish or self-sacrificing as it seemed.

Our obsession with egoism shows how we are still gripped by the problem of the inescapable self. Like Descartes, we begin both our ethics and our epistemology with the individual subject. This approach makes both solipsism and egoism perennial worries; but part of my point has been that there is no clear alternative to the individualist approach that does not simply beg all the important questions. I have shown how Hobbes's Cartesian philosophy tends towards both forms of the egocentric predicament, epistemological and ethical. And I have conjectured how the same fate might have befallen Descartes's own ethical philosophy, had he not censored this tendency out.

Other reasons for egoism's continuing grip on us today arise from another side of the problem of the inescapable self that we have not yet looked at. This is what in **0.2** I called the mind–world rift: it is a phenomenon which has been reinforced by the steady progress of the mechanical and scientific way of looking at humans and their actions and motivations. In this section and the next two, I will look at some of the intellectual influences that keep this rift wide open.

The first of these influences is *evolutionary thinking*. The conflict between evolutionary thinking and the idea of altruism is obvious, and is pointed out by Darwin himself. The problem is that it is hard to see how evolution could *select* in favour of self-sacrificing altruism:

It is extremely doubtful whether the offspring of the more sympathetic and benevolent parents...would be reared in greater number than the children of selfish and treacherous parents...He who was ready to sacrifice his own life...rather than betray his own comrades, would often leave no offspring to inherit his noble nature. The bravest men...who freely risked their lives for others, would on average perish in larger numbers than other men.[29]

Though modern Darwinistic biology is often popularly misunderstood, it has enormous and pervasive cultural power and influence in our society today. The phenomenon is not new. Hitler and Mussolini appropriated the Darwinian idea of 'the survival of the fittest' as early as the 1920s. (Or rather, they misappropriated it: Darwin's idea was that whatever creatures happened to survive were by definition the fittest, whereas Hitler's and Mussolini's idea was that certain creatures – most notably, themselves – deserved to survive because they were the strongest and most beautiful.) Again, writers such as Herbert Spencer

(1820–1903) and George Bernard Shaw (1856–1950) were writing solemn treatises on 'evolutionary ethics' many years before either Hitler or Mussolini. Indeed, some of Spencer's most important work actually predates Darwin's *Origin of Species* (1859).[30] It is not even certain that it was Darwin rather than Spencer who first used the phrase 'survival of the fittest'.

In recent years, evolutionary thinking has received a new impetus from a number of very widely read books that have popularized it. The most famous book of this sort is of course Richard Dawkins's *The Selfish Gene*:[31]

> The argument of this book is that we, and all other animals, are machines created by our genes. Like successful Chicago gangsters, our genes have survived, in some cases for millions of years, in a highly competitive world. This entitles us to expect certain qualities of our genes. I shall argue that a predominant quality to be expected in a successful gene is ruthless selfishness.[32]

Here the reader will naturally object that what goes for our genes does not necessarily go for us. Just because our genes are selfish does not mean that we are selfish. Dawkins agrees, pointing out that the biologist's use of terms like 'selfish' is in any case a metaphorical use:

> An entity…is said to be altruistic if it behaves in such a way as to increase another such entity's welfare at the expense of its own. Selfish behaviour has exactly the opposite effect. 'Welfare' is defined as 'chances of survival', even if the effect on actual life and death prospects is…small…It is important to realize that the above definitions of altruism and selfishness are *behavioural,* not subjective. I am not concerned here with the psychology of motives…that is not what this book is

about. My definition is concerned only with whether the *effect* of an act is to lower or raise the survival prospects of the presumed altruist and the presumed beneficiary.[33]

Still less, the reader may add, does the fact that we *are* selfish mean that we *should* be selfish. Again, Dawkins agrees: 'I am not advocating a morality based on evolution.'[32] Elsewhere, in a discussion of evolutionary conflicts between parents and children, he warns that some of his own phrases should not be misunderstood:

> I am not advocating this kind of behaviour as moral or desirable. I am simply saying that natural selection will tend to favour children who do act in this way, and that therefore when we look at wild populations we may expect to see cheating and selfishness within families. [My] phrase 'the child should cheat' means that genes that tend to make children cheat have an advantage in the gene pool.[34]

But now one begins to wonder whether Dawkins isn't really saying that we are selfish after all. If selfish genes do win out in evolutionary competitions, and if our individual behaviour is at least partly dictated by our genes, then surely the fact that our genes are selfish *will* mean that we ourselves are selfish?

This question has generated an extensive debate – some of it entertainingly overheated.[35] Dawkins's bottom-line reply to the question is a cautious concession. He admits that 'gene selfishness will usually give rise to selfishness in individual behaviour'.[32] However:

> as we shall see, there are special circumstances in which a gene can achieve its own selfish goals best by fostering a limited form of altruism at the level of individual animals.

Dawkins's phrase 'as we shall see' points us forward to his discussion of biological altruism in chapter 12 of *The Selfish Gene* (which has the delightful title 'Nice Guys Finish First'). There Dawkins stresses that 'biological altruism' is a technical term – and something of a misnomer. 'Biological altruism' refers to the kind of behaviour, often found in nature, where animals instinctively co-operate to help each other. (Two African examples: oxpecker birds groom rhinos for parasites; honey-birds help honey-badgers to track down beehives so that both can get a meal.)

Confronted with such cases, evolutionary scientists do *not* conclude that such behaviour is genuinely altruistic, in the strict sense of the word 'altruistic' that interests me here, and leave their inquiries at that. Instead, they look for a Darwinian explanation of why such apparently altruistic behaviour has evolved. A successful Darwinian explanation of a given individual creature's biologically altruistic behaviour means one that cashes out the behaviour's survival value for that individual creature. In other words, evolutionary scientists do not think that they have satisfactorily explained biologically altruistic behaviour until they have reduced it to self-interest. Hence the gloomy-sounding conclusion of Dawkins's previously quoted argument: '"Special" and "limited" are important words in the last sentence. Much as we might wish to believe otherwise, universal love and the love of the species as a whole are concepts that simply do not make evolutionary sense.'[32]

I have taken the trouble to spell out this point because it is important for my main argument about egoism and altruism. It is an interesting question (but not a philosophical one, so I won't address it) how strict altruism – genuinely unselfish and other-regarding behaviour – might have evolved in a world like ours. Obviously we can conjecture that it evolved from biological altruism – from patterns of behaviour that look unselfish but really work in the agent's own long-term interest. Such speculations should not obscure Dawkins's important observation that strict altruism is quite different from biological altruism. Biological altruism is simply smart egoism: it is egoism which has learned to use co-operation to secure its own interests more effectively. But strict altruism is not egoism at all: someone who is motivated by strict altruism is not aiming to secure his own interests in *any* way, not even a smart or cleverly disguised one. So if evolutionary biologists offer us a picture that systematically reduces strict altruism to biological altruism, they are offering us a picture like Hobbes's picture in **3.6** – a picture in which there is really no altruism, in the strict sense, at all. In such a picture, strict altruism will be what Hobbes thought it was – an impossibility. In the words of Michael Ruse, altruism – and more widely, morality itself – will be 'no more than a collective illusion fobbed off on us by our genes for reproductive ends'.[36]

However that may be, there can be no doubt of the importance of evolutionary ideas in reinforcing our society's scepticism about the possibility of altruism. I have just described three confusions that may often help to cause this scepticism: between describing selfishness and advocating it, between selfish genes and selfish people, and between biological altruism and strict altruism. With or without these confusions, the ways in which evolutionary ideas feed our doubts about altruism should be obvious.

3.8 Three great conspiracy theorists: Marx, Nietzsche, Freud

A second reason for egoism's continuing grip on us today is the influence of the three great 'conspiracy theorists' of the modern age.

A *conspiracy theory* is any theory that says that things are not as they seem. What's really going on is nothing like what most people think is going on; the truth makes a quite different, and much more sinister, pattern. Some conspiracy theories, like the theory that Elvis Presley was assassinated by the CIA and is now working on the till in Woolworth's, are obviously crazy, and are not taken seriously by many people in our society. Other conspiracy theories are not so crazy. Some of them are central to our society's world-view.

The evolutionary account of altruism that I've just described is, in this sense, a conspiracy theory. Its conspirators are our genes, which 'conspire' to give us the illusion of strict altruism. Three other conspiracy theorists – Marx, Nietzsche and Freud – also have a central place in our culture. In their different ways, all three of them offer theories of 'what's really going on' which, if they are true, make genuine altruism look just as unlikely as it seems to be in evolutionary theory.

A conspiracy theory can be crazy or not so crazy. It can also be influential or not influential, which is not the same thing. Unlike the theory of evolution, which remains enormously plausible, the theories of Marx, Nietzsche and Freud are no longer credible, not at least in their original forms. This fact has not stopped them from having a huge impact on our culture. Nor has it stopped them from continuing to influence the formation of many successor-theories, which are still widely believed. Moreover, Marx, Nietzsche and Freud remain important because of the continued plausibility of the general idea that all three, in their different ways, are developing. This is the idea that the development of scientific explanation undercuts the supposedly privileged human perspective. This idea is, of course, the same idea as the mind–world rift noted in **0.2**. The ideas of Marx, Nietzsche and Freud are, therefore, an important part of the story that I am telling, and need at least a brief look.

The thought of **Karl Marx** (1818–83) is dominated by the notion of *ideology*. An ideology is a structure of ideas which has been invented to justify a structure in society. Ideology changes as society changes, because new social structures need new kinds of justification.

Marx's position is developed in deliberately stark contrast to the position of his main philosophical influence, G. W. F. Hegel (1770–1831). Hegel thought that philosophical change was the source of all social, political and economic change. Marx, in his own proud phrase, 'stands Hegel on his head': Marx sees philosophical development as no more than a reflection of social, political and (above all) economic development. For Hegel, all history is really the history of ideas; for Marx, all history is really (in the opening words of *The Communist Manifesto*) 'the history of class struggle'.

Marx's view of human society is cynical and pessimistic: the new social structures that he means are new forms of *oppression*, and the new forms of justification that he means are new forms of *self-deception*. 'The ruling ideas of each age have ever been the ideas of its ruling class.'[37]

Religion, law and morality are prominent among the ideologies – the forms of self-deception – that a ruling class will use to reassure themselves, and their victims, of the justice of their oppressive social arrangements. These forms of ideology are nothing more than 'so many bourgeois prejudices behind which lurk just as many bourgeois interests'.[38]

So consider someone who thinks that he is moved to act by any moral motive, including the motive of strict altruism. We are not surprised to find that Marx claims that he is self-deceived. In the words of Marx's collaborator Friedrich Engels (1820–95): '[Ideology is] a process carried out by the so-called thinker with consciousness, but with a false consciousness. The real driving forces that move him remain unknown to him: otherwise it would not be an ideological process.'[39]

For Marx there is something fundamentally illusory about all morality, including altruism. It is not just that Marx thinks, like Hobbes, that no one is really motivated by strictly unselfish motivations. It is that even if some cases of strict and genuine altruism do exist, we still have to ask whose interests are served by the existence of genuine altruism. Since altruism is part of morality, Marx's answer is that altruism typically serves the class interests of the oppressors. Since class struggle is what is really going on in the world, it follows that what really drives the altruist to act altruistically is the ideological brainwashing that has been imposed on him by the bourgeoisie.

The Marxist view of morality (including altruism) deserves to be called a conspiracy theory, because it sees dark and sinister forces of class interest at work below the surface appearances of morality. **Friedrich Nietzsche** (1844–1900) too sees dark and sinister forces at work in morality – but different ones from Marx.

We've seen Marx argue that morality is a weapon which the ruling class use to maintain their grip over the working class; to put it another way, he thinks morality is a weapon which the strong use to oppress the weak. Nietzsche argues the exact opposite. Like Shakespeare's Richard III, he thinks that morality, at least as we have it today, is a weapon which the weak use to oppress the strong: 'Conscience is but a word that cowards use, Devised at first to keep the strong in awe.'[40] Historically, Nietzsche claims, there has been what he calls a 'slave revolt in morality', led by the Christian Church, and characterized by the motivation that Nietzsche calls *ressentiment* – the jealous hatred that weak, sickly, ugly individuals feel towards strong, healthy, beautiful individuals. The result of this 'slave revolt', according to Nietzsche, is the corruption and enslavement of all that is best, noblest and most beautiful in humanity:

Whoever knows what goes on in menageries is doubtful whether the beasts in them are 'improved'. They are weakened, they are made less harmful, they become *sickly* beasts through pain, through injuries, through hunger. – It is no different with the tamed human being whom the priest has 'improved'. In the early Middle Ages, when the Church was in fact above all a menagerie, one everywhere hunted down the fairest specimens of the 'blond beast' – one 'improved', for example, the noble Teutons. But what did such a Teuton afterwards look like when he had been 'improved' and led into a monastery? Like a caricature of a human being...There he lay now, sick, miserable, filled with ill-will towards himself; full of hatred for the impulses towards life, full of suspicion of all that was still strong and happy. In short, a Christian...[41]

It is only against this historical background, according to Nietzsche, that we can realistically hope to understand a phenomenon like altruism. For the key point about all moral demands, including the demand that we should be altruistic, is that 'morality is a piece of tyranny against nature', a 'protracted constraint'.[42] It is not *natural* to seek the well-being of others, rather than your own well-being (and perhaps the well-being of your nearest family or friends, or others with whom you closely identify):

To require of strength that it should *not* express itself as strength, that it should *not* be a desire to conquer, a desire to subdue, a desire to become master, a thirst for enemies and resistances and triumphs, is just as absurd as to require of weakness that it should express itself as strength. A quantum of force is an equivalent quantum of drive, will, operation – or rather it is nothing other than this driving, willing, operating itself...[43]

Rather, what is natural for us is to seek power:

What is good? – All that heightens the feeling of power, the will to power, power itself in man.

What is bad? – All that proceeds from weakness.

What is happiness? – The feeling that power *increases* – that a resistance is overcome.[44]

Nietzsche's psychology echoes Hobbes's (**3.5**): 'In the first place, I put for a general inclination of all mankind, a perpetual and restless desire of power after power, that ceaseth only in death.'[45] Nietzsche is not concerned primarily with *political* power; nor, come to that, is Hobbes. For both of them, the real point is about what we might call *personal* force. The basic human drive, which motivates the strong and the weak alike, is their will to become strong and flourishing human individuals: to overcome resistances. As I've already hinted, it might be part of this drive to care about *some* other people: Nietzsche never suggests that his ideal men, his 'blond beasts', cannot for example be affectionate parents or friends. But if a Nietzschean ideal man is a good parent or friend, his motivation to be so will derive ultimately from his will to power. It will have nothing to do with seeking the well-being of his children or friends as an end in itself. Still less will a Nietzschean ideal man have any interest in seeking the well-being of those outside his immediate circle of concern, for example the old and ill, or the starving in Africa: 'The weak and ill-constituted shall perish: *first* principle of our philanthropy. And we shall help them to do so.'[46]

For Nietzsche, altruism is never what the Christian and the moralist take it to be – simply impartial moral benevolence, innocent and transparent, with no murky depths to it. When we show altruism towards our families or our close friends, this is not what it seems to be, because it is a manifestation of the will to power. But when we show altruism towards complete strangers, this is not what it seems to be either. When this happens, it just demonstrates how we are gripped by the strictures of 'slave morality', with its debilitating and impossible demand that we should treat all people in line with the obvious lie (as Nietzsche sees it) that they are of equal value, and with its weapons of guilt and blame to enforce this demand. For Nietzsche, all cases of altruism have murky depths to them. This is what qualifies Nietzsche as my second great conspiracy theorist.

My third great conspiracy theorist is **Sigmund Freud** (1856–1939), that explorer *par excellence* of the murky depths of our minds. Freud fits the same pattern as Marx and Nietzsche: he refuses to take any moral or altruistic motivation at face value. This is just an instance of a wider pattern: Freud refuses to take any conscious motivation at all at face value. What Freud sees driving humans into action is not Marx's 'historical forces', nor Nietzsche's 'will to power', but the drives and instincts of the unconscious mind:

> We have been obliged to assume that very powerful mental processes or ideas exist…which can produce in the mind all the effects that ordinary ideas do…without themselves becoming conscious…Psycho-analytic theory [asserts] that such ideas cannot become conscious because a certain force is opposed to them…We obtain our theory of the unconscious, then, from the theory of repression.[47]

And what are the drives and instincts that work from the unconscious level, in ways complicated by 'repression' and 'neurosis', to provide us with the real motivation of everything we do? Freud's answer is usually supposed to be, in one word, sex:

> In the theory of psycho-analysis we have no hesitation in assuming that the course taken by mental events is automatically regulated by the pleasure principle. We believe, that is to say that the course of those events is invariably set in motion by an unpleasurable tension, and that it takes a

direction such that its final outcome coincides with a lowering of that tension – that is, with an avoidance of unpleasure or a production of pleasure.[48]

Certainly sex, or rather the Hobbesian duo of pleasure and self-preservation, is a big part of Freud's account of our basic motivations in his earlier writings, before *Beyond the Pleasure Principle*. Before that book, Freud's acceptance of the thesis that 'the course taken by mental events is automatically regulated by the pleasure principle' is fairly straightforward; he is fairly obviously a psychological hedonist, a believer in the thesis that everything we do is motivated by pleasure. (Not, of course, that this makes him any more sympathetic to the idea of genuine altruism: on the obvious conflict between psychological hedonism and altruism, see **3.9**.) By contrast, from 1920 on Freud is more inclined to balance the instinct for pleasure against a second group of instincts, which he gives the collective name of the 'death-instinct' – or 'death wish', as we call it today:

The second class of instincts was not so easy to define; in the end we came to recognise sadism as its representative. As a result of theoretical considerations, supported by biology, we assumed the existence of a death-instinct, the task of which is to lead organic matter back into the inorganic state...The appearance of life would thus be regarded as the cause of the continuance of life [through the instinct for pleasure], and also as the cause of the striving towards death [through the instinct for death]; and life itself would be a conflict and compromise between these two trends.[49]

This later account of our basic motivations seems more questionable. Freud's idea of an instinct for death faces an obvious, and I think decisive, evolutionary objection: it is no easier to see how evolution could *select* for an instinct for death than to see how it could select for an altruistic instinct. It also faces a second important objection, which is that Freud has simply given up on trying to *explain* unpleasant phenomena like sadism. To see sadism as the manifestation of an alleged instinct for death is, apparently, to admit that you cannot see how sadism might attract anyone in any positive way, for example – as seems to happen – by its seeming pleasant to them. A third problem is that Freud's claim that the death-instinct's 'task' is 'to lead organic matter back into the inorganic state' appears to rest on something like vitalism – a theory of the nature of life developed by Henri Bergson (1859–1941), which has now been universally rejected in science.

Freud's dubious science is – fortunately – not our problem. What is interesting about this Manichean struggle between the death-instinct and the pleasure principle is the way it leads Freud to an account of what is really going on in *morality*. Rather like Nietzsche, Freud takes the hallmark of morality to be the guilty conscience, about which he says this:

> An explanation of the normal conscious sense of guilt (conscience) presents no difficulties; it is due to tension between the ego and the ego-ideal [i.e. the agent's idealized self] and is the expression of a condemnation of the ego pronounced by its criticising function. The feelings of inferiority so well known in neurotics are presumably closely related to it.[50]

Notice first that, for Freud as for Nietzsche, a moral feeling is a way of *being sick*: morality is a kind of mental illness. To be sure, this illness is not very grave in 'normal' people. But it can easily become acute – and when it does, a crucial point about Freud's view of morality emerges:

> [In melancholia] the excessively strong super-ego which has obtained a hold upon consciousness rages against the ego with merciless fury, as if it had taken possession of the whole of the sadism available in the person concerned. Following our view of sadism, we should say that the destructive component had entrenched itself in the super-ego and turned against the ego. What is now holding sway in the super-ego is, as it were, a pure culture of the death-instinct…[51]

Here it becomes obvious that Freud, like Nietzsche, aligns morality with the urge for death. To be even a little 'moralized' is to be neurotic; to be highly moral, dominated in your character and thinking by the constraints of morality, is to be in the grip of a pathological death wish.

This conclusion leaves Freud about as far away from admitting the possibility of real altruism – without murky depths – as he could possibly be. Like Marx and Nietzsche, Freud always looks for the hidden forces at work in motivation. (Also like Marx and Nietzsche, Freud has a highly revisionary, and highly un-Cartesian view of the self; more about the self in chapter 5.) Freud joins Marx and Nietzsche as another principal reason why our society finds the idea of simple, straightforward altruism, with no ulterior motives and no murky depths, so hard to swallow.

3.9 The utilitarian tradition

Still more reasons why our society jibs at the idea of altruism can be found by looking at the utilitarian tradition. By this I mean principally the writings of Jeremy Bentham (1748–1832), John Stuart Mill (1806–73) and Henry Sidgwick (1838–1900). I also mean their philosophical descendants up to the present day, though I shall not explicitly refer to them much in this section. In this tradition, the problem is not good arguments against altruism, as you might think it is with Hobbes and Darwin, and perhaps also with Marx, Nietzsche and Freud; it is bad arguments for altruism.

To explain this remark, I must first say what utilitarianism is. Classical utilitarianism has at its heart a simple and appealing idea. This is the idea, most famously proposed by Bentham, that what matters morally is *pain and pleasure*:

> Nature has placed mankind under the governance of two sovereign masters, pain and pleasure...It is for them alone to point out what we ought to do, as well as to determine what we shall do. On the one hand the standard of right and wrong, on the other the chain of causes and effects, are fastened to their throne.[52]

John Stuart Mill agrees:

> If human nature is so constituted as to desire nothing which is not either a part of happiness or a means of happiness, we can have no other proof, and we require no other, that these are the only things desirable.[53]

If this is utilitarianism, how do we apply it? Well, suppose we are wondering how to decide some difficult moral issue. How, for instance, shall we settle whether Sunday trading or divorce should be allowed, what kind of lawcourts we ought to have, how animals should and should not be treated? All sorts of complicated answers may occur to us. But the utilitarians – who, incidentally, have historically had much to say on all three of these issues – say that we can ignore the complexities, and concentrate our attention on two very simple questions about our practices and institutions. These are: *What harm do they do?* and *What good do they do?*

Suppose the social institution of Sunday trading does no harm to anyone – causes no one any pain. In that case, say the utilitarians, there is no good argument against Sunday trading. Or suppose, again, that the social institution whereby judges wear silk stockings, suspenders and horsehair wigs does no one any good – causes no one any pleasure (not even the judges themselves). In that case, say the utilitarians, there is no good argument in favour of the traditional courtroom dress of British judges.

In practice, of course, there is likely to be some pain and some pleasure on both sides of any interesting moral issue. Some people will feel pain if Sunday trading is illegal – notably the shop-owners, who lose business if their shops can't open on Sundays. Other people will feel pain if Sunday trading is legal – notably the Sabbatarian protestants who see it as an offence against their religion for shops to be open on Sunday. The only question then, according to Bentham and the utilitarians, is which side feels *more* pain:

> Sum up all the values of all the *pleasures* on the one side, and those of all the *pains* on the other. The balance, if it be on the side of pleasure, will give the *good* tendency of the act [or practice] on the whole…if on the side of pain, the *bad* tendency of it upon the whole.[54]

If commerce is ubiquitous and Sabbatarianism is unusual, legalizing Sunday trading will lead to an overall balance of pleasure over pain. But if it's the other way round – if Sabbatarianism is ubiquitous and commerce is unusual – then legalizing Sunday trading will cause more overall pain than pleasure. So, the utilitarian will presumably say, Sunday trading should be legal in a commercial society like London, but illegal in a Sabbatarian society like Stornoway.

This utilitarian method of moral problem-solving looks simple. In fact it is not simple at all. A moment's thought will show how quickly perplexing questions arise about the idea of settling moral questions this way. How do we add up the pleasures and pains on either side? How do we measure the two sides against each other, once added up? How are we supposed to do all this moral accounting in the limited time we have to act? And what if we live in a racist society, where lynching Jews and blacks causes more overall pleasure than pain? Utilitarians and their opponents continue to debate these questions about the feasibility of utilitarianism, both as a 'decision procedure' (as a way of making decisions in real time) and as a 'criterion of rightness' (as a way of reviewing or criticizing decisions once made).

A further problem has to do with how Bentham and Mill move from facts to values. To see this problem, notice that both Bentham and Mill are saying two things together. First, they are stating the thesis of *psychological hedonism*. Like Freud (**3.8**), they both claim that each individual person does in fact act – unless confused or irrational – so as to promote pleasure or happiness, and minimize pain or unhappiness. In Mill's words, 'Happiness is the sole end of human action.'[53] Second, Bentham and Mill are also stating the thesis of *ethical hedonism*. They both claim that each individual *ought* to act so as to promote pleasure or happiness, and minimize pain or unhappiness. (Compare this distinction between psychological and ethical hedonism with the distinction between psychological and ethical egoism.[3])

Not only do Bentham and Mill argue both for psychological hedonism and for ethical hedonism. They also infer ethical hedonism directly from psychological hedonism. That is, they talk as if the claim that humans do in fact seek nothing but happiness or pleasure *logically implies* the claim that humans morally ought to seek nothing but happiness or pleasure. As G. E. Moore points out, this looks very suspect.[55] Just because humans do seek happiness, it doesn't follow that they *ought* to seek it. There is a general problem about how we get from a statement of fact – an 'is' – to a claim about value – an 'ought'. Mill and Bentham do not seem to deal satisfactorily with this problem.[56]

I won't pursue this fact–value problem here, though I will have more to say about it in **4.4**. Nor will I pursue the other questions that I have just raised about the feasibility of utilitarianism. For there is a deeper question about utilitarianism that we ought to be asking: *Whose pleasures count, and why?*

Whose happiness or pleasure does any individual human seek? At first sight, the obvious answer to that question seems to be 'His own'. So Mill:

> To think of an object as desirable and to think of it as pleasant are one and the same thing.[57]

And Bentham:

> The constantly proper end of action on the part of any individual at the moment of action is his real greatest happiness from that moment to the end of his life.[58]

The idea that the individual seeks his *own* happiness is what gives Bentham's and Mill's psychological claims their cogency. As we've already seen in this chapter, psychological hedonism – the idea that each individual is motivated exclusively by his own happiness or pleasure – is one that can easily feel irresistible. The trouble is, of course, that utilitarianism is not about each person promoting his own greatest happiness. It is about each person promoting 'the greatest happiness of the *greatest number*'.[59] How are we supposed to get from *individual* happiness – the notion that dominates utilitarian psychology – to the *general* happiness – the notion that is the keystone of utilitarian ethics?

Unlike Bentham (apparently, but more about him in a moment), John Stuart Mill at least sees this problem:

> The happiness which forms the utilitarian standard of what is right in conduct, is not the agent's own happiness, but that of

all concerned. As between his own happiness and that of others, utilitarianism requires him to be as strictly impartial as a disinterested and benevolent spectator. In the golden rule of Jesus of Nazareth, we read the complete spirit of the ethics of utility. To do as you would be done by, and to love your neighbour as yourself, constitute the ideal perfection of utilitarian morality.[60]

What Mill says here does not solve the problem; it just states it. Mill claims that utilitarian morality requires each agent to be 'strictly impartial' as between his own happiness and anyone else's happiness. But this utilitarian ethical claim only raises the question how any agent could possibly achieve such impartiality, if the utilitarian psychological claim is right that each agent is motivated only to pursue his own happiness. It also raises the question why on earth he should try. Just stating the Golden Rule – 'Do as you would be done by' – to a consistent egoist will tell him nothing that he recognizes as a reason to try to be impartial. If all my motivations are self-regarding, why *should* I seek to put myself in others' shoes?

To this question you might, of course, reply that I ought to treat the happiness of others as just as important as my own happiness, because others are not in any important way different from me. This is the reply given by both Mill and Bentham, and by many contemporary utilitarians as well, such as Peter Singer: 'My own interests cannot count for more, simply because they are my own, than the interests of others.'[61]

But this is a very weak response, and it will not impress any hard-nosed and clear-headed egoist. To begin with, the egoist can ask why his interests *shouldn't* count for more, simply because they are his. Utilitarians claim that the difference between your own interests and anyone else's is not a significant difference. The egoist retorts that this difference is certainly significant *to him*.

Similarly, the egoist can ask what Singer means by 'count for more'. 'Count for more' *to whom?* Maybe Singer is right that my interests don't 'count for more' to Mill's 'disinterested and benevolent spectator', or that they don't 'count for more' from what Sidgwick famously called 'the point of view of the universe'.[62] 'So what?' the egoist will reply: 'My interests *do* count for more from *my* point of view. And if you show me some other point of view from which my interests *don't* count for more, that just raises the question why I should be interested in this other point of view, or what could possibly motivate me to adopt it.'

The problem is nicely summed up in the words of an argument between Bertrand Russell and his daughter Kate:

'I don't want to! Why should I?'
'Because more people will be happier if you do than if you don't.'
'So what? I don't care about other people.'
'You should.'
'But why?'
'Because more people will be happier if you do than if you don't.'[63]

The utilitarian reasoner (such as, on this occasion, Bertrand Russell) has no knock-down argument against the egoist reasoner (such as, on this occasion, Kate Russell).

Mill tries to cover up this problem by recommending a little social conditioning. He has two proposals about how to make 'the nearest approach' to the ideal outlined by Jesus's golden rule. The first is to ensure 'that laws and social arrangements should place the happiness...of every individual, as nearly as possible in harmony with the interest of the whole'. The second is

that education and opinion, which have so vast a power over human character, should so use that power as to establish in the mind of every individual an indissoluble association between his own happiness and the good of the whole...so that not only he may be unable to conceive the possibility of happiness to himself, consistently with conduct opposed to the general good, but also that a direct impulse to promote the general good may be in every individual one of the habitual motives of action.[64]

These proposals are probably not feasible. But even if they were, the fundamental problem with them would remain. They only explain *how* to move from individual happiness to general happiness. They say nothing about *why* you should move from the one to the other.

Mill's proposals are methods of *motivating* individuals to seek the general happiness rather than their own individual happiness. Mill does little more than Hobbes (**3.6**) to *justify* anyone's decision to seek the general happiness rather than her own. Mill exhorts the legislator to bring it about that 'education and opinion' establish an 'indissoluble association' between individual and general happiness. It is an interesting question why the legislator himself should want to establish this association of ideas – after all, it is quite unclear how it serves *his* individual interest to do so. But the main point is that, for all Mill shows, this association might as well be a Pavlovian one. Our ingrained psychological tendency to move from individual to general happiness might be a simple mistake, a logical confusion. Mill, apparently, would still recommend that people in general should succumb to this confusion.

Anyone who remains clear-minded will still see the unbudgeable fact that the general happiness and the individual's happiness are, and remain, *different*. (If they were not different, why would Mill's first proposal highlight the need for the legislator to try to align them with each other?) Mill does nothing to show us how to move from the individual to the general happiness without making a philosophical mistake. In fact, his comments rather suggest that he privately thinks you can't make this move without making a philosophical mistake.

Bentham is more elusive than Mill on this question of why anyone should seek the general good rather than her own benefit. But Bentham does give some sort of answer to the question – an answer which, Henry Sidgwick suggests, is simply confused. For Bentham holds both the utilitarian doctrine that 'the greatest happiness of the greatest number' is the object of ethics, and also the view (which Sidgwick calls 'Egoistic Hedonism') that an individual's happiness or pleasure is his only motivation:

> Bentham adopted this doctrine [the greatest happiness principle] explicitly, in its most comprehensive scope, at the earliest stage in the formation of his opinions; nor do I think that he ever consciously abandoned or qualified it...At the same time I must admit that in other passages Bentham seems no less explicitly to adopt Egoistic Hedonism as the method of 'private ethics', as opposed to legislation.[65]

The only solution to this conflict that Sidgwick can find in Bentham is a gesture towards Adam Smith's (1723–90) famous doctrine of the 'invisible hand'. Smith had written that

> Every individual necessarily labours to render the annual revenue of the society as great as he can. He generally neither intends to promote the public interest, nor knows how much he is promoting it...He intends only his own gain, and he is in this, as in many other cases, led by an invisible hand to promote an end which was no part of his intention. Nor is it always the worse for society that it was no part of his intention. By pursuing his own interest he frequently promotes that of the society more effectually than when he

really intends to promote it. I have never known much good done by those who affected to trade for the public good.[66]

Smith's doctrine of the invisible hand is the claim that each individual's pursuit of his own interest is the best thing he can do for everybody's interests. Sidgwick finds the same equation, but made as it were from the other side, in Bentham's posthumous 'Deontology', where

the two principles [of morality and self-interest] appear to be reconciled by the doctrine, that it is always the individual's true interest, even from a purely mundane point of view, to act in the manner most conducive to the general happiness.[67]

Sidgwick is dismissive of Bentham's solution: 'This proposition...I regard as erroneous.'[67] He denies that Bentham succeeds in solving the utilitarians' problem of getting from the individual's to the general happiness, from the egoistic to the moral viewpoint. In fact, his own position is that nobody does or can solve that problem. In the concluding chapter to his *Methods of Ethics*, Sidgwick tells us that he regards the problem as insoluble:

We have discussed the rational process (called by a stretch of language 'proof') by which one who holds it reasonable to aim at his own greatest happiness may be determined to take Universal Happiness instead, as his ultimate standard of right conduct. We have seen, however, that the application of this process requires that the Egoist should affirm...that his own greatest happiness is not merely the rational ultimate end for himself, but a part of Universal Good: and he may avoid the proof of Utilitarianism by declining to affirm this. It would be contrary to Common Sense to deny that the distinction between any one individual and any other is real and fundamental, and that consequently 'I' am concerned with the quality of my existence as an individual in a sense, fundamentally important, in which I am not concerned with the quality of the existence of other individuals.[68]

3.10 **Conclusion**

The story of **3.9** was that the utilitarian first wins conviction by laying down what can look, in our culture, like an irresistible truth: the claim that each individual is motivated to act solely by his own happiness. The utilitarian then tries to transfer the force of conviction that this claim generates to a very different claim: the claim that each individual ought to be motivated to act solely by everyone's happiness. In the glaring difference between these two claims, and in the feebleness of the attempts that utilitarians have made (and are still making) to close the gap between them, lies another of the main reasons why our society continues to find altruism so hard to believe in. The badness of the utilitarians' influential arguments for altruism has brought altruism into disrepute just as effectively as the goodness, or at any rate sticking-power, of other philosophers' influential arguments against altruism. Or so, at any rate, I have been arguing in this chapter.

And what – the reader must be wondering – would be involved in a *solution* to the problem of altruism? Isn't there a way to show that we do really have reason to care about other people's happiness, and not just our own? Can't we shake off the doubts about genuine altruism that are intentionally raised by the conspiracy theorists, the evolutionary scientists and Hobbes, and unintentionally raised by the utilitarian tradition?[69]

I believe we could, provided we were prepared to believe that the sources of our reasons to act were not just our own desires and inclinations, but genuine realities that lie outside ourselves. To believe this would be to believe in *objective goods*: to believe in a list of real things that have ethical value in and of themselves, aside from our inclinations and desires – outside what Iris Murdoch bitingly calls the 'fat relentless ego'.[70] Other people, for instance, might be objective goods; so might the beauty of the world, or the goodness of truth and knowledge, or friendship, or life and health and pleasure. The point would then be that our reasons for action arose from *these* sorts of sources outside us, not just from our own desire for our own pleasure within us. This picture of our reasons for action would break the spell of egoism, because it would no longer be true that all our reasons for action and our motivations had to be rooted *within* us. On the contrary, our motivations would typically have their sources outside us – in the goods in the world.

The only trouble with this picture is that, to make it a credible one, we need to be able to solve the other part of the ethical problem of the inescapable self, about objectivity. And this, as we shall see in chapter 4, is far from easy.

1 Abridged from Plato, *Republic* 359c–360c, following my own translation in Chappell 1996.

2 Nozick 1974: 42–3.

3 It is usual to distinguish *psychological* egoism, the claim that agents are as a matter of fact motivated by self-interest, from *ethical* egoism, the claim that agents morally ought to be motivated by self-interest. Unless I say otherwise, my references here to 'egoism' will always refer to psychological egoism.

4 Descartes, *Discourse* 3, CSM I: 123. Cottingham 1998 argues interestingly that there is a more positive ethical theory to be found elsewhere in Descartes: in his *Passions of the Soul*, which gives us a picture of how to make peace with our emotions.

5 Hobbes, *Elements of Law* 1.3; *Leviathan* 1.2.

6 *Leviathan* 1.2; compare Descartes, Meditation 6, CSM II: 61.

7 Kant thinks the same: Kant 1929: 272.

8 Tuck 1989: 45.

9 Hobbes, *Leviathan* 3.34.

10 Hobbes, *Elements of Law* 1.11.

11 *Elements of Law* 1.2.

12 *Leviathan* 1.4.

13 *Leviathan* 1.13.

14 Tuck 1988.

15 Kavka 1986.

16 Another example is Ewin 1991: 114–15.

17 Boonin-Vail 1994.

18 Sorell 1986: 97 ff.

19 Hobbes, *Human Nature* 9.17.

20 Sorell 1986: 99 on *Leviathan* 1.14.8.

21 *Pace* Ewin 1991: 116, who oddly denies that it is egoistic to be ultimately motivated exclusively by a desire for self-preservation.

22 Hobbes, *Leviathan* 1.11.

23 *Leviathan* 1.13.5.

24 Joseph Butler, *Fifteen Sermons*, Sermon XI.

25 Hume, *Inquiry concerning the Principles of Morals*, section 5; compare *Treatise of Human Nature* 2.3.3: 'Men often act knowingly against their interest.'

26 Hobbes, *Leviathan* 1.17.13.

27 *Leviathan* 2.18.5; compare 2.21.14, where the subject allows the sovereign to kill him 'if he please'.

28 John Aubrey, 'Life of Hobbes', para. 16.

29 Darwin 1871: 163.

30 For instance, Spencer 1857.

31 Another example is Ridley 1996.

32 Dawkins 1989: 2.

33 Dawkins 1989: 4–5.

34 Dawkins 1989: 139.

35 Mackie 1978; Midgley 1979; Dawkins 1981.

36 Ruse 1991: 506.

37 Marx and Engels 1967: 102.

38 *Marx's and Engels' Works*, vol. 4, p. 472.

39 *Marx's and Engels' Works*, vol. 39, p. 97.

40 Shakespeare, *Richard III*, Act 5, Scene 3, 309–10.

41 Nietzsche 1968: 56.

42 Nietzsche 1977: 105.

43 Nietzsche 1977: 115.

44 Nietzsche 1968: 115.

45 Hobbes, *Leviathan* 1.11.

46 Nietzsche 1968: 116.

47 Freud 1947: 11–12.

48 Freud 1955: 7.

49 Freud 1947: 55–6.

50 Freud 1947: 73.

51 Freud 1947: 77.

52 Bentham 1970: 11.

53 Mill 1969: 292.

54 Bentham 1970: 40.

55 Moore 1993: 117.

56 Though it can be argued that Mill means only to argue that all the evidence we have of how people actually behave suggests that in practice people generally act as if they value pleasure; and that this fact is the best sort of evidence we can get that people *do* value pleasure. For this reading of Mill, see Skorupski 1989: 301.

57 Mill 1969: 293.

58 Bentham, *Memoirs*, in Bowring (ed.), *Bentham's Works*, Vol. 10, p. 560.

59 Mill 1969: 257; Bentham, *Works*, Vol. 10 p. 79.

60 Mill 1969: 268.

61 Singer 1993: 13.

62 Sidgwick 1874: 382, 420; on the implications of the phrase, see Williams 1995.

63 Tait 1975.

64 Mill 1969: 268.

65 Sidgwick 1874: 87–8.

66 Adam Smith, *The Wealth of Nations* [1776], Book 4, Ch. 2.

67 Sidgwick 1874: 88.

68 Sidgwick 1874: 498.

69 Another ethicist who faces a serious problem about the possibility of altruism is Kant: see **4.10**.

70 Murdoch 1970: 52.

4

Vanishing Values

4.1 **From altruism to objectivity**

The problem at the heart of this book is the problem of escaping
the self. The phrase is ambiguous, and is meant to be, between an
epistemological problem – or group of problems – and a related
ethical problem, or group of problems. The nub of the epistemological problem is, roughly, the question how I am to know that
the world is real and external to me, and comes to something
more than my own illusions. The nub of the ethical problem is,
roughly, the question how I am to know that there are reasons to
act which are real and external to me, and come to something
more than my own desires.

The ethical difficulty is partly a problem about egoism and
altruism. I've discussed that form of the problem in chapter 3 (and
will come back to it briefly in **4.10**). The problem is also a
problem about ethical objectivity – about how it could possibly
be that our reasons to act could be part of, or have their sources
in, objective, external reality. This is the form of the problem that
I shall discuss in this chapter.

If there are objective reasons with their sources in external
reality, that helps to explain how altruism is possible. If agents
regularly act on such reasons, then altruism is not only possible but
actual. This makes it clear that there is a connection between the
problem about altruism and the problem about objectivity. It also
makes it clear that this link between altruism and objectivity is not

an inevitable connection. Egoism is consistent with moral objectivity (all our objective reasons might be self-interested); altruism is consistent with moral subjectivity (all our desires and inclinations might be for others' well-being).

Not an inevitable connection; but a natural one. One reason why the connection is natural is because, if we want to show the possibility of altruism, part of what we want to show is that altruism is not just a motivation, but a justification too. We seek to show, not only that altruism happens, but also that it ought to happen: that being altruistic does not necessarily involve being duped, as the mother sparrow is duped into raising the cuckoo chick in her nest. Remembering Hobbes, Darwin, Marx, Nietzsche and Freud (**3.6** to **3.8**), we would like some reason to think that when someone acts altruistically, he is not just succumbing to an urge that he would really be better off ignoring. The clearest and most obvious reason we can have for thinking this will be that there are objective reasons for action that justify altruism.

What, then, are objective reasons for action? They are truths about what an agent ought to do, no matter what that agent wants or believes. So, for instance, if it is true that I ought to treat you kindly, then that remains true no matter whether I want to treat you kindly, or whether I even believe that you exist to be treated kindly.

It is natural to think that objective reasons for action arise from the presence of objective *value* or *goodness* in the world. So, for instance, my reason for treating you kindly might arise from the fact that the net amount of value or goodness in the world is increased by my treating you kindly. Or it might arise from the fact that you yourself are a value or a good existing in the world, or something like that. In this sort of way, the existence of objective *reasons* can seem to presuppose the existence of objective *goods*.

Doubts about reasons and about goods are logically separable: I shall spend some time in this chapter examining an attempt to separate them, namely Kant's (**4.6** to **4.10**). All the same, doubts about reasons and about goods are obviously connected too. One motive for doubting the existence of objective reasons is because you doubt the existence of the objective goods or values in the world that objective reasons are supposed to arise from. So let me begin with doubts about objective goods.

4.2 **Relativism and the argument from disagreement**

There are different kinds of doubt about the idea that there are objective goods or values out there in the world. One kind, moral relativism, is very familiar indeed. This is the view that ethical judgements – claims about the existence of objective goods or values, and claims about what it is right or wrong to do – are never objectively true or correct, because they are perspectival – relative to perspectives. Ethics looks the way it does to you, not because it is that way, but because of the viewpoint that you're looking at it from.

I have found, to my surprise, that sometimes the rhetorical question 'It's all relative, isn't it?' is apparently meant to invoke the authority of Einstein's theories of relativity. This is a striking testimony to the cultural influence of science in our society; but it's not a very good argument. Einstein's theories about the observer-relativity of measurements of space-time have nothing to do, one way or the other, with the claim that ethics is relative.

However, there is a venerable tradition of better arguments for relativism. For instance, something like relativism is clearly meant to be the moral of an anecdote told by the Greek historian Herodotus:

> When Darius was king of Persia, he summoned the Greeks who happened to be present at his court, and asked them what they would take to eat the dead bodies of their fathers.

They replied they would not do it for any money in the world. Later, in the presence of the Greeks, and through an interpreter, so that they could understand what was said, he asked some Indians, of the tribe called Callatiae, who do in fact eat their parents' dead bodies, what they would take to burn them (as was the custom of the Greeks). They uttered a cry of horror and forbade him to mention such a dreadful thing. One can see by this what custom can do and Pindar, in my opinion, was right when he called it '*king of all*'.[1]

In the 20th century, compare Heinrich Harrer's description of a Tibetan burial:

The body was taken, as usual, to a consecrated plot outside the town [Lhasa] where it was dismembered and given to the birds to dispose of. The Tibetans do not mourn for the dead in our sense of the word. Sorrow for the parting is relieved by the prospect of rebirth, and death has no terrors for the Buddhist.[2]

The relativist's point is not simply that Greeks and Callatians, or Germans and Tibetans, disagree about the right way to treat a corpse. Disagreement alone is no evidence for relativism. If I think that the chemical formula for water is HO_2, while you think that the formula is H_2O, then we disagree. It hardly follows that truth in chemistry is a perspectival affair, or that chemistry is 'all relative'. All that follows is that one of us is wrong (namely me). The same applies in ethics. Just because people disagree about ethics, it doesn't follow that ethics is 'all relative'. To argue straight from disagreement to relativism is a simple and uninteresting blunder.

However, there is a further point about ethics, which does not apply in chemistry. This is the point that Herodotus makes by quoting the poet Pindar's saying that 'Custom is king of all.' In chemistry, truths and falsehoods can be separated out by a massively successful and almost completely uncontroversial method of experiment and reasoning. It is because there is a clear method of proof for claims about chemistry that it is possible to say that one view about the chemical formula for water is straightforwardly wrong, while another is straightforwardly correct. There seems to be no corresponding method of proof for claims about ethics. Instead, it looks like our reasons for rejecting or accepting ethical claims all have to do with the set of customs and traditions that we happen to have inherited from our own society. As J. L. Mackie puts it:

> Disagreement about moral codes seems to reflect people's adherence to and participation in different ways of life...And the causal connection seems to be that way round...people approve of monogamy because they participate in a monogamous way of life, [not vice versa.]³

If Mackie is right about this, ethical disagreements are very different from disagreements about chemistry. If you are at all rational, your chemical views will be based on good reasons, which you will be able to appeal to in order to settle disagreements about chemistry. But if your views about ethics are based simply on your cultural background, there will be no point in appealing to that background to try to settle ethical disagreements. The person you are disagreeing with can appeal to his background too: to his own culture and/or to his own personal perspective. The only way forward then is for you to say that there is something *wrong* with his culture or his perspective, and something right about your own. But this looks to most people like an unattractive form of cultural imperialism or chauvinism.

In this way, Herodotus's claim that 'Custom is king of all' turns, when we spell it out, into Nietzsche's famous claim that ethical thinking is genealogically determined. According to Nietzsche, the way we think about ethics does not depend on the truth about ethics, for there is no such thing. Instead, it depends on our own backgrounds. It is conditioned by the history of our culture and society, and by our own biographies and experiences. As my students tell it, 'Everyone has a unique perspective because everyone has had a different life.' As Nietzsche tells it, in the Preface to *The Genealogy of Morals*:

> Our ideas, our values, our affirmations and denials, our *ifs* and *buts* – these grow out of us from the same necessity which makes a tree bear its fruit – totally related and interlinked amongst each other, witnesses of one will, one health, one soil, one sun...the question about where our good and evil really originated [is the question] 'Under what conditions did men invent for themselves these value judgments good and evil?'

Herodotus, Mackie and Nietzsche point us towards a way of understanding moral judgements. They suggest that we should see them as nothing more than outgrowths of the cultures in which they occur, to which they are entirely relative. How should the objectivist respond?

Well, the objectivist might respond that the relativist is exaggerating. Things aren't as hopeless as she paints them. There is lots of agreement about ethics – and far more agreement than disagreement. For instance, while societies often disagree over highly ritualistic questions like the treatment of corpses, apparently they never disagree about more basic and central ethical judgements, such as the judgements that pain and misery are bad, and that pleasure and happiness are good. Or at least, perhaps, they agree in the judgements that pain and misery are bad, and pleasure and happiness are good, other things being equal. (Most societies think that pleasure is bad when it is the pleasure of theft, and that pain is good when it is the pain of punishment.) All in all, it is not as hard as relativists often suppose to come up with ethical claims that no sane person would deny, whatever their culture.

These anti-relativist remarks seem undeniable to me. All the same, this response won't do on its own. It commits the same simple blunder as before, only on the other side. Just as disagreement on its own is no evidence *against* objectivity, so agreement on its own is no evidence *for* objectivity. The fact that cultures disagree about how to treat corpses does not prove that there isn't an objective moral truth about how to treat corpses. The fact that everyone in the world thinks that pain and misery are bad (other things being equal) doesn't prove that there is an objective moral truth about the badness of pain and misery.

The objectivist needs to back up his point about agreement by showing that ethical truth is based on something more than the dictates of custom. He needs to show at least that there is some method of arriving at ethical truth that is not completely culturally conditioned, and ideally that there is as clear a method of proof in ethics as there is in chemistry. The trouble is, of course, that claims about cultural conditioning are hard to refute; and we simply don't have any uncontroversially agreed method of ethical proof analogous to our method of chemical proof.

Neither of these difficulties need stop the objectivist in his tracks. Claims about cultural conditioning are more usually presupposed than argued. If you insist on looking at everything through the glasses of your presupposition that 'It's all culturally conditioned', then of course we won't get you to admit that anything you look at is more than a result of this conditioning. On the other hand, we might get you to take the glasses off – to abandon the presupposition.

Again, the fact that all proposed methods of proof in ethics are controversial does not show that none of them is right. To think that would be the same mistake as before. It would be another argument from disagreement to subjectivity. If it is fallacious to say 'There is disagreement about ethical claims; so no ethical claims can be objectively true', it must be equally fallacious to say 'There is disagreement about methods of proof in ethics; so no method of proof in ethics can be objectively correct.'

In short, the best objectivist response to the argument from disagreement is a robust one. It is to point out that while the argument from disagreement may be suggestive, there is nothing logically compelling about it. Herodotus, Nietzsche and Mackie – and many other writers along with them – are offering us a picture of what ethical judgements are like. We may find their picture a persuasive or attractive one. But there is nothing in the argument to force us to accept the picture. We can't be convicted of irrationality if we reject it. Despite the argument from disagreement for subjectivism, objectivism remains an option in ethics.

However, it is an option under considerable pressure. Since relativism is only one form of subjectivism, this pressure takes several other forms besides the relativist argument. Subjectivism is the view that ethical statements are never objectively true or correct; relativism is the view that ethical statements are never objectively true or correct *because ethical statements are perspectival.* Other forms of subjectivism will offer us other sorts of reason for thinking that ethical statements are never objectively true or correct. Among these other subjectivisms, the most important ones are versions of 'naturalism' or 'scientism'. I will consider these next.

4.3 **Values and the fabric of the world**
I have quoted J. L. Mackie in support of the argument from disagreement. Mackie also offers another argument for subjectivism – for the claim, as he puts it, that 'values are not objective, are not part of the fabric of the world'.[4] Mackie calls this 'the argument from queerness':

If there were objective values, then they would be entities or qualities or relations of a very strange sort, utterly different from anything else in the universe. Correspondingly, if we were aware of them, it would have to be by some special faculty of moral perception or intuition, utterly different from our ordinary ways of knowing everything else.[5]

Mackie's claim is that, if they exist, objective values, and our way of knowing about them, will have to be 'very strange'. To this we might of course object that strangeness alone is no bar to existence. Duckbilled platypuses are strange also – quite unlike any other mammals in existence. When you come to think about it, black holes, photons and atoms are all pretty strange entities too. Each of them is quite unlike anything else; the way we get to know about black holes, photons and atoms is pretty weird as well. This can hardly be a reason for thinking that they don't exist. (As it happens, there are philosophers of science who think that black holes, photons and atoms *don't* exist – or at least, they say that we have no reason to think they do. But their reason for denying this is not that these 'theoretical entities' are 'queer'; it is that we have no direct knowledge of them.[6])

Not surprisingly, Mackie has a better argument in mind. He is not saying merely 'Objective values are strange; therefore objective values can't exist.' Rather, his point is that, if objective values exist, they will have to combine different features that he sees no way of combining:

Plato's Forms give a dramatic picture of what objective values would have to be…[As with a Form], an objective good would be sought by anyone who was acquainted with it, not because of any contingent fact that this person, or every person, is so constituted that he desires this end, but just because the end has to-be-pursuedness somehow built into it.[7]

And again:

> Another way of bringing out this queerness is to ask, about anything that is supposed to have some objective moral quality, how this is linked with its natural features…The wrongness must somehow be 'consequential' or 'supervenient'; it is wrong because it is a piece of deliberate cruelty. But just what *in the world* is signified by this 'because'?[8]

Mackie's question is not just: how could there be such wacky things as objective moral values? Rather, his question is: how could anything combine *existing* with *being intrinsically to-be-pursued*? 'How much simpler and more comprehensible the situation would be', Mackie concludes, 'if we could replace the moral quality with some sort of subjective response…to natural features.'[8]

The reader might still not see the point of Mackie's argument. He might wonder what *forces* us to reject the notion of objectively existing moral qualities, and to prefer Mackie's 'simpler and more comprehensible' alternative. Why, in short, shouldn't there be things that combine existing with intrinsic to-be-pursuedness?

The answer to this question lies in Mackie's 'naturalism' or 'scientism', his belief that science tells the basic truth about the nature of the world, and that the story that science tells is essentially value-free (**2.6.4**). An explanation of why anyone should adopt this naturalistic or scientistic view takes us to the heart of the history of modern science. Here, of course, I can only put the explanation very briefly.

4.4 **A brief history of scientism**

From its beginnings in the work of Galileo, Descartes and Newton, our scientific tradition has consistently rejected Aristotle's teleology – his method of giving a scientific explanation of the world by appealing to the presence of inbuilt purpose and intrinsic directedness in things. For researchers in our tradition have consistently found that the appeal to teleology is neither helpful nor necessary to the construction of a successful science.

Aristotelian science is about an indefinite multiplicity of different kinds of 'substances', each with its own kind of inbuilt natural purpose, which it will naturally fulfil unless it is prevented. (So, for instance, the natural purpose of heavy bodies is to fall as far down as they can.[9]) This world of natures seeking their natural fulfilments includes, and indeed culminates in, *human* natures seeking *their* natural fulfilment. Aristotle calls human natural fulfilment *eudaimonia* ('well being'). For him, it is not only a biological concept, but also the key concept of his ethics. In fact, Aristotle thinks of the behaviour of all objects, including inanimate objects, on the model of the intentional and goal-directed action of human agents.

For all we can know, there might be indefinitely many different natural tendencies; Aristotle notoriously supposes, for example, that the basic physics of planet Earth differs from the basic physics of 'the heavens', the rest of the universe.[10] Moreover, Aristotle never makes it clear how, if at all, the operation of complex tendencies can be explained by the operation of simple tendencies. So Aristotelian scientific explanation is a cumbersome, local and ad hoc affair.

By contrast, Sir Isaac Newton, in the *Principia Mathematica* (1687), needs only two basic resources to give a simple, coherent and universal scientific explanation of why every physical body, however simple or complex, moves as it does. One of Newton's resources is classical mathematics. The other is the observable phenomena of nature, and in particular their action under a single force, the force of gravity.

'But what' – an Aristotelian might ask here – 'what *is* gravity?' Newton simply dismisses this question as unnecessary to science:

> I frame no hypotheses; for whatever is not deduced from the phænomena is to be called an hypothesis; and hypotheses, whether metaphysical or physical, whether of occult qualities or mechanical, have no place in experimental philosophy.[11]

Aristotelian science is about different kinds of things which will act in their different ways unless prevented; Newtonian science is about one kind of thing, physical matter, which will do nothing unless it is made to by some externally impressed force. Aristotelian science is, from the beginning, implicitly value-laden; Newtonian science is, from the beginning, explicitly value-free.

Over 100 years before Newton, Descartes's conception of science was already no less value-free:

> I recognise no matter in corporeal things apart from that which the geometers call quantity, and take as the object of their demonstrations, i.e. that to which every kind of division, shape, and motion is applicable. Moreover, my considerations of such matter involves absolutely nothing apart from these divisions, shapes and motions; and even with regard to these, I will admit as true only what has been deduced from indubitable common notions so evidently that it is fit to be considered a mathematical demonstration. And since all natural phenomena can be explained in this way…I do not think that any other principles are either admissible or desirable in physics.[12]

The basic picture of the subject-matter of science that our tradition recognizes, up to Newton and long beyond him, is essentially Descartes's conception as expressed in these words. The picture, as I've said before (0.2), is of a complete and exhaustive division between mind and matter: between a single physical reality whose essence is spatial extension, and a plurality of mental realities – minds – whose essence is thought. The picture, in short, is a divorce between the scientific and the humane perspectives; it is a picture of the mind–world rift.

Among other things, this picture is obviously a picture of the nature of persons; I shall consider it as such in **5.1** to **5.3**. It is also, perhaps less obviously, a picture of the nature of ethics – and this is what concerns us here. For Descartes just as for Newton, value is excluded from the physical world. The Aristotelian picture of a world of substances in process, each pursuing the value that fulfils its nature, is utterly denied. For Descartes, value has already become something that, as Wittgenstein put it 300 years later, has to lie *outside the world*: 'If there is any value that does have value, it must lie outside the whole sphere of what happens and is the case.'[13] The picture is, perhaps, most famously expressed in the words of Hume:

> In every system of morality, which I have hitherto met with, I have remarked, that the author proceeds for some time in the ordinary way of reasoning...when of a sudden I am surprized to find, that instead of the usual copulations of propositions, *is*, and *is not*, I meet with no proposition that is not connected with an *ought*, or an *ought not*. This change is imperceptible; but is, however, of the last consequence. For as this *ought*, or *ought not*, expresses some new relation or affirmation, 'tis necessary that it should be observed and explained; and at the same time that a reason should be given, for what seemed altogether inconceivable, how this new relation can be a deduction from others, which are entirely different from it.[14]

Hume's sardonic suggestion is that, if value is part of the fabric of the world, then we ought to be able to explain *how* we can derive this 'new relation' between propositions – the moral relation – from the relations between propositions that science knows about. In Hume's view, no one has ever offered any such explanation that stands five minutes' scrutiny. And no wonder, according to Hume: for value is not part of the fabric of the world at all. 'Ought' cannot be derived from 'is', because 'ought' is not given its content by reality, but by our reactions to reality. For Hume as for Descartes and Wittgenstein, there is an 'is–ought gap': value is excluded from the world.

As I said in the Prelude (**0.2**), this exclusion of value from the objective world is another manifestation of the problem of the inescapable self – a manifestation that will increasingly concern us in the rest of this book. For Descartes's retreat into the citadel of the certainties of self-consciousness not only puts everything else in doubt. It is also the ultimate explanation of his evacuation of all value from the external world of science. Not only does the problem of the inescapable self imply problems for what we can know, and what we can value, outside ourselves. It also implies the deep and problematic rift between the self's first-person perspective on things mental, and the scientist's third-person perspective on things physical, which I am calling the *scientific* and the *humane* perspectives.

4.5 **Varieties of subjectivism and varieties of response**
This mind–world rift will be a central focus from here on. For the moment, notice that we can now answer the question that launched us on our lightning tour of modern science. We can now identify the main problem about the notion of things 'out there in the world' that have objective moral value: things that, in J. L. Mackie's words (**4.3**), combine existing with intrinsic to-be-pursuedness. The problem is that, according to our standard scientific picture, *nothing* 'out there in the world' can possibly combine existing with intrinsic to-be-pursuedness. The rejection of Aristotle that inaugurates modern science is, as I've said, a

rejection of teleology. But teleology is just what intrinsic to-be-pursuedness is.

No wonder, then, that Mackie and others see a problem about admitting objective moral values into the 'fabric' or 'furniture' of the value-free world of post-Newtonian science. No wonder that Mackie is pushed to the conclusion that all ethical statements without exception are false, because they all embody the false presupposition that objective moral values are a part of the furniture of the world. (Since his view is that any ethical claim involves an error, this position is called Mackie's *error theory* of ethics.)

No wonder, either, that other ethical theorists, such as Simon Blackburn, have been led to develop subjectivist or non-realist theories designed specifically to 'avoid the metaphysical problems which [objectivist or] realist theories of ethics bring', and to explain 'the practice of moralizing in terms only of our exposure to some thinner reality'.[15] Given the way our scientific tradition has developed, the pressure on ethicists to believe in a thinner reality than Aristotle's – one that does not include objective goodnesses and badnesses as intrinsic qualities of the world – has become enormous.

As a result of this pressure, much recent discussion of subjectivist theories of ethics like Mackie's and Blackburn's takes this 'thinner reality' pretty much for granted. Consider, for instance, the important response to Mackie offered by Crispin Wright.[16] Wright does not query Mackie's claim that objective values are not real, 'out there in the world'. Instead, he queries whether it is appropriate, even on Mackie's own premisses, to call *every* ethical claim 'false'. There is, after all, *some* good distinction to be drawn between the claims that 'Genocide is morally abhorrent' and 'Genocide is morally admirable'. Wright asks: why not call this distinction the distinction between ethical truth and ethical falsity – even if Mackie is correct, and there really is no objective moral value as part of the fabric of the world?

Responses to Blackburn's rather different subjectivist theory of ethics often take a 'thin reality' for granted, too. Blackburn's view is *expressivism*. He does not hold, like Mackie, that all moral claims are false assertions, because they presuppose the objective existence of something that does not in fact exist. Instead, like Hume, Blackburn holds that moral claims are not assertions about the world at all. Rather, they are *reactions to* the world. To make a moral claim is not to state a fact, but to express my feelings about a fact: 'The [expressivist] theory asks no more than this: a natural world, and patterns of reaction to it.'[17]

Blackburn's view is the descendant of earlier expressivisms such as A. J. Ayer's:

If I say to someone, 'You acted wrongly in stealing that money', I am not stating anything more than if I had simply said, 'You stole that money'. In adding that this action is wrong, I am not making any further statement about it. I am simply evincing my moral disapproval about it.[18]

Here is how the view is put by David Hume, the father of all modern expressivisms:

[Reason] conveys the knowledge of truth and falsehood; [taste] gives the sentiment of beauty and deformity, vice and virtue. The one discovers objects as they really stand in nature, without addition or diminution; the other has a productive faculty, and gilding or staining all natural objects with the colours borrowed from internal sentiment, raises in a manner a new creation.[19]

I've noted that responses to Mackie's error theory have often left unquestioned his commitment to a 'thin reality'. The same is true of typical responses to expressivism, whether Blackburn's or some earlier version. Instead of querying the expressivists' commitment to a 'thin reality', critics have mostly focused on a technical difficulty for expressivism.

This technical difficulty, to put it very briefly, is the problem of explaining how any moral claim can have the meaning that expressivism gives it in every context where it occurs. For example, 'Murder is wrong' sometimes occurs on its own; and then the expressivist wants to treat its meaning as an expression of a feeling. So far, so good. But 'Murder is wrong' also occurs as a part of longer sentences, for instance:

A If murder is wrong, then Lee Harvey Oswald did something wrong.

It seems that the expressivist cannot claim that the meaning of *this* occurrence of 'Murder is wrong', inside **A**, is to express a feeling. (What would the feeling be?) But if not, then 'Murder is wrong' has two different meanings, depending on whether it occurs on its own or inside some longer sentence like **A**. All sorts of inconveniences will result from this. For example, it will turn out that I am guilty of the fallacy of equivocation if I argue (1) that murder is wrong, (2) that if murder is wrong, then Lee Harvey Oswald did something wrong, so (3) Lee Harvey Oswald did something wrong.

This problem – the 'Frege–Geach problem', as it is called – poses a nice technical challenge for the expressivist.[20] I do not want to say any more about it here; I simply want to point out that a robust and resolute realist might respond differently to Blackburn (perhaps, of course, alongside the Frege–Geach objection). This different response – developed, for instance, by John McDowell – is to question Blackburn's and Mackie's commitment to a thin reality, their naturalism.[21]

The point made by resolute realists such as McDowell is not simply the obvious historical observation that, in fact, neither

Descartes nor Newton ever intended that their views about *physical* reality should be taken – as moderns like Blackburn and Mackie are inclined to take them – as views about the *whole* of reality, including moral reality. That historical remark is true. But it is undermined by the stark contrast between the lightning progress that science has made in describing physical reality, and the very dubious, controversial and apparently non-progressive status of all available attempts to describe moral reality. McDowell's point is rather that the thin picture of reality, irresistible though it may seem to many of us today, is nonetheless only a picture. It is a presupposition of modern subjectivism, rather than something that modern subjectivism proves. If we can find, and defend, credible alternative pictures of reality that are less thin, we may be able to cut off the 'scientistic' motivation for moral subjectivism at its source. For in a thicker picture of reality, there may be less difficulty in understanding what it might be like for objective moral values to exist.

Maybe something like what McDowell has in mind here is possible. However, it has to be said that McDowell's own attempts to spell out a thicker picture of reality have seemed, to many philosophers, exceedingly sketchy. Even would-be proponents of moral objectivism have often found the idea of a thicker picture of reality too much to swallow. Or at least, they have not found it a credible idea that our picture of reality could be thick enough to include the existence of objective moral goods, out there in the world, providing a grounding for objective moral reasons.

The trouble is that – whether moral subjectivism is stated as an error theory or as some form of expressivism – there is something fundamentally unsatisfactory about moral subjectivism too. Bertrand Russell puts the basic problem with his customary elegance and brevity:

I am not, myself, satisfied with what I have read or said on the philosophical basis of ethics. I cannot see how to refute the arguments for the subjectivity of ethical values, but I find myself incapable of believing that all that is wrong with wanton cruelty is that I don't like it.[22]

As many writers have pointed out, it is very hard to combine a seriously thought-through subjectivism with serious moral commitments like Russell's own to the wrongness of bull-fighting, Nazism and nuclear war. For subjectivism says either that all moral assertions are false (this is Mackie's error theory). Or else it says that all moral assertions are neither true nor false, because they are not really assertions about the world at all: they are just reactions to the world (this is expressivism).

Since the error-theorist holds that all moral assertions are false, he can't say that any moral assertions are true. As we have seen Crispin Wright point out, this is deeply unsatisfactory. It means that the error-theorist must say that even the assertion 'Genocide is morally abhorrent' is false – just as false, in fact, as the assertion 'Genocide is morally admirable'. But this is surely crazy. If this is a consequence of the error theory, then the error theory is powerless to prevent a deep rift appearing between our use of moral assertions and our theory of what moral assertions are. (A rift which is, of course, just another manifestation of the rift between the personal and the scientific perspectives.)

It is supposed to be the great merit of expressivism that it avoids this sort of crazy conclusion. But does the expressivist really do any better? I don't believe he does. Expressivism, remember, works with 'no more than this: a natural world, and patterns of reaction to it'.[17] So all our moral assertions are reactions to reality: none of them is a *representation* of how reality is. To say that 'Genocide is morally abhorrent' is not to report a fact about genocide: it is to express my own strong negative reaction to genocide. (As we might also put it: 'Boo to genocide!') Of course, I might add that 'It's right (or true) to say that genocide is morally abhorrent.' But if I do that, I still won't be reporting a fact about genocide: I will just be expressing my own positive reaction to my own strong negative reaction to genocide. ('Hurray for: "Boo to genocide!"') The same will apply even if I say that 'It's right to say that it's right to say that genocide is morally abhorrent.' This utterance does not report a fact either; it just expresses my own positive reaction to my own positive reaction to my own strong negative reaction to genocide. ('Hurray for: "Hurray for: 'Boo to genocide!'"')

Is this really an adequate view of everything that is involved in moral assertion? When we make moral assertions, do we normally think that all we're doing is expressing reactions, however complex? I don't believe so: we also think that the reactions we express are *justified*. And, it seems to me, this sense that moral reactions can be justified – or fail to be justified – is simply not captured by expressivism. If I may be excused for quoting myself:

> According to the expressivist there is no deeper level of fact at which it is simply and non-attitudinally true that the Nazi *is* evil...This puts in doubt our right to say anything more about our basic moral attitudes, to determined and consistent rejecters of those attitudes, than to utter a series of variations on the uninteresting theme that we accept them and think it would be nice if everyone else accepted them too. Despite Blackburn's repeated protests, this just does not seem enough to prevent the corrosion of our moral confidence and competence by moral scepticism.[23]

Suppose you and I are arguing about the morality of fox-hunting. When I say 'Fox hunting is wrong' and you retort 'No, it isn't', do we imagine that we are just exchanging reports on the state of our own psychology? Of course not. We think, instead, that we are trying to get something right about the way the world is, no matter what our own psychological kinks may be. Our ordinary moral discourse is world-directed, not self-referential. However many bells and whistles are added to the basic model of expressivism, this world-directedness in our ethical talk always seems, somehow, to go missing. This means that expressivism is, in the end, no more satisfactory as an account of the meaning of moral assertions than the error theory is. (At least the error theory recognizes the world-directedness of ethical talk – even if it claims that this is precisely the feature of our ethical talk that makes it all false.)

So far, then, the conclusion of this chapter is that both moral subjectivism and moral objectivism are deeply problematic positions. Is there any other alternative?

It seems that there is. Apparently, there can be a middle way between outright moral subjectivism – subjectivism about both goods and reasons – and outright objectivism – objectivism about both. In one form, this middle way is the position that we will develop if we find a way of arguing for objective moral reasons *without* objective moral values. On this view, the idea will not be that moral reasons derive from moral goods which are themselves part of the 'furniture of the world'. Rather, the idea will be that our moral reasons derive from reason itself. Hence we simply don't need to suppose that, besides objective moral reasons, there are objective moral goods as well, out there in the world. According to this middle way, we can reconstruct the whole of ethics without supposing that there are objective goods: we need appeal only to objective reasons. This way we can avoid the objectivist claims about the existence of goods out there in the world that the naturalist, with his 'thin' picture of reality, finds so objectionable.

This middle way between moral objectivism and moral subjectivism is *constructivism* – a view that was invented by Kant. Kantian constructivism is, perhaps, the most sophisticated attempt there has ever been to finesse the dilemma that I have just described, between ethical objectivity and ethical subjectivity. It therefore deserves close examination, which I shall give it in **4.6** to **4.10**.

4.6 **Kantian ethics: from form to content**

In **2.6.3** I gave a brief outline of Kantianism as a theory of knowledge. The reader might like to bookmark that section while reading this one. For as we will now see, Kant's ethical theory develops a striking parallel with his theory of knowledge.

As I put it in **2.6.3**, Kant's theory of knowledge stands epistemology on its head. Instead of the vain attempt to conform our knowledge to objects, he proposes conforming objects to our knowledge; instead of the vain question 'What can we know about the world out there?', he proposes asking 'What kind of minds must we have to know anything?' Thus Kant's epistemology makes a simple but dazzlingly audacious reversal. Instead of first looking for the content of our knowledge, and then determining what the form of our knowledge must be given that content, Kant first looks for the form of our knowledge, and derives the content of our knowledge from its form.

This *formalism* – this strategy of deriving content from form, not form from content – dominates Kant's ethics just as it dominates his epistemology. Kant's theories of ethics and of knowledge develop in close parallel, as Kant himself notes: 'There is really no other foundation for a metaphysics of morals than the critique of a *pure practical reason*, just as [the foundation] of metaphysics [of nature] is the critique of pure speculative reason already published.'[24]

The original motivation for Kant's formalism in epistemology is, simply, scepticism about the external world. Kant is a formalist in epistemology because he thinks that the sceptics are right about the objective world that Descartes and Locke tried to get at: it is simply not accessible by any direct route. (Perhaps he thinks it isn't accessible by *any* route: it depends how you read Kant.) Kant is a formalist in ethics too, and, again, because of scepticism. It is because Kant thinks the objective world is hopelessly inaccessible, at least by the direct route, that he thinks that objective goods or values in the world must be inaccessible too. In general, we cannot start our epistemology with 'the things out there that we know'. In particular, then, we cannot start our moral episte-mology with 'the values out there that we know'.

In general epistemology, Kant's sceptical starting-point leads him to say that knowledge depends on the structure of universally applicable rules for the understanding that we apply to the chaos of our experience. We order and structure that chaos so that it becomes an intelligible coherent picture of the world. Similarly in ethics, Kant's sceptical starting-point – his denial of the possibility of knowing about objective goods out there in the world – leads him to say that moral knowledge depends on developing a structure of universally applicable rules for decision-making: rules which we can apply to the chaos of our desires and inclinations, to find a rational way of responding to those desires and inclina-tions.

In epistemology, our experience begins in a hurly-burly of attraction, repulsion, to and fro, motion and rest, sensation and perception, delusion and profusion and confusion – and can only be made sense of by principles imposed on that hurly-burly 'from above'. Likewise in ethics, our thinking about what to do begins in a hurly-burly of desires and inclinations, preferences and attrac-tions, aversions and perversions – and it too can only be made sense of by principles imposed on that hurly-burly 'from above'.

What are these principles imposed from above? In episte-mology, we saw, they were *concepts*, rules for the understanding that can be applied anywhere and everywhere, in just the same way, with complete consistency. In ethics, they are *universalizable maxims*: rules for the will that can be applied anywhere and everywhere, in just the same way, with complete consistency.

Hence Kant's famous test for the permissibility of any proposed action – the *Categorical Imperative*:

> *Act only in accordance with that maxim through which you can at the same time will that it become a universal law.*[25]

For Kant, the question in epistemology is 'How can reason apply to what I experience?' For Kant, the question in ethics is 'How can reason apply to what I do?' The answer in both cases is that the key to rationality is *consistency*. In epistemology this means consistency in our thinking; in ethics it means consistency in our actions.

Clearly, then, Kant believes that some particular ethical content can be derived from the form that he offers us. This form, as we've seen, is the form of consistency. What is its content?

4.7 The content of practical consistency

At first sight, it might seem that consistency alone could give us almost no particular ethical content at all. An ethics that requires you only to be consistent in your actions seems to have nothing to say about which actions should be yours. Some people torture every cat, or molest every child, or lynch every Jew who comes their way. (As the quip goes: 'I'm not prejudiced – I hate everybody.') Surely people like these don't count as good moral agents just because they're consistent!

Another worry about the ethical emptiness of the formal notion of consistency arises here, too. Presumably you are acting consistently if and only if you act in the same way in the same circumstances. But until we know what 'same way' means, and what 'same circumstances' means, this requirement of consistency looks completely empty.

Illustration: suppose that, like Hobbes (**3.6**), I give a beggar sixpence every time I see one. Then I always keep the rule 'If you see a beggar, give him sixpence.' So I am consistent. Fine. But I am equally consistent if I give a beggar sixpence every time I see one, except on Thursday 24 July 2003, when I give him a kick in the face. For then I always keep the rule 'If you see a beggar, give him sixpence if it is not Thursday 24 July 2003; otherwise, kick him in the face.' Indeed, I can be equally consistent if my treatment of the beggar is completely different every time I see him. For perhaps I am keeping the rule 'Do something different every time you see a beggar', or the rule 'Do whatever you feel like doing'; or perhaps I am keeping an extremely long and complicated rule which has, as its contents, everything that I in fact do throughout the course of my life. This is our paradox: no course of action can be determined by the criterion of consistency, because every course of action can be made to accord with *some* sort of consistency.[26]

From Hegel onwards, a long line of critics of Kant have pushed something like this criticism, accusing him of what Hegel called an 'empty formalism'. Does the criticism hit its target?

It does not, because Kant has a clearer notion of consistency in action than these critics realize. Kant is not merely giving us the advice to make sure that whatever we do is consistent with some rule or other. That advice really would be an 'empty formalism'. But this is not Kant's advice, and not his notion of consistency either. He has a special notion of consistency, which goes beyond mere logical consistency, and so needs a special label; I shall call it *practical* consistency.

Kant's point about practical consistency is this. He thinks that there is something definite that everything we do *has* to be consistent with, if it is to make any kind of rational sense at all. This definite something is *the phenomenon of our own agency*. Kant believes that to act at all is to show that you value something. No matter what you are trying to bring about by your action, it must be something that you think is *worthwhile* to bring about. (Why else would you try to bring it about?) So every action implies a view about value: it implies that you think something or other is valuable, and worth trying to achieve by acting.

Hence every action also implies a second view about value. To act at all implies that you value the aim of your action. So it also implies that you value your capacity for action. For unless you had a capacity for action, you could not achieve your aim. If the aim of your action is valuable as an end, then your capacity for action must be valuable as the only possible means to that end.

So no matter what different things different people may value, there is one thing that everybody has to value if they are to count as rational (as practically consistent). This is our capacity for action itself – as Kant calls it, our *will*. We may disagree about all other claims about value, and so find ourselves enmeshed in the kind of problems about relativism that I sketched in **4.2**. But for all the values that breed disagreements that no argument can solve, there is always one sort of value that no rational person can reject. This is the value of the good will itself. Hence Kant's famous opening claim in *The Groundwork of the Metaphysics of Morals*: 'It is impossible to think of anything at all in the world, or indeed even beyond it, that could be called good without limitation except a good will.'[27]

No matter what else you value, you must value your own good will, your own capacity for valuing things. No matter what else you take as your aim in action, you must take it as your aim to protect and promote your own capacity for *having* aims in action. This is Kant's notion of practical consistency – a notion that he arrives at via what Kantian scholars call a *transcendental argument*. The central idea is that you must not act in a way that destroys or undermines your own status as an agent. Any action you can possibly do will always presuppose that you think it is worthwhile to be an agent.

The actions that Kant wants to rule out as practically inconsistent are the ones that involve contradicting this presupposition.

And which actions are these? In the *Groundwork* Kant gives us four examples: suicide, a lying promise, laziness and lack of charity.[28] In Kant's view, these four cases between them exemplify every kind of practical inconsistency. (There are other examples of practical inconsistency, of course – but these are the four examples that Kant concentrates on.) Kant thinks that there are only two relations in which an agent can act so as to deny the worthwhileness of action: in his relation to himself, and in his relation to others. And he thinks that actions in these two relations can go wrong in just two ways: either they *destroy* the presupposed worthwhileness of action, or else they merely *undercut* it. They destroy it when they make it impossible for there to be any agency at all; they undercut it when they hamper the chances of agency's achieving anything much. So we have what Kant calls a 'perfect duty' not to destroy agency, and an 'imperfect duty' not to hamper or hinder it:

	In relation to ourselves	In relation to others
we have a **perfect duty** not to	commit suicide	make lying promises
we have an **imperfect duty** not to	fail through laziness to develop our own talents	refuse to help others when they need it

So why, to take the first of these four examples, is suicide practically inconsistent? Because suicide is the action of destroying my own capacity for action. But every action I do – suicide included – comes with the presupposition that my own capacity for action is valuable, and so not to be destroyed. Suicide is practically inconsistent because suicidal agency contradicts its own presuppositions: 'a nature whose law it would be to destroy life itself, by means of the same feeling whose destination it is to impel towards the furtherance of life, would contradict itself and would therefore not subsist as nature'.[29]

And why is it practically inconsistent to act in ways that preclude developing my own talents? Because these lazy actions handicap and thwart my own capacity for action, by preventing me from widening the scope of that capacity as I might if I did develop my talents. But whatever action I do – lazy ones included – comes with the presupposition that my own capacity for action is valuable, and so not to be handicapped or thwarted. Thus laziness is practically inconsistent, because lazy agency contradicts its own presuppositions: 'As a rational being, [each person] necessarily wills that all the capacities in him be developed, since they serve him and are given to him for all sorts of possible purposes.'[30]

These two examples are enough to show that Hegel's charge of 'empty formalism' is mistaken. Someone might disagree with Kant's claim that suicide and laziness are morally wrong, or with his claim that the reason *why* they are morally wrong is because they involve practical inconsistency; or with both of these claims. What a critic cannot reasonably do at this point is just carry on insisting, without further argument, that Kantian ethics is empty of any particular content.

However, there are of course plenty more problems for Kantian ethics with the particular content that these examples spell out. In **4.8** I shall look at two relatively small and technical problems. **4.9** will examine a larger problem for Kant that is raised by Bernard Williams. **4.10** will conclude my discussion of Kant's ethics by raising one further problem – a simple problem but, as I think, the largest of all.

4.8 **Two small problems for Kant**
First small problem If I am right to tabulate Kant's four examples as I have above, then the lying-promises example does not fit with

the other three examples. What we ought to have in this box in the table is a case of destroying someone else's agency, and a perfect duty not to do so. We might perhaps say that a lying promise, like any lie, undercuts other people's agency, by depriving them of the freedom to deliberate against the background of the true facts, and substituting a false reality that we have presumed to choose for them. At a stretch, we might even call this partially destroying others' agency. Even so, however, a lying promise clearly does not destroy anyone else's agency in the comprehensive way that, say, killing or lobotomizing them does.

Moreover, at least as Kant presents the case in the *Groundwork*, the inconsistency involved in a lying promise seems like a different sort of inconsistency from the practical inconsistency involved in the other three cases. It is not an inconsistency between the aim of the action and the presupposition that agency is valuable. It is an inconsistency between accepting and rejecting the social institution of promising. Or apparently so, though Kant's actual words are far from clear:

> [A policy of making lying promises] could never hold as a universal law of nature and be consistent with itself, but must necessarily contradict itself...[if] everyone, when he believes himself to be in need, could promise whatever he pleased with the intention of not keeping [his promise, then this] would make the promise and the end one might have in it itself impossible, since no one would believe what was promised him, but would laugh at all such expressions as vain pretences.[29]

The point here, apparently, is that I must accept the social institution of promising, if I am to get my promise believed; but I must reject the social institution of promising, if I am going to break my promise. If there is a real inconsistency here, it is quite different from the other three cases of inconsistency.

But perhaps there isn't a real inconsistency here anyway. I can get my promise believed without accepting the promising institution, and I can break my promise without rejecting it. You don't have to accept an institution to use it, and you don't reject an institution the moment you break its rules. (At least sometimes, all of us break the rules of nearly every social institution. It doesn't follow that we all reject nearly every social institution.)

Thus Kant's third example of practical inconsistency looks like a blunder. It does not make the point that it ought to make (namely, a plausible point about the practical inconsistency of destroying someone else's agency), and it ought not to make the point that it does make (namely, an implausible point about the alleged practical inconsistency of exploiting a social institution that you don't accept). This blunder does not show that Kant's ethics is mistaken as a whole. It has been widely discussed and has caused much confusion; but it should be noted as a distraction from the real point, and set on one side.

So let me leave it, and turn to the *second small problem* about Kant's notion of practical consistency. As we've seen, Kant says that suicide is practically inconsistent with protecting and promoting my own agency, because suicide involves accepting the destruction of my own agency; and he says that lazy living is practically inconsistent, because laziness involves doing less than I might to develop the scope of my own agency.

However, we might retort, it isn't only suicide that involves accepting the destruction of my own agency. I accept the destruction of my own agency if I allow myself to die at all. So apparently Kant must say that I am guilty of practical inconsistency if I refuse to take any life-prolonging treatment whatever. And similarly, we might retort that it isn't only lazy agency that involves doing less than I might to develop the scope of my own agency. I do less than I might to develop the scope of my own agency if I leave any talent undeveloped to any degree. So apparently Kant must say that I am guilty of practical inconsistency if, say, I could pass 13 Open University degree courses, yet refuse to take more than 12. But these conclusions are ridiculous. So Kant had better have a way of blocking them, if his notion of practical consistency is to yield an ethical content that is not ridiculous.

I believe Kant could block these sorts of conclusions – but does not himself do very much to explain how. Most people's intuitions tell them that there is a big moral difference between committing suicide and deciding to accept no further medical treatment. Similarly, most people's intuitions tell them that there is a big moral difference between doing nothing at all to develop your talents, and doing some things to develop them but not others. To explain these moral differences would be to explain why (as many would accept) it is permissible for a sick person to refuse further treatment, but wrong for him to commit suicide; why it is permissible not to do everything to develop your talents, but wrong to do nothing to develop them; why it is permissible not to send all your money to the starving in Africa, but wrong to send them poisoned food; and so on. The classic way to explain these differences is to draw two moral distinctions:

(a) between what you intend to bring about by your action, and what you foresee your action will lead to, although you do not intend it (the *double-effect* distinction)
(b) between what you do and what you allow to happen (the *action/omission* distinction)

So, for instance, poisoning people is a doing, whereas their starving to death is something you allow to happen; and again, committing suicide involves intending your own death, whereas dying because you refuse treatment need only involve foreseeing your own death.

I have defended the double–effect distinction and the action/omission distinction elsewhere.[31] Here, I simply want to note that it looks like Kant needs to deploy both these distinctions, if he is to prevent his notion of practical inconsistency from yielding the conclusion that the only things we are morally permitted to do are the ones that maximize the promotion of our own agency. But that conclusion needs to be blocked; for it is plainly ridiculous.

In passing, it is worth noting that utilitarians (**3.9**) have no general rejoinder to this problem, precisely because utilitarianism is basically a maximizing theory – one that, in its most basic form, says that 'Only the best is good enough', and that to do anything less than the best is always wrong. So utilitarianism, at least in its basic form, does commit us to such absurd conclusions as the view that, if life is a good, then it is wrong not to seek to prolong life as long as possible. There have been many attempts to modify the basic form of utilitarianism so as to avoid these absurd conclusions, most of them quite unconvincing. Since Kant is vehemently anti-utilitarian, we might expect him not to follow the utilitarians by making his own theory a maximizing one too. Since the double-effect and action/omission distinctions are very helpful tools for anyone who wants to avoid making their theory a maximizing one, this is another reason why we might expect Kant to find them useful, despite the fact that he nowhere explicitly deploys them (unless something like this is supposed to be the point of Kant's distinction between 'perfect' and 'imperfect' duties[32]).

4.9 A bigger problem for Kant: Williams on external reasons

These two points, as I say, are relatively unthreatening to Kant's overall project. There is nothing to stop his followers from repudiating the lying-promises example and invoking the double-effect and action/omission distinctions. A bigger threat to Kant's project arises from Bernard Williams's attack on the idea of an 'external reason'.[33]

An external reason is a reason to act such that, if you come to believe that such a reason applies to you, then you will be motivated to act as the reason dictates – no matter what desires you may already have, and no matter what your other beliefs may be. Williams argues for the conclusion that there can be no external reasons.

The relevance of this argument to Kant's account of ethics should be fairly clear. As we saw in **4.6**, the whole point of Kant's ethics is to base motivation not on the hurly-burly of our desires and inclinations, but on our reason and our reason alone:

> All imperatives command either *hypothetically* or *categorically*. The former represent the practical necessity of a possible action as a means to achieving something else that one wills (or that it is at least possible for one to will). The categorical imperative would be that which represented an action as objectively necessary of itself, without reference to another end.[34]

If there is a purely rationally based source of motivations – a Categorical Imperative – then this imperative will itself be an external reason, and a source of further external reasons.

Why does Williams think there can be no external reasons? He thinks this on two grounds. First, he does not see how someone's belief that 'He has a reason to do something, no matter what else he wants or believes' can ever be true. Second, he does not see how this belief, even if it is true, can ever motivate. Let me consider these points in turn.

The first point is that no one could have a reason to do something such that the reason still applied, no matter what else they wanted or believed. The problem is well brought out by (Williams's example) talk about needs. Suppose someone is sick, and needs to drink a certain medicine if he is to recover. But then we find that he simply does not want to recover, and so does not want to drink the medicine. Does he still need to drink the medicine? Williams denies that he has any internal reason to drink it:

> I take it that, insofar as there are determinately recognisable needs, there can be an agent who lacks any interest in getting what he indeed needs. I take it, further, that that lack of interest can remain after deliberation, and also that it would be wrong to say that such a lack of interest must always rest on false belief…[in such a case] I think we do have to say that in the internal sense he indeed has no reason to pursue these things.[35]

What would be the corresponding external sense, in which someone in this position would still have reason to drink the medicine that he needs to get well? Interestingly enough, I think his external reason to drink the medicine would have to rest on something like an Aristotelian teleological view (see **4.4**). It would have to rest on a general view that said something like 'Humans have reason to do whatever makes them flourish.' In rejecting such a view, Williams falls into place within the post-Cartesian tradition of rejecting Aristotelian teleology.

But remember here that Kant too is a card-carrying adherent of this post-Cartesian tradition. If Kantian objective reasons are anything like the kind of reasons that Aristotelian teleology gives us, then they are undermined by Kant's own scepticism about the possibility of knowledge of value in the external world. We might have expected Kant to agree with Williams that it is hard to see how statements of such reasons can ever be true, and it will be a surprise if Kant does not take Williams's line.

And yet Kant doesn't take that line. In an important way Kant's moral reasons – reasons to act which we are given purely by our rationality – *are* like Aristotelian teleological reasons – reasons to act which we are given purely by our nature as human organisms. And this brings us to Williams's second point, the claim that no one could be motivated by his belief that 'He has a reason to do something, no matter what else he wants or believes.' For what Kant's and Aristotle's conceptions of practical reasons have in common is this: on either conception, there have to be beliefs which motivate in this way. Both for Kant and Aristotle, it has to be possible that the belief *that I have an external reason to do X* will motivate me *to do X*.

But it is a well-known philosophical puzzle how a belief – including the belief that I have a reason to do something – can possibly motivate, in and of itself. The puzzle is most famously expressed by David Hume:

> Reason [which for Hume means 'the discovery of truth or falsehood', and so includes belief] is perfectly inert, and can never either prevent or produce any action or affection...Reason, in a strict and philosophical sense, can have influence on our conduct only after two ways: Either when it excites a passion by informing us of the existence of something which is a proper object of it; or when it discovers the connexion of causes and effects, so as to afford us means of exerting any passion. These are the only kinds of judgment, which can accompany our actions, or can be said to produce them in any manner.[36]

Hume's point is that beliefs alone do not motivate us. What motivates us is always the combination of beliefs – such as my belief that the house is on fire – with desires – such as my desire not to be burned alive. Given the belief alone, we have little chance of guessing what a reasonable person will do. Given the belief *and* the desire, we can predict very confidently that the reasonable person will get out of the house.

If Hume is right about this, and if there is a general problem about how any belief could motivate without the presence of a desire as well, then this general problem will apply, in particular, to my beliefs about what I have reason to do. Of course, if I *want* to do what I believe I have reason to do, then no doubt I will go ahead and do it. But that is beside the point, since it won't be a case where my belief motivates me. The real problem is this. Suppose a case where you do have the thought that you have reason to act a certain way, but where you do not also have a *desire* to act that way; nor do you have a more general desire to do whatever you have a reason to do. How could you be motivated to act *just* by the thought?

Kant's best response to this question, it seems to me – and perhaps the same goes for Aristotle – is just for him to insist that even if beliefs *in general* don't motivate in their own right, it doesn't follow that beliefs *about my reasons* can't motivate in their own right. Beliefs about reasons, Kant can say, are an exception to Hume's generalizations, precisely because they have this special feature: that believing that you have a reason to do something does motivate you to do it (insofar as you are rational).

But here remember Mackie's 'argument from queerness' (**4.3**). If Kant does make the move just suggested, won't beliefs about reasons, on his account of them, be infected with precisely the kind of queerness that Mackie complained of? If Kant is right, then our typical beliefs about reasons will have to say things like this: that some action has to-be-doneness built into it, or that some state of affairs has to-be-brought-aboutness built into it. But these beliefs, of course, are precisely the kinds of beliefs that Mackie rejects, because he denies that they could possibly be true. If they were true, moral values, or moral properties, would be part of the 'furniture of the universe'. This straightforward moral objectivism is precisely the picture that Mackie feels obliged to reject, because of the anti-teleological pressure of the Western scientific tradition to which Mackie is heir (**4.4**).

As we have already noted (**4.6**), Kant too rejects this straight-forward version of moral objectivism, and hopes to do better than it does, by finding a way for objective moral reasons to exist without depending on objective moral goods existing out there in the world. Our examination of Williams's critique of the idea of external reasons now suggests that the problem for Kant's project is that objective, intrinsically motivating moral reasons are just as problematically mysterious as objective, intrinsically motivating moral goods.

This point spells the collapse of Kant's 'middle way'. As I said at the end of **4.5**, Kant's strategy in ethics is to find a way between a dogmatic moral objectivism, which just helps itself to a list of objective goods, and a sceptical moral subjectivism, which condemns all objective moral entities as infected with what Mackie calls 'queerness' – incompatibility with Cartesian scientific naturalism. Kant's middle way between queerness and scientific naturalism asserts only that there are objective moral reasons, based not on any spooky external entities but simply on reason itself. (This is part of the point of the parallel between Kant's epistemology and his ethics: **4.6**.) But the whole point of this middle way will be lost, if it turns out that objective moral reasons are just as incompatible with scientific naturalism as objective moral goods are. And that is precisely what has just turned out. The upshot of Williams's critique of external reasons is that believing in objective moral reasons is just as metaphysically committing as believing in objective moral goods. Therefore Kant's compromise between moral objectivism and moral subjectivism fails.

4.10 Another big problem: Kant's ethics and the problem of other agents

The last and most important question I want to raise about Kant's ethics can be put very quickly and simply. The question is this. Kant's argument, as I stated it in **4.6**, may give me decisive reason to value my own agency, if I value anything. But how does it give me decisive reason to value anyone else's agency?

Remember how I set up the case for Kant's notion of practical consistency (**4.7**). I said that 'To act at all implies that you value the aim of your action. So it also implies that you value your capacity for action.' I said that 'No matter what else you value, you must value your own good will, your own capacity for valuing things; no matter what else you take as your aim in action, you must take it as your aim to protect and promote your own capacity for *having* aims in action.' I argued, in short, that each of us has reason to value his or her *own* capacity for agency. But how is that supposed to show that anyone has reason to value anyone else's capacity for agency?

Kant does, of course, have an answer to this. His answer is that what we value in ourselves is not *our* capacity for agency, but *the* capacity for agency. To quote the slogan again, 'It is impossible to think of anything at all in the world, or indeed even beyond it, that could be called good without limitation except a good will.'[27] This does not mean my good will particularly, or yours, or anyone else's. It means good will itself, the capacity for agency itself, wherever it occurs. As Kant puts it in one of his various formulations of the Categorical Imperative, 'humanity' is something that we are obliged to respect, no matter whether it occurs in our own person, or somebody else's.[37]

But this reply, it seems to me, is unconvincing. What I have reason to value, as the precondition of my pursuing any of my particular ends, simply isn't the capacity for agency *in general*. For the capacity for agency in general isn't the precondition for *my* pursuit of those ends. *My* capacity for agency is. So Kant's argument only shows that I am obliged to respect my own capacity for agency.

Can we block this difficulty by appealing to principles of consistency? No, we can't; because as I have shown (**4.7**), the way we establish principles of consistency already presupposes the value of my capacity for agency.

Can we block the difficulty by simply pointing out that there are other agents like me, whose value is equal to mine? Not without begging a number of questions. One of these is chapter 2's question of scepticism about the external world. Another is our present question: 'What reason do I have to give equal value to others' capacity for agency?' Simply to assert that others' capacity for agency has equal value with my own capacity for agency is not a solution to this problem, but a rejection of it. Such an answer is no better than Peter Singer's utilitarian response to the egoist (**3.9**): 'My own interests cannot count for more, simply because they are my own, than the interests of others.'[38]

Thus a perplexing problem for Kant's ethics appears in the place where we might least have expected it. Not only does Kant's ethics fail to find a stable compromise between objectivism and subjectivism, of the sort that would solve this chapter's problem about moral objectivity. Despite its stress on impartiality and consistency, Kant's ethics also fails, surprisingly enough, to solve chapter 3's problem about altruism.

Perhaps, on reflection, this is not such a surprise after all. It is often remarked that, in the last analysis, Kant's epistemology has no good defence against solipsistic idealism. If Kant's ethics and epistemology develop in as close a parallel as I suggested in **4.6**, and if I am right in my more general thesis (**0.2**) that the 'egocentric predicament' names both a problem about knowledge and a problem about ethics, then it ought to be no surprise if, in the last analysis, Kant's ethics turns out to be equally undefended against the danger of solipsistic egoism.

4.11 Conclusion

I have looked in this chapter at the problem of ethical objectivity, a problem that gets its bite both from the egocentric predicament that the problem of the inescapable self leads us into, and also from the mind–world rift that the problem of the inescapable self creates. My conclusion has been pessimistic. Both moral objectivism and moral subjectivism are deeply problematic views (**4.5**); but the best attempt to mediate a compromise between objectivism and subjectivism – Kant's – turns out to be a failure (**4.9**). For Kant's diluted objectivism shares the central feature that the subjectivist finds unacceptable in more standard and robust forms of objectivism. This is the metaphysical queerness of supposing that the world contains objective moral entities of any sort – not just objective moral goods, as in straightforward objectivism, but objective moral reasons as well.

In **4.10**, we saw that Kantianism also proves no better equipped than utilitarianism (**3.9**) to find an effective answer to the egoist. Although the Kantian has a plausible story to tell about why I should value *my own* capacity for agency, he cannot explain why I should value capacity for agency *as such* – not just my own, but anyone else's too. This leaves chapter 3's problem of egoism just as much unanswered as chapter 4's problem of objectivity.

In chapters 5 and 6 I shall look at some further aspects of the problem, to do with the philosophy of mind.

1 Herodotus, *Histories* 3.38.

2 Harrer 1953: 233.

3 Mackie 1977: 36.

4 Mackie 1977: 15.

5 Mackie 1977: 38.

6 e.g. van Fraassen 1982.

7 Mackie 1977: 40.

8 Mackie 1977: 41.

9 Aristotle, *de Caelo* 308a29–33.

10 Aristotle, *de Mundo* 392a9.

11 Newton, *Principia Mathematica*, Book III, General Scholium.

12 Descartes, *Principles of Philosophy* 2.64; CSM II: 247.

13 Wittgenstein, *Tractatus Logico-Philosophicus* 6.41.

14 Hume, *Treatise of Human Nature* 3.1.1.

15 Blackburn 1984: 167, 169.

16 Wright 1996.

17 Blackburn 1984: 182.

18 Ayer 1936: 107.

19 Hume, *Enquiry concerning the Principles of Morals*, Appendix 1.

20 Brief bibliography on the Frege–Geach problem: Geach 1960: 221–5; Blackburn 1984, chs. 5–6; Blackburn 1993, ch. 10; Gibbard 1990, ch. 5; Hale 1993: 337–63; Miller 2003, chs. 4–5.

21 McDowell 1985.

22 Russell 1960: 165–6.

23 Chappell 1998: 57–8.

24 Kant 1998: 5.

25 Kant 1998: 31; italics in original.

26 I am echoing Wittgenstein, *Philosophical Investigations* I, 201: 'This was our paradox: no course of action could be determined by a rule, because every course of action can be made to accord with the rule.'

27 Kant 1998: 7.

28 Kant 1998: 31–3.

29 Kant 1998: 32.

30 Kant 1998: 33.

31 Chappell 2001a. I have also argued against suicide (and euthanasia), using an argument that has some parallels with Kant's: Chappell 2003.

32 Kant 1998: 31, footnote.

33 Williams 1981.

34 Kant 1998: 25.

35 Williams 1981: 105.

36 Hume, *Treatise of Human Nature* 3.1.1; compare 2.3.3.

37 Kant 1998: 38.

38 Singer 1993: 13.

5

Problems of the Self

5.1 Descartes's 'thinking things'

The moment Descartes has proved his own existence in the second Meditation by arguing 'I think, therefore I am', he turns to the obvious next question: 'But what am I?'

> I do not yet have a sufficient understanding of what this 'I' is, that now necessarily exists. So I must be on my guard against carelessly taking something else to be this 'I', and so making a mistake in the very item of knowledge that I maintain is the most certain and evident of all.[1]

This leads Descartes to re-assess his own 'previous opinion' about what he is: 'What then', he asks, 'did I formerly think I was?' Well, obviously (he answers), he thought he was a human being. So what is a human being? In Descartes's time the standard answer to this question was the Aristotelian definition: 'Man is a rational animal.' But Descartes rejects this answer at once. It raises, he tells us, more questions than it answers: what does 'rational' mean, what does 'animal' mean? It is not that the Aristotelian answer is *false*: Descartes thinks that there is a sense in which it is perfectly correct to say that any human is a rational animal (see **5.4** below). It is rather that the Aristotelian answer can only be known to be true once we have already answered a swarm of other questions. And in the *Meditations* – the 'Meditations', remember, 'on *First* Philosophy' – Descartes is looking for an account of what he is that he can know to be true *immediately*, without knowing anything else first.

If he wants this sort of answer to the question 'What am I?', where should he look? As usual, Descartes looks within himself: 'I propose to concentrate on what came into my thoughts spontaneously and quite naturally whenever I used to consider what I was.'[1] When he looks in this direction, he quickly discovers that he can't know immediately that he is a human, because to be a human is to have a human body. And he can't know immediately that he has a body of any sort – let alone a human body. On both questions, he could be deceived by the evil demon:

> But what shall I now say that I am, when I am supposing that there is some supremely powerful and, if it is permissible to say so, malicious deceiver, who is deliberately trying to trick me in every way he can? Can I now assert that I possess even the most insignificant of all the attributes which I have just said belong to the nature of a body?[2]

The answer is 'No'. I can conceivably be fooled by the evil demon into supposing that I have a body when really I don't, or supposing that I am a human when really I am a crocodile. But what the evil demon can't fool me about is my own existence. It follows that I can conceive *my own* existence, without conceiving the existence of a human or the existence of my body. I can also conceive my own existence, as Descartes goes on to note, without conceiving the existence of my powers of nutrition, locomotion, perception, and even 'imagination' (Descartes's term for internal visualization).

However, there is one power of mine that I can't conceive of apart from my own existence. This, of course, is the one power that the evil demon can't fool me about – my power of conceiving itself:

> At last I have discovered it – thought: this alone is inseparable from me. I am, I exist – that is certain. But for how long? For as long as I am thinking...I am then in the strict sense only a thing that thinks.[2]

The existence of Descartes's self *is* the existence of a power of conceiving: there is a Cartesian self if, and only if, there is some thinking going on. As Descartes restates the argument in the sixth Meditation, there is nothing else that is identical with the self, because everything else can be conceived as existing apart from the self:

> My essence consists solely in the fact that I am a thinking thing. It is true that I...have a body that is very closely joined to me. But nevertheless, on the one hand I have a clear and distinct idea of myself, insofar as I am simply a thinking, non-extended thing; and on the other hand I have a distinct idea of body, insofar as this is simply an extended, non-thinking thing. And accordingly, it is certain that I am really distinct from my body, and can exist without it.[3]

In this passage, Descartes's criterion for the existence of the self also shows us how he wants to draw the line between mind and world. On one side of this line, the idea of my own self is made manifest to me by the *cogito*. On the other side of the line, the existence of the external world (and my own body as part of it) is established much later in Descartes's argument. And it is established by a route which – as we saw in **1.4** – is much more complicated and problematic than the route to self-knowledge.

Thus Descartes divides the universe into two separate parts: the immaterial self and the material world. Once this division is made – and Descartes does not see how we can avoid making it – we face the problem of bringing the two parts back into contact.

As I've shown, in epistemology this is the problem of *knowledge*: the problem of how an immaterial self can know anything about a material external world. In normative ethics, it is the problem of *altruism*: the problem of how the self can be motivated to act for the benefit of, or on a reason arising from, anything in the world out there. And in metaethics, it is the problem of *objectivity*: the problem of how altruistic, or other moral, action can be justified.

Chapters 1 to 4 examined these three problems. Descartes's division raises other problems too. One is the problem what this self *is*. Another is the problem how, if at all, such a self can fit into the world. The nature of the self, and the self's place in nature: these are my questions, respectively, in this chapter and the next.

5.2 **Descartes's exclusive selves**

Descartes's account of the self is an extreme and radical one. As Fergus Kerr points out,[4] it is completely alien to our ordinary thinking to follow Descartes in reducing the self to a pinpoint of consciousness, 'a hermit in the head', 'a solitary intellect locked within a space that is inaccessible to anyone else'. Obviously, there are other ways of answering questions like 'What am I?' or 'Who am I?' Each of us uses these alternatives all the time, in contexts where it would never occur to us for a moment to give Descartes's answer: 'I am a thinking thing.'

The point is nicely brought out in an anecdote told by Martin Hollis:

> I well recall having my identity tested in California fifteen years ago. Candidates were faced with a sheet of lined foolscap paper, topped with the single question 'Who am I?'. They had to respond with whatever truths about themselves they thought important, broadly either descriptions of their inner being or lists of their significant roles...Having been nurtured in arctic regions of English society, where upper lips

are stiff and chins up, the whole show seemed dreadfully bad form. Having been polished off on Oxford analytical philosophy, it appeared incomprehensible. At any rate I wrote my name and then could think of nothing to add. Even that was a mistake, as the test was supposed to be anonymous.[5]

Hollis answers 'Who am I?' with his name – and feels nonplussed by the idea that more might be required. Similarly, Aristotle answers 'What am I?' with 'A human, a rational animal' – and clearly has little time for the idea that any other answer might be more metaphysically correct than his own. But obviously, both Hollis and Aristotle could, in principle, be wrong to give these answers. It is conceivable that my name might not really be 'Timothy Chappell'. Perhaps there was a mix-up in the maternity ward, and my real name is 'Elvis Presley II'; or perhaps I have simply been hypnotized to think that I am called 'Timothy Chappell'. And it is conceivable that I might not be a human: perhaps I am like the ugly duckling, the cygnet who grows up with ducks, and have come to think that I am human merely because everyone around me is human.

In the light of these sceptical possibilities, Descartes concludes that neither my (alleged) name nor the (alleged) fact that I am human can possibly be part of my essence – what I most truly am. For if some property is part of my essence, then I cannot conceivably exist without it.

If my name and my being human are excluded from my essence, how much more so are the kinds of properties listed by the sociologist Anthony Giddens in his account of our 'self-identity':

Self-identity is not something that is just given, as a result of the continuities of the individual's action-system, but something that has to be routinely created and sustained in the reflexive activities of the individual...A person's identity is not to be found in behaviour, nor – important though this is – in the reactions of others, but in the capacity *to keep a particular narrative going*. The individual's biography...must continually integrate events which occur in the external world, and sort them into the ongoing 'story' about the self.[6]

Compare the proposal of the American philosopher Josiah Royce (1855–1916): 'A person, an individual self, may be defined as a human life lived according to a plan.'[7]

Descartes would disagree with Giddens and Royce. By Cartesian standards, the self cannot be a narrative or a lived-out plan. After all, my memory can conceivably fail me; and when it does, I can be mistaken about what 'narrative' or 'plan' I am in (or what narrative or plan I *am*).

Nor can the self be what Martin Heidegger (1889–1976) takes it to be – *being in the world*: human existence essentially constituted by the body, the biography, and a context of relationships and roles (see **0.2**). (As Heidegger puts it: 'Being-in-the-world is a basic state of *Dasein*, and one in which *Dasein* operates not only in general but pre-eminently in the mode of everydayness.'[8]) Heidegger's main purpose in *Being and Time* is the destruction (his word) of post-Cartesian philosophy. So it comes as no surprise that Heidegger's whole philosophy of the self fails if Descartes is right. The person cannot be essentially 'being in the world', if the existence of the world is in doubt when the existence of the person is not.

Still less, then, can the self be what Royce's contemporary and compatriot William James (1842–1910) sometimes suggests it is:

A man's Me is the sum total of all that he CAN call his, not only his body and his psychic powers but his clothes, his house, his wife and children, his ancestors and friends, his reputation and works, his lands and horses and yacht and bank account...[9]

At other times, of course, James's view of the self is more restrictive. (The whole point of his approach is to contrast restrictive and non-restrictive views of the self, and to wonder about how these views are related.) What James sometimes says about the nature of the self is guided by his own, rather Cartesian, method of doing psychology by introspection:

Whenever my introspective glance succeeds in turning round quickly enough to catch one of these manifestations of spontaneity in the act, all it can ever feel distinctly is some bodily process, for the most part taking place within the head...In a sense, then, it may be truly said that, in one person at least, the 'Self of selves', when carefully examined, is found to consist mainly of the collection of these peculiar motions in the head or between the head and throat.[9]

But here too Descartes will repeat that none of this apparatus can possibly be part of the essential me; for I can lose it all and *still* be me. There is always a separation between me and such properties of mine as a feeling in my throat; even more so between me and such properties of mine (excuse the pun) as a yacht or a horse. The self cannot be both a narrative of Giddens's sort, and the agent who 'keeps this narrative going'; still less can the self be both a network of relationships, projects and possessions, and the agent who operates within that network. The Cartesian self is, in the most extreme possible sense, an *exclusive* self. Perhaps this extreme sense of exclusiveness is less well captured by the psychologist William James than by the poet Gerard Manley Hopkins:

my self-being, my consciousness and feeling of myself, that taste of myself, of *I* and *me* above and in all things, which is more distinctive than the taste of ale or alum, more distinctive than the smell of walnutleaf or camphor, and is incommunicable by any means to another man…Nothing else in nature comes near this unspeakable stress of pitch, distinctiveness, and selving, this selfbeing of my own.[10]

Hopkins's remarks show the influence of Descartes as clearly as William James's. Yet Descartes's self is even more exclusive than Hopkins's is: for Descartes would say that even this 'feeling of myself' could conceivably be removed from me, or imitated by a deceiving demon, without my ceasing to be myself. As both Hopkins and James knew, Descartes's view of the self is deeply seductive. It is also deeply puzzling. In **5.3** to **5.5**, I look at some of the puzzles.

5.3 **The puzzles of the Cartesian self; and Locke's response**

The first and most obvious puzzle is one that William James discusses in chapter 10 of *The Principles of Psychology*; it is a puzzle that I have already noted, in **1.4**. Simply, the puzzle is the relationship between the exclusive Cartesian self just described, and the rest of the capacities, properties, social roles and relationships that I might, in a less exclusive mood, think of as constituents of me. If I am not identical with my body, or my character, or my narrative, or my friendships, or my place in society, then what is my relation to all of these attributes?

Part of the problem here is to square Descartes's answer to 'What is the self?' with our answer to a related question. This is the question of *personal identity over time* – the question of what makes it true (if it is true) that I am the same person now as I was yesterday, or 10 days ago, or 80 years ago. As we have seen,

Descartes's doctrine is that 'if I should wholly cease to think, then I would at the same time altogether cease to be'. As John Locke caustically commented, 'every drowsy Nod' shakes this doctrine:[11] if I exist only as long as I am thinking, then it looks as if I will cease to exist as soon as I go to bed tonight. In which case Descartes not only has some work to do to explain how the mind relates to the body and the rest of its environment. He also has some work to do to explain what makes it true that we have the *same* mind at any two times.

Locke's own response to this last problem inaugurates a long and still-vigorous tradition in discussions of personal identity over time. Locke defines a person as 'a thinking intelligent Being, that has reason and reflection, and can consider it self as it self, the same thinking thing in different times and places'. On the basis of this definition Locke goes on, in the same passage, to claim that we have the same person just so long as we have a continuity of consciousness, sustained by memory:

> For since consciousness always accompanies thinking, and 'tis that, that makes every one to be, what he calls *self*; and thereby distinguishes himself from all other thinking things, in this alone consists *personal Identity*, *i.e.* the sameness of a rational Being; And as far as this consciousness can be extended backwards to any past Action or Thought, so far reaches the Identity of that *Person*.[12]

In this passage Locke offers a criterion of *personal* identity, a criterion for sameness of person. Locke makes it explicit that there is a different criterion for sameness of human being: 'the Identity of the same *Man* consists…in nothing but a participation of the same continued Life, by constantly fleeting Particles of Matter, in succession vitally united to the same organised Body.'[13] This approach makes it possible for Locke's theory to get out of at least some of the problems that Descartes faces. For it enables him to say something constructive about the puzzle noted above – the puzzle about the relationship between the self in the thinnest sense, and the variety of properties that go to make up the self in a wider sense, including, of course, our bodily properties. Locke's distinction between sameness of human and sameness of person can be used to give the beginnings of an account of how the self and the human relate to each other.

5.4 **Five problems for Locke**

On the other hand, Locke's theory raises new problems in its turn. One problem was immediately pointed out by Locke's contemporary Joseph Butler (1692–1752): 'Consciousness of personal identity presupposes, and therefore cannot constitute, personal identity.'[14] The memory criterion looks circular, because it seems to say 'I am the same person as X if and only if I remember being the same person as X' – a remark which leaves the key concept 'being the same person as' entirely unanalysed.[15]

Another problem that Locke faces is a question of a technical logic, about what is called 'the relativity of identity'. Is it possible for something, X, to be the same F, but not the same G? For example, is it possible for me now to be the same man, but not the same person, as Timothy Chappell 20 years ago? Philosophers continue to disagree about this. On the one hand, we have a strong intuition that identity is true of *things*, not of *descriptions* of things – and it is hard to square the doctrine of relative identity with this intuition. On the other hand, there are obvious cases that at least look like cases of relative identity. For example, I can, over time, remain the same *human being* without remaining the same *toddler* (because I am no longer a toddler at all); and someone can be the same *office bearer* (e.g. Prime Minister) but not the same *person* (e.g. because Tony Blair has been replaced by Ken Livingstone).[16]

A third, related, problem for Locke is another technical puzzle about identity. To put it very crudely, the problem is this. Locke is committed to all three of these claims: (1) I am, by definition, a person; (2) I am, by definition, a human being, (3) what it is to be a person is different from what it is to be a human being. But these claims are incompatible with each other. Why? Because, putting it crudely again, you can only be *one* thing by definition. So if I am by definition a person, and by definition a human, being a person must be *the same thing* as being a human. The only way to avoid this contradiction is to drop either (1) or (2). Maybe I am a person, but not by definition a person. Or maybe I am a human being, but not by definition a human being.

If we drop either (1) or (2), the contradiction doesn't arise. There is no contradiction in my being, for instance, both a philosophy lecturer and a human being, because nobody thinks that I am by definition a philosophy lecturer; hence there is no temptation to say, absurdly, that being a philosophy lecturer and being a human are the same thing. Likewise, there is no contradiction in my being, by definition, a human animal, while I am only a person in some weaker sense than by definition. And conversely, there is no contradiction in my being, by definition, a person, while I am only a human animal in some weaker sense than by definition.

Someone who drops (2), and holds that I am by definition a person but only a human animal in some weaker sense, is of course Descartes. Someone who drops (1), and holds that I am by definition a human animal but only a person in some weaker sense, is Aristotle. Plenty of recent philosophers have developed both Aristotle's and Descartes's options. For example, the view that I am *identical with* a person, but *constituted by* a human being, is a common view in modern philosophy.[17] And the view that I am by definition a human animal, and only a person in a weaker sense (like the sense in which I am a philosopher or a mountaineer), has been revived in modern philosophy under the name *animalism*. Animalism is defended, for example, by Eric Olson:

> I believe that we are animals: human organisms. That means that our identity is animal identity. What it takes for me to persist through time is what it takes for this organism to persist through time. I began when this organism began, and I shall cease to be when this organism ceases to be...

Why should we adopt the animalist view? Olson offers three reasons:

> Well, first, there is a human animal standing here where I am. When I look in a mirror, I see a human animal. For each one of us, there is a human animal. Second, this human animal can think. It can talk. It is thinking and talking now. In fact this animal seems to be thinking the very thoughts that I am thinking...Third, there are not two thinking things standing here. There is only one: me. I am the being that thinks my thoughts. It follows from these three assumptions that I am an animal. There is an animal here; it thinks my thoughts; I am the one – the only one – who thinks my thoughts. I must be that animal.[18]

The problem for Locke is that, unlike the constitution theorist or the animalist, he doesn't seem to drop either (1) or (2): and this leaves him with the original contradiction.

Two other problems about Locke's account of personal identity are ethical problems. One is the problem of *responsibility*. We naturally assume that I can't normally be held responsible for what *I* didn't do. If it wasn't me who burnt down the Reichstag building, but some other person, then it is wrong to blame me and not this other person. But now: what counts as me, and what counts as other people? Suppose we accept Locke's memory criterion of personal identity, and think that responsibility is attributed to persons, not to men. Then if I can't remember starting the Reichstag fire, I am not the same person as the person who started it – even if I am the same man as the man who started it. So I am not responsible, simply because I can't remember doing it. But this seems very strange. It is also not how courts of law in fact assign responsibility. At least in most cases, they take sameness of human, not sameness of person, to be what counts. Maybe, of course, the Lockean can show that the courts are wrong; but at any rate, there is a problem for him here.

The other ethical problem is related; it is the problem of the *criterion of moral status*. What makes someone *count*, morally speaking? Is it being a human, or being a person? If the criterion is being a person, then apparently, any human who has no continuous chain of memories – say a small baby, or someone with serious amnesia – does not count, morally speaking. This seems an outrageous conclusion, though there are plenty of philosophers nowadays who are prepared to accept it.[19] If, on the other hand, the criterion of moral status is being a human, we will get other controversial conclusions. For example, it seems reasonably clear that, as a matter of biology, unborn babies are no less human beings than born ones are. In which case abortion will be just as bad as infanticide – a view which, even if it is right, certainly does not seem to be mirrored in the practices of our society.

Whether or not we accept Locke's account of personal and human identity, we may be grateful to him for usefully raising some big and perplexing questions about the relation of the person or self to the human animal, and for giving us at least an inkling of how we might address these questions. Descartes, by contrast, is much less useful, and in fact rather evasive, on these issues. Pretty well all he says about them is this: it is not sufficient, he tells us in the sixth Meditation, to suppose only that 'I am not merely present in my body as a sailor is present in a ship'.[20] For this idea, though true, is only a partial truth: 'I am very closely joined, and, as it were, intermingled with it, so that I and the body form a unit.' (This is why, as I noted in **5.1**, Descartes thinks that the Aristotelian definition 'Man is a rational animal' is true, even if it is not really a *definition* of man.)

As evidence of this intimate conjunction, Descartes cites the familiar experience of pain. If my relation to my body was only that of pilot to ship, damage to the ship could never be pain to me. It could only be information received, as when the captain of the *Titanic* hears back from a sailor whom he has sent off to look for perforations in the hull.

But if the relation of mind to body is not only that of sailor or helmsman to ship, what is the extra element, the left-over element that is not captured by the helmsman image? Just to say, as Descartes does, that mind and body are 'very closely joined, and, as it were, intermingled' is hardly to offer a *theory* of their conjunction and intermixture. Despite some bold efforts to clarify what their interrelations might be,[21] the issue remains mysterious.

5.5 **The self as a limit of the world**

Perhaps a little further reflection will show why the issue is bound to remain mysterious. Our first puzzle is about the relationship between the 'thin' Cartesian self and the 'thick' self of social interaction – the self that includes body, psychology, personal history, and personal and social relationships. But really, this first puzzle is just a special case of a second, more general puzzle. This is the puzzle of the relationship between the Cartesian self and everything else: between the Cartesian self and the world.

Part of this puzzle has to do with the problem of chapters 1 and 2: the problem of knowing about the world, when scepticism is always a possibility. But the puzzle is also created by the mind–world rift (**0.2**), the clash between the scientific and the humane perspectives that the problem of the inescapable self also leads to.

To explain. For Descartes, we might say, the self is essentially a viewpoint on the world. But then it apparently follows that the self cannot be identified with anything that might be *seen* from that viewpoint. Moreover, everything in the world can of course be seen from the viewpoint of the self. And so it becomes hard to see how the self can be in the world at all.

This thought has been developed, in different ways, by thinkers as diverse as Aristotle, Wittgenstein and Sartre. Aristotle believes that thinking about things is, in a certain way, taking on their natures. He also believes that everything is a possible object of thought. From these premises he infers that the thinking self can have no nature of its own:

> Since everything is a possible object of thought (*nous*), mind, in order…to know, must be pure from all admixture…it…can have no nature of its own, other than that of having a certain capacity. Thus mind…is, before it thinks, not actually any of the things that are.[22]

Somewhat similarly Wittgenstein, in the *Tractatus Logico-Philosophicus*, tells us that 'the subject' – the self – 'does not belong to the world; rather, it is a limit of the world.' By this he means that the subject could not be included in an inventory of the world, precisely because it is the subject who performs the inventory:

> If I wrote a book 'The world as I found it', I should have to include a report on my body, and should have to say which parts were subordinate to my will and which were not, etc.,

this being a method of isolating the subject, or rather of showing that in an important sense there is no subject: for it alone could *not* be mentioned in that book.[23]

We may compare Sartre's contrast between, as he calls them, *l' en-soi* ('the in-itself') and *le pour-soi* ('the for-itself'). Roughly, this is a contrast between the physical world and the conscious mind:

[In the in-itself,] being is what it is…The in-itself is full of itself, and no more total plenitude can be imagined, no more perfect equivalence of content to container…The distinguishing characteristic of consciousness, on the other hand, is that it is a decompression of being…The for-itself is a being which is not what it is, and which is what it is not.[24]

Sartre's paradox is that *le pour-soi*, consciousness, exists only as directed onto something in the world. Moreover, like Aristotelian *nous*, Sartrean consciousness can be directed onto *anything* in the world. But then, if consciousness is a directedness onto anything in the world, how can consciousness itself *be* anything in the world? Sartre himself, like Heidegger, seeks to overcome this paradox by invoking the notion of *engagement*: 'The point of view of pure knowledge is contradictory; there is only the point of view of *engaged* knowledge.'[25] But it is not clear how much difference this addition makes. The problem remains that the self, engaged or not, seems simultaneously to be both within and outside the world.

The idea of selves as subjects, points of view on the world, thus becomes a deeply problematic notion. Besides the paradox just noted, the problems arise partly because it is hard to know how to combine the self that is a point of view on the world, with the self that is (apparently) a human animal, a living breathing physical object engaged in all sorts of social and interpersonal contexts and commitments. The problems also arise because selves that are subjects are conscious; and it is difficult to know how to fit consciousness into a world that is – according to science – a wholly physical world. We face not only the question of what selves or persons are, but also the question of how subjectivity – the property of being a subject – can be fitted into an objective world: on which more in chapter 6. As with chapter 4's question about ethical objectivity and subjectivity, what all these questions raise is a clash of perspectives.

5.6 **Deconstructing the self**

One way with these clashes is simply to dismiss the idea that there are, really, any selves or persons. As noted by Daniel Dennett, this 'deconstruction of the self' has been 'a hot theme among the deconstructionists' – literary and cultural theorists and philosophers under the influence of Jacques Derrida (1930–2004) – for quite a while.[26] Dennett quotes the English author David Lodge's description of Robyn, one of the main characters in Lodge's novel *Nice Work*:

> According to Robyn (or, more precisely, according to the writers who have influenced her thinking on these matters), there is no such thing as the 'Self' on which capitalism and the classic novel are founded – that is to say, a finite, unique soul or essence that constitutes a person's identity; there is only a subject position in an infinite web of discourses – the discourses of power, sex, family, science, religion, poetry etc. – and by the same token, there is no such thing as an author, that is to say, one who originates a work of fiction *ab nihilo*[27]…in the famous words of Jacques Derrida, *il n' y a pas de hors-texte*, there is nothing outside the text.[28] There are no origins, there is only production, and we produce our 'selves' in language…

Dennett complains ruefully that the deconstructionists have beaten him to it with the enunciation of this view. But then, of course, David Hume got in before either of them:

> For my part, when I enter most intimately into what I call *myself*, I always stumble on some particular perception or other, of heat or cold, light or shade, love or hatred, pain or pleasure. I can never catch *myself* at any time without a perception, and never can observe anything but the perception...If anyone, upon serious and unprejudiced reflection, thinks he has a different notion of *himself*, I must confess I can reason no longer with him. All I can allow him is, that he may be in the right as well as I, and that we are essentially different in this particular. He may, perhaps, perceive something simple and continued, which he calls *himself*; though I am certain there is no such principle in me...But setting aside some metaphysicians of this kind, I may venture to affirm of the rest of mankind, that they are nothing but a bundle or collection of different perceptions, which succeed each other with inconceivable rapidity, and are in a perpetual flux and movement.[29]

Indeed, Heracleitus in Greece and the Buddha in India (both 5th century BC) both seem to have got there long before Hume:

> [Heracleitus holds that] nothing is one, in and of itself...Everything that we say *is*, in reality *comes to be* from motion and process and blending-together...Our way of speaking is inaccurate, because there never *is* any *thing*: it is always coming-to-be. [In a perception, the perceiver and the thing perceived] only exist or come to be *relative to each other*...necessity binds our essences to each other, even though it does not bind our essences to anything else.[30]

O brethren, actions do exist, and also their consequences, but the person that acts does not. There is no one to cast away this set of elements and no one to assume a new set of them. There exists no individual, it is only a conventional name given to a set of elements.[31]

Such views have not only influenced literary theory; they have affected historians too. As Simon Schama remarks at the beginning of *Citizens*, his magisterial study of the French Revolution, a related form of scepticism about persons has often come, under Marx's influence, to dominate much of modern historiography:

the Marxist-scientific claim [was] that the significance of the Revolution was to be sought in some great change in the balance of social power…[so, for instance,] the utterances of orators were little more than vaporous claptrap, unsuccessfully disguising their helplessness at the hands of impersonal historical forces…Weighty volumes appeared…documenting every aspect of [the *ancien régime*'s] structural faults. Biographies of Danton and Mirabeau disappeared…and were replaced by studies of price fluctuations in the grain market…[32]

According to Marxist historians, selves, persons, personalities are a superficial phenomenon. They are not part of the real story about what happened in history. Persons are not causes; social and economic structures are causes, and persons are *results* of those causes. So a historian who analyses events such as the French Revolution by talking about Danton, Mirabeau and the other persons involved – as, for instance, Hilaire Belloc and Thomas Carlyle do[33] – is taking a superficial approach. Such talk explains nothing important about what happens in history, or how it happens.

The great novelist Leo Tolstoy thought just the same:

> What is the power that moves nations? To this the [personal] school [of historians] laboriously replies either that Napoleon was a great genius or that Louis XIV was very arrogant, or else that certain writers wrote certain books...All that might be very interesting if we recognised a divine power governing the nations by means of Napoleons, Louises and philosophical writers; but we acknowledge no such power...The life of nations cannot be summarised in the lives of a few men, for the connexion between those men and the nations has not been discovered.[34]

Humean, deconstructionist, Buddhist, Heracleitean, or Marxist historian: all of these different schools of thought move, in their different ways, towards the same conclusion about the self. The conclusion is that selves are causally and explanatorily inert because they do not actually exist, as parts of the 'fabric of the world' (to borrow a phrase from **4.3**). Selves cannot, as Carlyle thought, explain anything, because selves are not, as Descartes thought, substances with an essence that does not change over time. Rather, they are historically conditioned social constructs. Insofar as we exist at all, *we make ourselves up*, and the way we make ourselves up is conditioned and determined by the way our society is.

Dennett quotes Lodge to approve the Derridean view that Lodge satirizes: 'this jocular passage is a fine parody of the view I'm about to present.'[35] Dennett's own view of the self also claims that there is something illusory about it. There is no 'brain–pearl', no inmost and essential self, and the hope that there is is a 'pathetic bauble'.[36] All there is, according to Dennett, is an intelligent brain engaged in 'multiple draftings' of experiential input – draftings which include, at the higher levels, something very like Derrida's narrative construction of the self:

[We should recognise] the importance of drama, storytelling, and the more fundamental phenomenon of make-believe in providing practice for human beings who are novice self-spinners...we build up a defining story about ourselves, organised around a sort of basic blip of self-representation. The blip isn't a self, of course; it's a representation of a self...what makes one blip the *me*-blip and another blip just a *he* or *she* or *it*-blip is not what it looks like, but what it is used for. It gathers and organises the information on the topic of me in the same way other structures in my brain keep track of information on Boston, or Reagan, or ice-cream.[37]

A welter of attractive and suggestive ideas fall out of passages like this. (Dennett's book is full of such passages.) The idea that our lives, or our personalities or characters, are in some sense narratively constructed, and that the way such narratives are constructed is affected by the societies we find ourselves in – these ideas are surely correct.

Yet if Dennett's (or Hume's, or Derrida's, or the Buddha's) central thesis is that there is really no such thing as subjectivity, no such thing as the subject's or self's own point of view, this thesis looks as manifestly false as any thesis could be. The question that Descartes would surely ask here is surely the right one to ask: what do I know better than my own point of view? It is one thing to deny a particular account, say Descartes's, of what it is to be a self or a subject; it is quite another to say that there *are* no subjects. But Dennett, like Derrida and many another author (though not, I think, Hume), seems to move surreptitiously between these two claims without sufficiently pausing on the difference between them.

What has happened here, perhaps, is that Dennett – again, like many another author – has been so drawn to acknowledge the demands of the scientific perspective on the question what the self is, that he has failed to do enough to acknowledge the demands of the personal or humane perspective on that question. The attractions of his multiple-draft account of the self – whether that particular account is right or wrong – are precisely the attractions of the scientific perspective. The incredulity inspired by his claim that there are no selves – when that claim is not obscured by Dennett's masterly rhetoric – is precisely the incredulity of the personal perspective denied. (I'll say more about Dennett in **6.3.3**.) We are back in a position of intellectual dilemma; and as before, the source of the intellectual dilemma is the mind–world rift. Somehow, we want to find a way of accepting the picture that we are animals *plus* subjectivity – that we are both conscious subjects, and also (in Olson's phrase) human animals. The mind–world rift splits this picture right down the middle.

But our question 'What is a person?' is now reshaping itself, under the stress of examination, as a rather different question: the question how consciousness can be fitted into the world of science. A similar intellectual dilemma, with similar sources, will arise when we look in more detail at the puzzle of consciousness, in chapter 6.

1 Descartes, CSM II: 17.

2 CSM II: 18.

3 CSM II: 54.

4 Kerr 1986: 57.

5 Hollis 1977: 87.

6 Giddens 1991: 52–4.

7 Royce, *Philosophy of Loyalty*, Lecture IV.

8 Heidegger 1962: 86.

9 James 1890, ch. 10.

10 Hopkins 1959: 123; cited both by Glover 1988: 59 and by Galen Strawson 1997: 405–28.

11 Locke, *Essay Concerning Human Understanding* II.1.10.

12 *Essay* II.27.9.

13 *Essay* II.27.6.

14 Butler, First Dissertation to *The Analogy of Religion* [1736].

15 One good discussion of the circularity objection is Wiggins 2001: 197–207.

16 For defences of relative identity, see Geach 1962, sections 31–4, and Griffin and Routley 1979. For a defence of absolute identity, see Wiggins 2001.

17 e.g. Baker 2000.

18 Olson 2002; compare Olson 1999.

19 e.g. Singer 1993, ch. 4 and Tooley 1996. For contrary views, see Oderberg 2000 and Chappell 1998a.

20 Descartes, CSM II: 56; compare the 'helmsman' of *Discourse* 5, CSM I: 141.

21 See particularly Cottingham 1998, who does much to draw a Cartesian answer to this question out of Descartes's work *The Passions of the Soul.*

22 Aristotle, *de Anima* 429a18–24.

23 Wittgenstein, *Tractatus* 5.631, 632.

24 Sartre 1958: 74, 77.

25 Sartre 1958: 308.

26 Dennett 1991: 410–11.

27 *Sic.* The Latin for 'out of nothing' is actually *ex nihilo.*

28 This slogan is frequently used by Derrideans, but it is ironically hard to track down to its original occurrence. Derrida 1977: 105 comments thus on the slogan: 'La phrase qui, pour certains, est devenue une sorte de slogan en général si mal compris de la déconstruction ('il n'y a pas de hors-texte') ne signifie rien d'autre: il n'y a pas de hors-contexte. Sous cette forme, qui dit exactement la même chose, la formule aurait sans doute moins choqué.'

29 Hume, *Treatise of Human Nature* 1.4.6.

30 Plato, *Theaetetus* 152d, 160b.

31 Said to be the Buddha's own words; quoted from a Buddhist text in Parfit 1984: 502–3.

32 Schama 1989: xiii–xiv.

33 Belloc 1911 and Carlyle 1906.

34 Tolstoy 1957: 1404, 1416.

35 Dennett 1991: 411.

36 Dennett 1991: 430.

37 Dennett 1991: 428–9.

Minds in a Mindless World

6.1 **The mind and its place in nature**

As David Chalmers points out at the beginning of his wonderful book *The Conscious Mind*, the existence of consciousness is 'at once the most familiar thing in the world and the most mysterious':

> Why should there be conscious experience at all? It is central to a subjective viewpoint, but from an objective viewpoint it is utterly unexpected...When someone strikes middle C on the piano...sound vibrates in the air and a wave travels to my ear. The wave is processed and analysed into frequencies inside the ear, and a signal is sent to the auditory cortex. Further processing takes place here: isolation of certain aspects of the signal, categorisation, and ultimately reaction. All this is not so hard to understand in principle. But why should this be accompanied by an *experience*?[1]

Everyone – even Daniel Dennett (**5.6**) – knows that they have minds: that they are conscious beings. But where does consciousness appear in the scientific picture of reality? Why, indeed, as Chalmers asks, should it appear anywhere?

> Consciousness is *surprising*. If all we knew about were the facts of physics, and even the facts about dynamics and infor-

mation processing in complex systems, there would be no compelling reason to postulate the existence of conscious experience. If it were not for our direct evidence in the first-person case, the hypothesis would seem unwarranted…Yet we know, directly, that there is conscious experience. The question is, how do we reconcile it with everything else we know?[1]

Or as Jerry Fodor puts it:

Nobody has the slightest idea how anything material could be conscious. Nobody even knows what it would be like to have the slightest idea about how anything material could be conscious. So much for the philosophy of consciousness.[2]

It seems that we could imagine a world exactly like ours, only without consciousness in it. (Call it the 'Zombie World'.) What difference does this subtraction make? No difference at all – and all the difference imaginable!

Scientifically speaking, it looks as if the Zombie World is simply indiscernible from our world (the Conscious World). Consider Chalmers's middle-C case, for example. In the Zombie World, what happens when someone strikes middle C on the piano? There is vibration, followed by sound-processing, followed by signal, followed by reaction. In short, there is everything, except the experience that I have in the Conscious World. Striking middle C in the Zombie World will lead me to exactly the same actions that I do in response to that sound in the Conscious World. Exactly the same equations of physics will capture the whole process equally well in either world. From a scientific point of view, what more could you want?

But now suppose *you* are given the choice of being in the Conscious World or the Zombie World. And suppose that you like music, and would enjoy the sound of a sonorous middle C, deftly struck on a well-made period instrument. Which world would you rather be in? In either world, remember, your publicly visible reactions will be as indiscernible as everything else. So in either world, you will smile, or sigh with satisfaction, or exclaim 'What a delightful timbre', or do whatever else one does to express appreciation of fine performances on fine instruments. But in the Zombie World you react like this simply because that's the reaction that your system naturally makes to this stimulus; whereas in the Conscious World you react like this *because the striking of middle C causes you to experience pleasure.* In the light of this, the question 'Which world should I choose?' is a no-brainer. If hearing middle C is your thing (and it is some people's), you have *every* reason to want to be in the Conscious World, and no reason whatever to want to be in the Zombie World. From the first-person point of view, there is a *huge* difference between the two.

Compare another choice that goes the other way. Suppose you are about to be tortured, and can choose whether this is to happen in the Conscious World or the Zombie World. As before, your publicly visible reactions will be the same in both worlds. In either world, you will scream, struggle and try to escape from the slab where you are being tortured. But also as before, in the Zombie World you react like this because aversion is the reaction that your system naturally makes to the physical stimuli involved in torture; whereas in the Conscious World you react like this *because it hurts.* Here too, which world to choose is a no-brainer. If avoiding pain is your thing (and whose thing isn't it?), you have *every* reason to prefer to be tortured in the Zombie World, and no reason whatever to prefer to be tortured in the Conscious World. Once again: from the first-person perspective, the difference between the two worlds is about as big as it possibly could be.

Or consider a third choice. Here your choice between the Conscious and Zombie Worlds is permanent. Whichever world you choose, from now on you'll be in that world, not just for the time it takes for you to be tortured or hear a pleasant sound, but for the rest of your life. (So the choice is like the choice whether or not to go on Nozick's Experience Machine: **3.1**.) We might be unsure which way we would choose between these alternatives. The Zombie World guarantees us freedom from all future pain, which seems a consummation devoutly to be desired; on the other hand, in the Zombie World we will never experience any more pleasure, either. So how should we choose? I'll leave that question for the reader to answer. My point is simply that, however you choose, this is no small choice. The choice is a momentous one; because – from the first-person perspective – the difference between the two worlds is a momentous one.

So what is it that makes this difference? Well, it's consciousness; but what is that? You might think – indeed some modern philosophers have thought – that consciousness is simply the capacity to self-refer. The idea is an interesting one, and the capacity to self-refer deserves some discussion in its own right. (Even though, as I'll argue, consciousness is not simply the capacity to self-refer.)

The modern debate about self-reference is rich, sophisticated, and quite impossible to summarize properly here: for more about it see for example Perry 1993. The debate begins with the great German logician Gottlob Frege (1848–1925). In his famous essays *Begriffsschrift* and 'On sense and reference', Frege proposed that a perfect representation of the meanings of our language would eliminate all self-referring terms. It would replace, for instance, 'me' (used in the way that I use it, and only I can use it) with 'Timothy Chappell' (a term that anyone can use in exactly the same way, including me).

Pretty well everyone since has thought that there is something wrong with Frege's proposal, because – for a start – the capacity to self-refer seems crucial to agency. 'A piano is about to fall on Timothy Chappell's head' has a quite different impact on my motivations from 'A piano is about to fall on *my* head'. If I don't realize that Timothy Chappell is *me*, all I know is that *someone's* head is about to be crushed, and this might not affect my choices of action at all.

As Arthur Prior points out, the same is true of some other words too, 'now' and 'here' for example.[3] Knowing that a gruelling exam that I have to sit ends at 5.30 on 6 June 2000 has quite different implications for agency from knowing that that gruelling exam ends *now*, or that it ended *five minutes ago*. No one would say 'Thank goodness that the exam ended at 5.30 on 6 June 2000', but anyone might say 'Thank goodness that the exam is over *now*.' All terms of this sort – demonstratives or indexicals, as philosophers call them – have the crucial feature that they bear directly on our agency in a way that less relative and more objective terms just cannot do.

In the light of all this, it is tempting to make a connection (as Dennett does, for example) between self-reference and consciousness to help explain the evolutionary origins of consciousness. The suggestion would be that a capacity for self-reference is evolutionarily desirable for an obvious reason. Creatures that can have thoughts like 'A piano is falling on *my* head', not just thoughts like 'A piano is falling on Timothy Chappell's head', have much better prospects of survival. So that's why self-reference evolved; and consciousness is just the same thing as the capacity for self-reference.

The trouble is, though, that consciousness plainly isn't the same thing as the capacity for self-reference. To see this, it is only necessary to consider my printer, or the drinks machine in the hall. My printer is capable of issuing error messages that say things like 'System malfunction #45'; and the drinks machine currently has a read-out which says 'No money inserted'. What my printer means by its message is, of course, that *it* is suffering from system malfunction #45; and what the drinks machine means by its message is that *it* has had no money inserted in it. So drinks machines and printers have the capacity for self-reference. But if anything lacks consciousness, drinks machines and printers do. Patently, as Thomas Nagel puts it,[4] there is 'nothing it is like' to be a drinks machine or a printer. So self-reference is not consciousness. QED.

A capacity to self-refer could exist in the Zombie World; but consciousness couldn't. This fact just adds to our reasons for saying that, from the scientific perspective, the difference between the Conscious and the Zombie Worlds is pretty well invisible. From the personal perspective, the difference between the Conscious and the Zombie Worlds is – as I've argued – momentous. The ambition of science is to explain *everything*; but it looks as if science cannot explain the way things look and feel from the personal perspective.

What we have here is an example of that philosophical phenomenon *par excellence*: a clash of perspectives. This particular clash of perspectives is a manifestation of the mind–world rift that I described in **0.2**: the gap between the world as science describes it and the world as it is for subjectivity.

How are we to make sense of this clash of perspectives? How should we respond to it? Broadly speaking, three responses are possible:

(a) 'If the explanatory ambitions of science can't be extended to cover the personal perspective, so much the worse for science.'

(b) 'If the personal perspective clashes with the explanatory ambitions of science, so much the worse for the personal perspective.'

(c) 'The apparent clash is only apparent, so we can keep hold of both perspectives.'

In **6.2** to **6.4**, I will consider each of these responses in turn.

6.2 **'So much the worse for science'**

The position that most clearly expresses the explanatory ambitions of science is naturalism. As I said in my discussion of naturalized epistemology at the end of **2.6.4**, naturalism is the view that the subject-matter of science is the whole of reality, and that the only world there is is the natural or scientific world. Science will be complete when it has explained everything; and there is nothing real that it can't explain.

Naturalism in the philosophy of science – the general view that the only facts are the scientific facts – implies physicalism in the philosophy of mind – the more specific view that the only facts about any human are the facts about his or her body. So we can discuss naturalism and physicalism together.

Thomas Nagel is one prominent philosopher who has noted the apparent incompatibility of the naturalists' or physicalists' explanatory ambitions with the personal perspective:

> If the facts of experience – facts about what it is like *for* the experiencing organism – are available only from one point of view, then it is a mystery how the true character of experience could be revealed in the physical operation of that organism.[5]

Frank Jackson goes further than Nagel. He infers from the clash of perspectives not merely that physicalism is mysterious, but that it is false. His argument for this conclusion, sometimes called the Knowledge Argument, features a famous thought-experiment. This is the story of Mary the colour scientist:

> Mary is confined to a black-and-white room, is educated through black-and-white books and through lectures relayed

on black-and-white television. In this way she learns every-thing there is to know about the physical nature of the world. She knows all the physical facts about us and our environment, in a wide sense of 'physical' which includes everything in *completed* physics, chemistry and neurophysiology...[6]

As a scientist, Mary is maximally well informed. But how well informed is that? Not as well informed as she might be, says Jackson:

If physicalism is true, [Mary] knows all there is to know. For to suppose otherwise is to suppose that there is more to know than every physical fact, and that is just what physicalism denies...It seems, however, that Mary does not know all there is to know. For when she is let out of the black-and-white room or given a colour television, she will learn what it is like to see something red...This is rightly described as *learning*...Hence, physicalism is false.[6]

What is shown by the story of Mary, if the story is a possible one? The story shows that there is more to the world than the physical world, and more to the facts than the physical facts. For there are facts about consciousness, for example facts about what it is like to see the colour red. These facts are not captured in physical theory; and, Jackson thinks, they *cannot* be captured in physical theory. (This is why Jackson emphasizes that the physics, chemistry and neurophysiology that Mary knows are 'completed'.) Mary's story shows that there are facts about Mary that are not physical facts. But physicalism is precisely the thesis that the only facts about persons are the physical facts about them. So, Jackson concludes, the story of Mary the colour scientist is a disproof of physicalism. The conflict between the scientific perspective and the personal perspective cannot be resolved in favour of the scientific perspective. Therefore physicalism is false; which means that naturalism is false too.[7]

6.3 'So much the worse for the personal perspective'

The Knowledge Argument claims to prove that the scientific perspective is not as all-encompassing as it makes itself out to be. Clearly this is a conclusion that would be welcomed not only by modern dualists and their allies, such as Nagel and Colin McGinn,[8] but also by traditional dualists like Descartes. To some extent it is a common-sense conclusion, too. Surely, the voice of common sense will say (speaking as usual in clichés, but still convincingly), there are plenty of things that we can't expect a scientific account of: why we are moved by sunsets or symphonies, what made Shakespeare write the way he did, why this wine is good and that wine bad, how many roads a man must walk down before you can call him a man... So why shouldn't the personal perspective be just one more of the things that, from the scientific perspective, simply can't be explained?

The line of thought is familiar to the point of platitude. Many philosophers will say that it totally underestimates the power and ambition of the continuing project of science. For a start, these philosophers will say, it is a mistake to talk about the scientific *perspective*. The whole point about science is that it is precisely not a perspective, but the truth – truth absolute and freed from all perspectives. To give up the personal perspective in favour of science is not to move from one perspective to another. It is to move from a biased and partial subjectivity to a hygienic and complete objectivity. So, for instance, Israel Scheffler:

> A fundamental feature of science is its ideal of objectivity, an ideal that subjects all scientific statements to the test of independent and impartial criteria, recognising no authority of persons in the realm of cognition.[9]

Bernard Williams describes this ideal of objectivity as science's aspiration to 'the absolute conception of reality'.[10] It is of course no coincidence that Williams's discussion of the theme occurs in his book on Descartes. As Williams shows, Descartes's philosophy is itself one of the principal sources of the idea that science pursues the 'absolute conception of reality'. As I have argued in this book, the clash between the personal and scientific perspectives that afflicts us today is rooted, via the mind–world rift, in Descartes's own thought.

Naturalism, then, prompts an austere and inhospitable approach to the personal perspective: an approach which may well prompt philosophers to take Ockham's Razor to the phenomenon of consciousness, treating it as explanatorily superfluous and therefore non-existent. This naturalistic austerity has reappeared a number of times in the last century of philosophy. I shall review four forms (or perceived forms) of this hostility to the personal perspective in this section: the later Wittgenstein (**6.3.1**), behaviourism (**6.3.2**), functionalism (**6.3.3**), and eliminativism (**6.3.4**).

6.3.1 The later Wittgenstein Wittgenstein is often thought to be hostile to the personal perspective; but wrongly. We saw in **2.3.2** that Wittgenstein does argue against the idea that the contents of our inner mental lives are, or could be, essential to our ability to mean anything: this is the upshot of his famous Private Language Argument. However, it is clearly a mistake to think that the later Wittgenstein denies that we *have* inner mental lives. It is even more of a mistake to think that the later Wittgenstein would deny this in order to further the ambitions of science and quash the pretensions of the personal perspective. In fact, no philosopher is *less* inclined to push a scientific agenda than Wittgenstein. In a way, the whole point of his later work is to insist that philosophy is precisely not science.

6.3.2 Behaviourism Part of this confusion about Wittgenstein's attitude to the personal perspective arises from reading him as a behaviourist. This is also a mistake, as Wittgenstein himself points out: 'And now it looks as if we had denied mental processes. And naturally we don't want to deny them.'[11] Wittgenstein is no behaviourist; though behaviourism certainly is a form of hostility to the personal perspective. Behaviourism, the classic expositions of which are those of B. F. Skinner and Gilbert Ryle,[12] is the view that talk about our mental life is completely analysable into talk about what we actually do – how our bodies behave – plus talk about how our bodies *would* behave in certain circumstances.

Skinner's version of behaviourism can be called *psychological* behaviourism. This is a way of doing psychology which makes everything depend on overt behaviour, and nothing depend on the alleged contents of minds. In the words of Skinner's mentor, J. B. Watson: 'Psychology as a behaviorist views it is a purely objective experimental branch of natural science. *Its theoretical goal is…prediction and control*.'[13] One standard objection to psychological behaviourism is its rather sinister political implications, which are clear enough from the words italicized in that quotation. In any case, as a research methodology for psychologists, behaviourism has proved hopelessly restrictive: there just isn't much prospect of getting very far in cognitive psychology without allowing ourselves to look at people's mental processes in an essentially non-behaviourist way.

Ryle's version is *logical* behaviourism. This is a way of giving truth-conditions for sentences about psychology in purely behavioural terms: 'the styles and procedures of people's activities *are* the way their minds work.'[14] A standard objection to logical behaviourism is to point out its dependence on logical positivism, the now-refuted view that sentences can have no meaning unless there is a way of verifying them.

If either of these versions of behaviourism were plausible, that would give us a way of understanding the workings of the mind that made consciousness and the personal perspective pretty marginal phenomena. But neither form is plausible; and there are reasons to think that no form of behaviourism could be plausible. One standard objection is that behaviourism makes the workings of my mind more accessible to you than they are to me myself. (As in the joke about the two behaviourists after sex: 'It was great for you, how was it for me?') This consequence of behaviourism seems to conflict with an intuition central to Descartes's philosophy: that each of us knows about the workings of his own mind in a uniquely direct and authoritative way. I may not be infallible about my own mind; but surely I at least have privileged access to my own mind? Philosophers continue to debate whether this is in fact so, and what form our privileged access might take.[15] But that we do have privileged access to our own minds is surely the most natural assumption – and one that the behaviourist denies.

A second standard objection to behaviourism is more decisive. This objection, which apparently was first noted by Peter Geach and Roderick Chisholm,[16] we may call the *umbrella problem*. The problem is this. Behaviourism claims to be able to translate mental phenomena such as beliefs into patterns of behaviour. So, for instance, my believing that it is raining is supposed to translate into something like a propensity for me to pick up my umbrella on the way out of the building. However, I won't have this propensity unless I also have a desire not to get wet; and desires are mental phenomena too. So my propensity to pick up my umbrella on the way out of the building can't be the behavioural translation of my belief that it is raining *on its own*. It will have to be the behavioural translation of the combination {my belief that it is raining + my desire not to get wet}.

By this point the behaviourist has already lost the crucial battle. It is already clear that he can't provide individual behavioural translations for individual mental phenomena, one to one. It follows that the non-behaviourist has a way of picking out individual mental phenomena which the behaviourist can't imitate. The whole point of behaviourism was to enable us to say everything that needs to be said about the world of the mental by referring only to the world of behaviour. So behaviourism looks dead in the water already.

Even if the behaviourist can recover from this defeat, worse defeats lie ahead for him elsewhere. Notice, for one thing, that the combination {my belief that it is raining + my desire not to get wet} won't make me pick up the umbrella either, unless I also have still more beliefs: for example, that 'This here is an umbrella', 'Umbrellas protect you from the wet', 'I am not going to get wet *whatever* I do', etc. Presumably, the same is true with my desires. So it turns out that my propensity to pick up the umbrella is, at best, a behavioural translation of a whole complex of mutually interacting desires and beliefs. In Donald Davidson's phrase, there is a 'holism of the intentional'.[17] It is impossible to separate out the behavioural consequences of individual mental phenomena, because individual mental phenomena never appear in atomistic isolation. They are always interrelated in a web of great complexity.

Notice, for another thing, that even if we did manage to pin down one specific web of desires and beliefs which translated behaviourally into my picking up my umbrella, there would still not be a one-to-one correlation between the mental phenomena and their behavioural translation. It is child's play to think up other complexes of desires and beliefs that might equally lead me to pick up the umbrella. For instance, a desire to get wet plus a false belief that umbrellas attract water could have this effect.

Finally, notice this: behaviourism proposes to offer a reductive analysis of the mental processes of intelligent beings by reference to their actual or hypothetical behaviour. But to follow through on this proposal, we need to know which beings are the intelligent ones. That is, we need to know which beings are the ones with a mental life that needs to be reductively analysed in terms of their behaviour. But it seems very difficult to indicate which beings these are without presupposing *non*-behaviourism. Why are vacuum cleaners, spirogyras, sunflowers and robots not targets for the behaviourist project – if not because they do not have minds that are *more than* behaviour?

In the light of these and other problems, behaviourism has been fairly thoroughly refuted, and fairly widely abandoned. However, the basic behaviourist programme was to analyse mental processes in a way that links them inextricably to the world around them, and minimizes mysteries about the nature of consciousness. And this programme is still being pursued, principally by the functionalists, to whom I turn next.

6.3.3 Functionalism The central idea of functionalism is one with a recognizably behaviourist ring to it. It is that *mental states are essentially functional states*. In other words, what identifies some mental item X as a belief that it's raining is the role that X plays in mediating between inputs and outputs to my mental life. On the input side: does X tend to come about when the subject is awake in a rainy environment, and/or when he can't see a window and you drum your fingers on a tin roof? On the output side: does X tend to lead the subject to make such assertions as 'Not a good day for cricket', 'I'm glad I'm not going for a picnic today', or (most obviously) 'It's raining'? Again, does X make the subject pick up his umbrella on the way out of the building when the subject doesn't want to get wet (and believes that umbrellas keep off rain, etc.)? For the functionalist, there is no question of trying to identify the belief that it's raining with any *single* type of behaviour; so the functionalist avoids the first two objections that I posed to behaviourism above. All the same, for the functionalist as for the behaviourist, whether I have a belief depends on where I stand in various causal networks.

The most obvious feature of functionalism is its flexibility about what might count as a mental state. Although functionalism is usually deployed in the interests of physicalism, there is no reason why a functionalist *must* be a physicalist. He might be, for example, a Cartesian dualist, and believe that mental states are to be found in an entirely non-physical parallel universe of mental substance, ectoplasm, or some other mysterious immaterial stuff. For the functionalist, it simply doesn't matter what mental states are in themselves, just so long as they regularly stand in the right place relative to their causes and effects.

In particular, then, it doesn't matter to the functionalist whether the world – this world, our world – contains consciousness or not. The way the characteristic functionalist approach to the workings of the mind develops, questions such as 'What is consciousness?' are simply bypassed. This has often been supposed to be a merit of functionalism – just as it was thought, in earlier times, to be a merit of behaviourism. After all, when you get stuck on the puzzles created by one question, it is often a sound tactic to leave it and try asking a different question.

However, there are real problems here for functionalism. To begin with, it should be obvious already that no position in the philosophy of mind can be entirely unproblematic, if it has the upshot that there is no important difference between the Zombie World and the Conscious World. But since, as I have just said, it doesn't matter to the functionalist whether or not our world contains consciousness, this is precisely the upshot of functionalism. Indeed, for some functionalists, such as Daniel Dennett, the eliminativists might as well be right – there might as well be no such thing as consciousness:

Are zombies possible? They're not just possible, they're actual. We're all zombies. Nobody is conscious – not in the systematically mysterious way that supports such doctrines as epiphenomenalism![18]

Dennett's view – perhaps the most sophisticated version of functionalism extant – is what he himself calls a 'Multiple Drafts theory of consciousness'. As we saw in **5.6**, where we discussed its implications for our account of the person, Dennett's multiple-drafts view says that what we call consciousness is not the unitary thing that we – like Descartes – imagine it to be. There *is* no central focus, no single viewpoint on the world, that can be identified as a Cartesian 'I', a self that is anything more than 'a Centre of Narrative Gravity'.[19] Rather, there is only a hierarchy of functional systems in our brains: simple ones at the lower levels with nothing remotely like consciousness 'in' them; complex ones at the higher levels with all sorts of different phenomena 'in' them that fit different aspects of the Cartesian template with more or less deceptive accuracy. The 'multiple drafts' are what we get during the ascent from the lower levels to the higher. We are constantly tempted to put our finger on some particular level in this hierarchy of functions, and say '*Just here* is where consciousness first appears.' But, Dennett insists, there is no such first level where consciousness is present. Rather, what consciousness is, if it is anything, is the sound of the whole machine at work. Perhaps an illusion; and certainly an overall effect that does not need to be fitted into our ontology if we are trying to explain the fine detail of the workings of the machine. To recycle an old joke, Dennett's picture makes the soul no more than the hum of its parts.

Even if this is right, it does not banish the mystery. Why should consciousness – or something very like it that fits Dennett's terms: some high-level, high-definition, late-in-the-process draft –

emerge as we ascend through the levels of the multiple-drafts model? Remember that every level in the model is a level of more or less complex *functions*; and that, as we've already seen, the functions that interest the functionalist can, in the simpler cases, operate equally well *with or without* consciousness. Well, why should it be any different in more complex cases? How can adding complexity, on its own, be enough to get us from non-consciousness to consciousness? And why should we buy Dennett's idea that, where it doesn't seem enough, that's because we are suffering from philosophical illusions?

To put it very simply, the basic troubles of functionalism are not fixed by adding complexity. Most of these troubles are neatly encapsulated by John Searle's famous Chinese Room Thought-Experiment. Before I can describe that, I need to say a little to flesh out the context of Searle's argument. The context is a tradition of thinking about artificial intelligence (AI) which goes back at least as far as Descartes's *Discourse on the Method*. This tradition begins with the question: what would we have to do to create a machine that could genuinely *think* – think in just as strong and full-blown a sense of the word 'think' as applies to humans?

In the *Discourse*, Descartes himself replies that we could never create such a machine. Why not? Because, he says, there are 'two very certain' tests whereby we could know that 'machines [which] bore a resemblance to our bodies and imitated our actions as closely as possible for all practical purposes' were nonetheless 'not real men', i.e. did not really have minds.[20] Both of Descartes's tests have to do with *versatility*. What humans have is *reason*, 'a universal instrument which can be used in all kinds of situations'; machines, on the other hand, 'need some particular disposition for each particular action'. So you can make a machine that performs one task even better than humans do. But (the first test) you can't make a machine that will convincingly mirror the whole range of human skills and abilities; and in particular (the second test), you can't make a machine that will convincingly mirror the whole range of what humans talk about. For the source of this wide range is the human capacity to reason, which no mechanical contrivance can match.

In the 1950s, the famous mathematician Alan Turing (1912–54) suggested a way of updating Descartes's tests for having a mind.[21] Turing proposed that a machine would count as a genuine thinking machine if it passed a 'blind-interview' test. Suppose I ask questions of two respondents who are hidden from me behind a curtain. One of them is human and the other is a computer. If I can't tell from their answers which of them is the computer and which of them is the human, then the computer has passed the 'Turing Test'. If any machines can be made which pass this test, then Descartes was wrong: we *can* make a machine that can genuinely think.

Searle's Chinese Room Thought-Experiment is designed to show that the Turing Test does not do the job it is supposed to do – discriminate thinkers from non-thinkers. Searle describes a particular experiment in artificial intelligence, conducted by Roger Schank and colleagues at Yale, where a computer was developed that could be 'fed' simple narratives like bar-room yarns, and produced responses to them that certainly did pass the Turing Test. Does this mean that Schank's computer was really thinking, or really understanding?

Searle thinks not. To explain his denial, Searle asks us to picture an English-speaker who can neither read nor write Chinese. He is locked in a room, into which are posted a series of batches of Chinese writing, plus rules (in English) about 'how to give back certain Chinese symbols with certain sorts of shapes' as a response when particular Chinese symbols are posted into the room. 'After a while', our Anglophone gets so good at giving the right responses back that, 'from the external point of view – that is, from the point of view of somebody outside the room in which [the Anglophone] is locked – [his] answers are absolutely indistinguishable from those of native Chinese speakers.' And yet, by hypothesis, the Anglophone *understands no Chinese at all*:

> I produce the [right] answers by manipulating uninterpreted formal symbols...I have inputs and outputs that are indistinguishable from those of the native Chinese speaker, and I can have any formal programme you like [as my means of deciding which symbols to output], but I still understand nothing. For the same reasons, Schank's computer understands nothing of any stories, whether in Chinese, English or whatever, since in the Chinese case the computer is me, and in cases where the computer is not me, the computer has nothing more than I have in the case where I understand nothing.[22]

If this argument works, it doesn't only show that computers can't think. It also shows that functionalism is false. For the sense in which some researchers (the proponents of 'strong AI') claim that computers do think is just this: computers think in that they succeed in manipulating inputs so as to produce the right output. If Searle is right, this isn't thinking or understanding at all, because not just any reliable route from input to correct output counts as thinking or understanding. Now the whole point of functionalism is to define thinking or consciousness as *whatever* goes on between input and reliably produced correct output. So if Searle is right, functionalism is false too.

Searle's opponents have come up with all sorts of responses to this argument. The most effective replies put pressure on Searle to explain why it is so important to *our* thinking that it should involve the special kind of understanding and consciousness that is isolated by the Chinese Room argument. They can turn the tables on Searle by pointing out that, at least if you go by results, the Anglophone does just as well as the Chinese speakers, and Schank's computer does just as well as the man in the bar that you tell the same yarn to. If the difference between the Anglophone and the Chinese speakers is, as Searle claims, understanding, then we should ask: so what's so great about understanding? Why should we want it, if it doesn't make us any better at producing the right results?

'What's so great about it?' Searle might perhaps retort: 'Well, what's so great about not being a zombie?' Searle's opponents seem to be suggesting that we might simply dispense, in our account of the mind and its workings, with the sort of consciousness that is central to Searle's account. We have already seen (**6.1**) why this is no small step to take. To eliminate that sort of consciousness from our theory is to eliminate the aspects of our own minds that we know best and care most about. In a moment, I shall turn to consider a group of philosophers of mind – the eliminativists – who propose to bite this bullet, and do actually eliminate consciousness from their theory of mind. But first, let us close our discussion of Searle by noting two interesting features of the debate about the Chinese Room.

The first interesting feature is a parallel. Compare the standoff in the philosophy of mind between Searle and the functionalists with the standoff in epistemology between the internalist and the externalist (see **2.3.4** on externalism and **2.5.4** on reliablism). Externalist epistemology typically cares more about getting at the truth than about *knowing* that you have got at the truth: what it looks for is a *reliable* method of finding out truths, not a subjectively transparent one. (This is why reliablism is the paradigm expression of externalism in epistemology.) Likewise, functionalists think that understanding and thinking are a matter of getting things right *as seen from an external standpoint*. It doesn't matter to the functionalist *how*, 'on the inside', the understander does his understanding, provided (as I put it above) he follows *some* 'reliable route from input to correct output'.

By contrast, Searle's approach looks thoroughly internalist – and when you think about it, thoroughly Cartesian too. By Searle's lights, no one is going to count as a thinker or understander unless they are the subjects of certain 'inner processes'. This is just the kind of view that Wittgenstein, the arch anti-Cartesian, takes exception to. As I said above, I don't think that Wittgenstein objected to the idea that there *are* inner processes. But he surely would object to Searle's view that understanding is one of them:

> We are trying to get hold of the mental process of under-standing which seems to be hidden behind those coarser and therefore more readily visible accompaniments. But we do not succeed; or rather, it does not get as far as a real attempt. For even supposing I had found something that happened in all those cases of understanding – why should *it* be the under-standing?...Try not to think of understanding as a 'mental process' at all.[23]

The second interesting feature – noted by Searle himself[24] – is that the problem of other minds does not look much easier for Searle than it did for Descartes. For Searle, presumably, the problem of other minds is the problem of knowing whether other people are actually conscious understanders, and not merely symbol manipulators like computers, or the Anglophone in the Chinese Room. But on his view, apparently, our evidence that other people have minds is *exactly as good* as our evidence that high-powered computers have minds! In both cases, we only have behaviour and functional evidence to go on; and in principle, both humans and computers can pass the Turing Test with equal success rates. So what justifies Searle in attributing minds to other humans, but not to computers?

Searle replies that the problem 'is not about how I know that other people have cognitive states, but rather what it is that I am attributing to them when I attribute cognitive states'.[24] But this reply is unconvincing, since Searle is offering to refute functionalism, which is a theory that ties together the nature of mental states and the evidence for them. If Searle wants to replace functionalism, he cannot simply skip the question why we should ascribe mental states to some things but not others. Searle goes on to say that 'in "cognitive sciences" one presupposes the reality and knowability of the mental'. But this sounds less like an argument than an admission that Searle has no argument.

In any case, there are some cognitive scientists who do not presuppose 'the reality and knowability of the mental'. These are the eliminativists, to whom I now turn.

6.3.4 Eliminativism This approach begins with the observation that, in the history of science, conservatism and obscurantism are consistent losers. The ideas that certain things are simply off-limits to scientific explanation (obscurantism), or that there are some parts of our world-view that science just couldn't dislodge (conservatism), have had a poor time of it since the age of Descartes. Plainly enough, this observation applies to the more mysterious features of our mental lives, such as consciousness and the personal perspective, as much as to anything else. The fact that the personal perspective is a central part of our world-view may be *some* sort of evidence in its favour. But it can hardly be decisive evidence. After all, once upon a time, alchemy was a central part of our world-view, too.

Alchemy collapsed because it faced insuperable scientific objections. Paul Churchland and others have argued that very similar scientific objections can be made against our beliefs, not just about the reality of the personal perspective, but more generally about the whole of our commonsense conceptual framework for mental phenomena.

Churchland calls this conceptual framework by the resounding name 'folk psychology'. This term, which first emerged in discussion in the 1980s, is a significant one. Apparently 'folk psychology' is coined on analogy with 'folk etymology', which means the usually mistaken and misleading guesses about the origins of words that gain popular currency in the absence of proper scientific research into the origins of words. (Three examples: (a) the English name 'Iceland' comes from the Norse *Island*, which means, not 'land of ice', but simply 'island'; (b) 'outrage' is not 'out' + 'rage', but the French *outrage,* 'going beyond (*outre*) the limits'; (c) modern English-speakers increasingly admit the existence of a strange implement called 'a fine tooth-comb', but the original cliché referred rather to 'a fine-toothed comb'.)

The point of the name 'folk psychology', then, is that 'our commonsense conceptual framework for mental phenomena' is just as ill-founded, unscientific and misleading as folk etymology. The way we naturally think about our own minds, including our natural belief in the personal perspective, is no more off-limits to scientific assessment than anything else is. Indeed, Churchland's striking suggestion is that folk psychology actually *fails* this assessment.

As Churchland points out, the sciences of man have in general been making spectacular progress:

If we approach *homo sapiens* from the perspective of the…physical sciences, we can tell a coherent story of his constitution, development, and behavioural capacities which encompasses particle physics, atomic and molecular theory, organic chemistry, evolutionary theory, biology, physiology, and materialistic neuroscience. That story, though still radically incomplete, is already extremely powerful [and] coherent…the greatest theoretical synthesis in the history of the human race is currently in our hands.[25]

However, Churchland goes on, 'folk psychology is no part of this growing synthesis':

> Its intentional categories stand magnificently alone, without visible prospect of reduction to that larger corpus [of physical science]…Folk psychology's explanatory impotence and long stagnation inspire little faith that its categories will find themselves neatly reflected in the categories of neuroscience. On the contrary, one is reminded of how alchemy must have looked as elemental chemistry was taking form, how Aristotelian cosmology must have looked as classical mechanics was being articulated, or how the vitalist conception of life must have looked as organic chemistry marched forward.

According to Churchland and other eliminativists, the way we think about our own minds has been superseded by science. In our interactions with other humans, we make constant use of concepts like 'desire', 'belief', 'pain', 'experience' – and indeed 'personal perspective'. But, as tools for understanding one another, these concepts are in no better scientific shape than concepts like 'bewitched', 'possessed by the devil', or 'under the influence of Saturn in the Twelfth House'. The only serious science of the mind that we have is neuroscience – the science of the brain. What we should do is develop that – and simply eliminate folk psychology as unscientific. Until we have found some scientific basis for them, all serious references to desires, beliefs, pains, experiences and so on, should just be avoided as ill-founded, misleading and unscientific mumbo–jumbo.

When the explanatory ambitions of science clash with the apparent reality of the personal perspective, the eliminativist thinks the same as the behaviourist: it is the personal perspective that must give way. If the personal perspective is not explicable by science, that does not mean, according to the eliminativist, that there is something wrong with science; for we know from experience how well science has succeeded everywhere else. Rather, it means that the personal perspective, like the rest of folk psychology, is likely to be a nest of just the sort of confusions and illusions that the progress of science has exposed in so many other places.

So when science makes the progress necessary to replace folk psychology completely, what will happen, according to the eliminativists? The answer is that folk-psychological concepts like consciousness, belief, desire and personal perspective will either be replaced or else simply abolished. If they are replaced, they will be replaced by scientifically credible surrogates – as happened in the history of chemistry, when Joseph Priestley's concept of 'pure air' was replaced by Lavoisier's concept of 'oxygen'. If the concepts of folk psychology are abolished, this will be because science has shown that there is no need for any concept *anything like* such current concepts as consciousness, belief, desire and the personal perspective – as happened in the history of chemistry, when, after Lavoisier, the 17th-century concept of 'phlogiston' was simply abandoned.

What would it be like to live in a world where folk-psychological concepts had been abandoned as unscientific? Churchland gives us an entertaining picture of what it might be like:

These people do not sit on the beach and listen to the steady roar of the pounding surf. They sit on the beach and listen to the aperiodic atmospheric compression waves produced as the coherent energy of the ocean waves is audibly redistributed in the chaotic turbulence of the shallows…They do not observe the western sky redden as the sun sets. They observe the wavelength distribution of incoming solar radiation shift towards the longer wavelengths as the shorter are increasingly scattered away from the lengthening atmospheric path they must take as terrestrial rotation turns us slowly away from their source...[26]

This is a perfectly credible picture of how things might be in a world that had banished or replaced unscientific concepts. No doubt the most scientifically literate members of our own community are already inhabiting such a picture. But the extension of this process of concept-replacement to the working of our own minds: is that conceivable?

Here is a tempting argument against its conceivability. (Churchland himself describes this argument as 'very popular', though he gives no citations.) The argument is this: 'The eliminativist is denying the existence of, among other things, beliefs. This means that he's advising us to adopt the belief that we have no beliefs. But this advice is obviously incoherent.'

Indeed it is incoherent. However, as Churchland points out,[27] it need not be the eliminativist's advice. If our present concept of belief is ill-formed, scientifically speaking, what follows is not that we should believe that we have no beliefs. What follows is only that we should replace our concept of belief with something more scientifically respectable *as soon as we are in a position to do so*. The eliminativist's point is that our concept of belief is a bad instrument for understanding ourselves, just as a chalk and slate are bad instruments for writing with. The solution is not to refuse to write anything, or to throw away every instrument immediately; it is to get a better instrument as soon as we can. While we are still waiting for one, it is no more incoherent for me to have the belief 'In the end, my concept of belief will be superseded', than it is for me to write 'A slate is a bad medium for writing' on my slate.

A parallel argument against the conceivability of eliminativism, in the case of the personal perspective, is no more successful. You might think that eliminativism, as it applies to the personal perspective, tells each of us to conclude that the personal perspective is an unscientific illusion. But this conclusion about my own perspective is, of course, one that *I* have to reach – from my own perspective. So it looks as if I have to adopt the personal perspective even to abandon the personal perspective – which seems self-contradictory. This 'reflexive' argument against eliminativism might, perhaps, have appealed to Descartes, or to Kant. All the same, it fails for just the same reason as the argument about belief in the last paragraph. As before, the eliminativist conclusion is not that I ought to decide, from my own perspective, that my own perspective is an illusion. More modestly, the eliminativist conclusion is, rather, that there is something creaky and suspect in our current concept of the personal perspective; so we should upgrade our concept as soon as we can. And it is not hard to see how that might be right.

So eliminativism is conceivable. It's perfectly possible to imagine that we might do without the folk psychology that we currently have. At some time in the future, our current concepts of belief and desire might very well be replaced by more scientifically sophisticated concepts. If and when more scientifically sophisticated alternatives to desire and belief as we know them become available, will it be time to trade in the folk-psychological concepts? Of course it will. Refusing this conceptual upgrade would be – in Churchland's own progressivist rhetoric – as bad as preferring Aristotelian mechanics to Newtonian, or Newtonian to quantum mechanics. However, though eliminativism is conceivable, there are good reasons for thinking it false; as I shall now explain.

A crucial part of the eliminative materialists' case against folk psychology is that it is a theory that doesn't work very well. Here is Churchland again:

Consider...mental illness, creative imagination, or the ground of intelligence differences between individuals. Consider our utter ignorance of the nature and psychological functions of sleep...reflect on the common ability to hit a moving car with a snowball...On these and many other mental phenomena, folk psychology sheds negligible light.[28]

Churchland's accusation that folk psychology is a theory that doesn't work very well is often countered by the riposte that folk psychology is not a scientific theory at all. One reason for doubting that it is a scientific theory is that it's hard to see how we could test folk psychology experimentally. What sort of evidence would we accept as evidence *against* folk psychology?

Some writers, perhaps under the influence of Wittgenstein, think that our ways of understanding one another are not so much a scientific theory, as parts of an unscientific tradition of what the Germans call *Verstehen*. This is a form of mutual understanding that resists formulation: a 'form of life', in Wittgenstein's phrase.[29]

Other philosophers have debated the merits of two alternative approaches to our ways of understanding one another, which have acquired the inelegant names 'simulation theory' and 'theory theory'. (I am, as it happens, the proud owner of a hobby-horse about unhelpful terminology in philosophy; but I won't ride it here.) Theory theory says that folk psychology is indeed a scientific theory, which we use to interpret each other; its exponents tend to be eliminativists. By contrast, simulation theory says that folk psychology is not a scientific theory, but an aptitude for simulating what it's like to be in someone else's shoes and imagining what we would do there; so folk psychology is not a theory, and the usual argument for eliminativism can't even start.[30]

This choice between simulation theory and theory theory looks like a false dilemma. It is hard to see how you could be good at simulating others' mental processes without having, at least implicitly, the materials for a good theory of mind. There is no reason to think that understanding others by simulation is incompatible with understanding others by theory. Moreover, the dilemma is not only false but unimportant. Eliminativism can be run without the assumption that folk psychology is (in any strict sense) a scientific theory: an eliminativist might complain that folk psychology – like various other superstitions – isn't *even* a theory. Therefore, eliminativism can't be refuted by showing that folk psychology is not a theory.

In any case, the best response to the eliminative materialists' complaint that folk psychology is 'a theory that doesn't work very well' is not the apologetic response that folk psychology isn't meant to be a theory at all. The best response is a robust one: folk psychology *is* a theory, and a very successful one.[31]

Churchland claims that folk psychology does not work very well, and comes up with a short list of hard questions for believers in folk psychology. The friends of folk psychology can respond in kind, with a much longer list of much harder questions for Churchland. Folk psychology not work very well? Then how do Inspector Morse and Sherlock Holmes get such good results? And why do so many of us get so much pleasure from novels, plays and soap operas? And why is there a Prisoners' Dilemma, or a skill of controlling a classroom, or such a thing as being good at charades or telling jokes? (And so on, almost indefinitely.) To put the point at its most general: if folk psychology does not work very well, then how is it that nearly all of us, except for a few unfortunates who are autistic or the like, are so good at predicting and explaining what other people are doing and thinking? The eliminativist claims that folk psychology lacks the predictive and explanatory power that a good scientific hypothesis ought to have. But this charge strikes me as extraordinarily unconvincing. If folk psychology is really, as the eliminativists say, no better than mumbo-jumbo – well, it is mumbo-jumbo that makes remarkably accurate predictions.

Even if the charge that folk psychology doesn't work was a convincing one, the eliminativist would still have to show that there is a serious alternative to folk psychology that works better than it does. This is something that the eliminativists have, so far, completely failed to do. To date, the question of replacing our current folk psychology's concepts with better, more scientifically respectable surrogates remains completely hypothetical. No such surrogates have been made available by the eliminativists, nor by anyone else; nor is there any sign that they soon will be. In the absence of such surrogates, the eliminativist project has not even begun. Until they begin to be produced, eliminativism is a harmless speculation that we need not even reject.

I conclude that neither behaviourists nor eliminativists – nor anyone else – has shown us good reason to reject the personal perspective in favour of the scientific perspective. So does the clash between science and the personal perspective remain? Or are there any promising ways of reconciling them? That is the question of the next section.

6.4 **Keeping hold of both perspectives**

Confronted with a clash between science's explanatory ambitions and the personal perspective, some philosophers reject the ambitions of science (**6.2**). They either make the familiar claim that science does not really aim to explain literally everything (contrary to what naturalists and physicalists say). Or else they argue, like Frank Jackson, that even if science really does have this aim, it fails to achieve it.

Other philosophers reject the personal perspective (**6.3**), either because they misunderstand Wittgenstein (**6.3.1**); or because they are behaviourists and think that only third-personal observations count (**6.3.2**); or because they are functionalists and think that we can do good philosophy of mind without saying anything much about the nature of consciousness (**6.3.3**); or because they are eliminativists and think that the apparent mysteries of the first-person perspective are a nest of illusions that will eventually be exposed by the progress of science (**6.3.4**).

A third group of philosophers deny that there is really a clash between the two perspectives after all. These philosophers probably form the majority in contemporary philosophy of mind. I shall now look at four versions of their position: Rorty's version (**6.4.1**), the ability approach (**6.4.2**), supervenience (**6.4.3**), and dual-aspect theory (**6.4.4**).

6.4.1 Richard Rorty A first way of denying that there is really any clash between the scientific and the personal perspectives comes down, in effect, to something like a version of eliminativism. This is the position developed by Richard Rorty in *Philosophy and the Mirror of Nature*. Rorty begins his argument by sketching a picture of a race of aliens, in many ways rather similar to us, whom he nicknames 'the Antipodeans'. These aliens, he tells us, 'did not know that they had minds. They had notions like "wanting to" and "intending to"…But they had no notion that these signified *mental* states – states of a peculiar and distinct sort':

Neurology and biochemistry had been the first disciplines in which technological breakthroughs had been achieved, and a large part of the conversation of [the Antipodeans] concerned the state of their nerves. When their infants veered towards hot stoves, mothers cried out, 'He'll stimulate his C-fibres'…Their knowledge of physiology was such that each well-formed sentence of the language…could easily be correlated with a readily identifiable neural state…Sometimes they would say things like 'It looked like an elephant, but then it struck me that elephants don't occur on this continent, so I realised that it must be a mastodon.' But they would also sometimes say, in just the same circumstances, thinks like 'I had G-412 together with F-11, but then I had S-147, so I realised that it must be a mastodon.'[32]

Rorty's story has both an eliminativist bit and a conciliatory bit. Here's the eliminativist bit: in the world of the Antipodeans, folk psychology, as a scientific theory, has been completely superseded. But – here comes the conciliatory bit – it is still possible for the Antipodeans to talk the language of folk psychology if they want; or at least, they can do this wherever the language of folk psychology corresponds to the language of neuroscience. (The Antipodeans have abandoned the folk-psychological concepts that do *not* correspond to neuroscientific concepts.) But, the Antipodeans will tell us, the language of folk psychology is not the one that 'wears the trousers'. The neuroscientific language is the one that accurately represents what is really there, and the one that provides us with all the real explanations.

The moral of Rorty's Antipodean fable is this. We have the idea that the concepts of folk psychology are a wholly different class of concepts – 'mental concepts' – from the concepts of neuroscience – 'physical concepts', and that there is a huge problem about the relation between the two sorts of concepts – the 'mind–body problem'. The Antipodeans do not face our problem about the relation of the mental to the physical, because they do not have our idea that the mental and the physical are radically different categories. And that, Rorty suggests, is all the better for them:

If there is no way of explaining to the Antipodeans our problems and theories about mind and body – no way of making them see that this is the paradigm case of an ontological divide – then we ought to face up to the possibility that [the Antipodeans] are right: we have just been reporting neurons when we thought we were reporting raw feels.[32]

Where the mind–body problem is concerned, says Rorty, the Antipodeans have it right and we have it wrong. There just isn't a mind–body problem, because the sort of mental items that could give rise to such a problem simply don't exist. There just aren't any 'raw feels' whose relationship to the stimulation of neurons is problematic and mysterious. As the Antipodeans have learned, 'raw feels' *are* neuron-stimulations. If we could learn to think the same way as the Antipodeans, we could give up the mind–body problem as a mare's nest. And then there would no longer be a clash between the scientific and personal perspectives. What is a raw feel from the personal perspective is the very same thing as what is a neuron-stimulation from the scientific perspective. The difference between the mental and the physical is then purely perspectival; moreover, the relationship between the two perspectives is fully explained by science. And so the mysteries and problems simply evaporate.

Thus Rorty proposes a theoretical identification between neuron-stimulations and raw feels and other mental items – a theoretical identification that, he thinks, will fully explain the relationship between the personal and scientific, the mental and physical, perspectives. One problem with Rorty's proposal is that the identification he suggests seems implausible. Neuronal states (such as 'S-147') could not possibly correspond, one on one, with mental items like thoughts (such as 'Elephants don't occur on this continent'). Let me briefly explain some familiar reasons why not.

For a start, there is good scientific evidence of a very simple sort against any such correspondence. Patients can suffer physical damage to the thinking areas of their brains without suffering any loss in their capacity to think. What usually happens in the case of small brain-lesions, apparently, is that other areas of the brain take over the cognitive functions of the areas that have been damaged. The moral is *multiple realizability*: there isn't only one way a given brain can think a given thought.

Moreover, different people acquire different concepts, such as 'elephant', in different ways and on the basis of different experiences. If we are going to tell a thoroughly physical story about what it is to have thoughts about elephants, these different histories of concept-acquisition presumably ought to be relevant. But if the story of how you got hold of the concept of an elephant is quite different from the story of how I got hold of the concept of an elephant, then it seems virtually inevitable that different neurons will end up carrying the concept of an elephant in you and in me. (Or do I have any takers for the hypothesis that the human brain is hard-wired with elephant-thinking neurons?) This shows that our shared capacity to think about elephants cannot depend on our sharing exactly the same neuronal architecture. The *mental* is the *environmental*: most of the time,[33] our thought and conscious experience cannot depend exclusively on the state of our neurons, but must also be externally determined. It must depend also on what is present in the environment around us.

This point is, of course, another manifestation of something like semantic externalism. As I pointed out in **2.3.4**, semantic externalism is not in itself a refutation of scepticism. The facts (1) that I have thoughts about trees, and (2) that mental content about trees is externally determined (by trees), do indeed show (3) that there are trees. But that does not get rid of scepticism. It merely relocates it, as a problem about whether (1) is really true – a problem about whether my thoughts that *seem* to be about trees really *are* about trees. These thoughts will have entirely different contents, depending on whether or not there really are trees. But exactly what contents they do have, precisely because it is not determined solely 'from inside our heads', need not be transparently accessible to us 'from inside our heads'.

Rorty can't get round these two problems by restricting himself to claiming only that for every mental state there is *some* physical state. His project was to show that there could be people like the Antipodeans, who talk about mental states by talking about physical states (neuronal states). But if mental states are multiply realizable, a given state of our neurons could correlate with all sorts of mental states. So we can't possibly know which mental state someone is talking about, when they refer to it only via a neuronal state that could be almost any mental state. And if mental states have their content determined at least partly by their environment, then things like the following might happen: (neuronal state N + an elephant) could equal the thought 'This is not a mastodon', while (neuronal state N + a mastodon) could equal the thought 'This is not an elephant'. We will then have two quite different mental states with the very same neuronal state, N. This will be a second way in which a given state of our neurons can correlate with all sorts of mental states; and a second reason why Rorty's proposal cannot possibly work.

A third problem with Rorty's proposal echoes the problem facing the other eliminativist proposals already considered. This is that a proposal is all it is. Is it true that 'what is a raw feel from the personal perspective is the very same thing as a neuron–stimulation from the scientific perspective'? Who knows? Perhaps it is. But if it is true, we have as yet no notion of how or why it comes to be true. As Jerry Fodor and David Chalmers point out (**6.1**), we have no explanation whatever of *why* raw feels and neuron-stimulations are related in this way; indeed, we have no explanation of why there are any raw feels at all. But this is precisely where the mystery lies that Rorty is trying to banish. Even if he could overcome the first and second problems, he would not succeed in banishing this mystery. Nor, therefore, does he succeed in showing that there is no clash between the personal and scientific perspectives.

Rorty's way of denying that there is a real clash between the personal and scientific perspectives tends to bring us down on the side of the scientific perspective. A second way of denying the clash also has this effect. This is the ability approach.

6.4.2 The ability approach This proposal is a response to the story of Mary the colour scientist (**6.2**). About her, you remember, Jackson said that she learns new facts when she first encounters colours other than black and white. And this point was crucial to Jackson's argument. For the whole point of these facts was that they were not *physical* facts, and hence were a counterexample to naturalism – the thesis that the physical facts are the only facts there are.

We might say that Rorty's response to the tale of Mary would be, in effect, to allow that the 'facts' that Mary learns are indeed facts, but deny that they are non-physical facts. Rather, as Rorty might have put it, they are neuronal facts disguised as facts about raw feels. The ability approach's response to the tale of Mary is the other way around. It is to allow that the 'facts' that Mary learns are indeed non-physical, but deny that they are genuine facts. To quote David Lewis quoting Laurence Nemirow:

Some modes of understanding consist, not in the grasping of facts, but in the acquisition of abilities...I understand the experience of seeing red if I can at will visualise red. Now it is perfectly clear why there must be a special connection between the ability to place oneself in a state representative of a given experience and the point of view of experiencer: exercising the ability just *is* what we call 'adopting the point of view of experiencer'...We can, then, come to terms with the subjectivity of our understanding of experience without positing subjective facts as the objects of our understanding.[34]

For Lewis and Nemirow, what Mary learns may be non-physical, but it is not facts: it is an *ability*. Compare what Mary learns if she learns to ride a bike (of whatever colour). Is Mary learning facts here? Should we posit a category of special cycling facts, necessarily inaccessible to non-cyclists, and undergirded by a mysterious ontology? Of course not. Knowing how to ride a bike is — as Ryle's old distinction has it — knowledge *how*, not knowledge *that*.[35] There are no stateable facts, physical or non-physical, about what Mary learns when she learns to ride a bike. Nor are there any stateable facts, physical or non-physical, about what Mary learns when she learns to visualize red. And so, Lewis and Nemirow conclude, Jackson's argument fails.

Undoubtedly Lewis and Nemirow are on to something here. To see this, consider how hard it is for Jackson to say what the fact is that Mary learns when she comes out of the black-and-white room and sees red for the first time. According to Jackson, Mary learns 'what it is like to see red'. But how do we state this new knowledge of Mary's as a *fact*? The fact in question will have to be something along the lines of: 'Seeing red is like *this*.' But what sort of fact is caught by that utterance?

It all depends on what kind of performance accompanies the utterance of 'Seeing red is like *this*'. You might say these words while pointing at something. Or you might say these words while grabbing me by the shoulders and steering me round so that I am facing a red object. The latter sort of performance, the steering, is just what Lewis and Nemirow think it is — your putting me in a position to acquire a perceptual ability — and so, according to their argument, not a real case of my acquiring a new *fact*. As for the former sort of performance, the pointing, the question here is what you point at. If you point at something *public*, like a red surface over there, then your pointing is not significantly different from the case where you steer me towards something. If on the other hand you point at something *private*, such as your own experience of redness, this seems like a nonsensical thing to do as a way for *you* to communicate something to *me*. For, of course, I cannot have your experience of redness.

This line of thought suggests that Wittgenstein is lurking in the wings of Lewis and Nemirow's argument. It was just this sort of worry about defining public properties, such as redness, by pointing to private properties, such as my experience of redness, that set the Private Language Argument in motion (**2.3.2**). Jackson needs to explain what '*this*' refers to in 'Seeing red is like *this*'. Apparently the Lewis–Nemirow strategy is to block off the alternative that '*this*' might refer to a private object, perhaps with the help of an implicit appeal to Wittgenstein; and then to insist that the other alternative – that '*this*' is just what you say as you steer my eyes towards a public instance of redness – involves no more than what they say it involves: namely that you are teaching me an ability, not a fact.

If so, Lewis and Nemirow's response may perhaps show that Jackson's argument about Mary the colour scientist fails to refute physicalism. However, their response certainly doesn't show that there is no clash between the physical and personal perspectives. To see this, we may switch from the question 'What sort of facts is Jackson talking about?' to the question 'What sort of abilities are Lewis and Nemirow talking about?' The answer to that, irresistibly, is that Lewis and Nemirow are talking about abilities to have experiences. (See the Nemirow quotation above, which identifies knowing what it's like to see red with the ability to 'visualise red'.) I submit that the idea that physical objects such as human beings should have any such ability remains as difficult to explain from the scientific perspective as ever.

What's more, it seems likely that the objects of experience are not *physical* objects. I've already shown why this is likely in my discussion of Rorty's Antipodeans (**6.4.1**). The reason is that the objects of experience are *mental* items, and there seems no chance of identifying the great majority of mental items (e.g. thoughts of mastodons) with any particular kind of physical items (e.g. neuronal states such as S-147). This means that we can replace Jackson's argument about Mary the colour scientist with this argument: (1) physicalism entails that there are no non-physical objects, (2) but the objects of experience are non-physical objects, (3) therefore physicalism is false. So long as both physicalism and this argument continue to look plausible, nothing like the Lewis–Nemirow ability approach to experience will be able to resolve the clash between the physical and the personal perspectives.

6.4.3 Supervenience So will anything else resolve that clash? Let us consider the notion of supervenience. Many philosophers with physicalist inclinations – and a fair number with dualist inclinations too – often find it comforting to say that the mental *supervenes* on the physical. The basic idea here is that the relation between the mental and the physical is like the relation between, for instance, physics and chemistry. Physics isn't chemistry, and chemistry isn't physics. But physics underlies chemistry: if there were no physics, there couldn't be any chemistry either. And physics explains chemistry: the reason why chemical reactions happen the way they do is because physical particles behave the way they do. Hence we can say that chemistry supervenes on physics, meaning that – although chemistry is not the very same thing as physics – there can be no change or state of rest in chemistry without there being some change or state of rest in physics. Likewise, the friends of supervenience hold, we can say that the mental supervenes on the physical, meaning that – although the mental is not the very same thing as the physical – there can be no change or state of rest in the mental without there being some change or state of rest in the physical.

I don't wish to dispute the possibility of saying this. But I do wonder about its usefulness. Three disanalogies with the case of physics and chemistry will help to explain my doubt.

The first disanalogy is that the supervenience of chemistry on physics is tightly local: that is, the change or state of rest in physics that accompanies any change or state of rest in chemistry is nearly always right there where the chemical change or state of rest is. By contrast, the supervenience of the mental on the physical is very loosely global: that is, the change or state of rest in the physical that accompanies any change or state of rest in the mental need not be (so to speak) anywhere near the mental change or state of rest. As I said in discussing Rorty, 'the mental is the environmental': the content of my thoughts about Australia, for example, has among its determinants Australia itself, a large physical object right on the other side of the world from me.[36] So my mental state of thinking about Australia is, so to speak, right here where I am; but the physical state that it supervenes on includes a landmass on the other side of the world. (My mental states when I think about Andromeda, or the origins of the cosmos, will be even more extreme cases of global supervenience.)

The second disanalogy is that chemistry is not just supervenient on physics; it is actually reducible to physics. Every chemical change or state of rest is not just accompanied by some change or state of rest in physics; it is, in literal truth, nothing more than some change or state of rest in physics. You can express every chemical reaction as a physical event: the only reason not to is that it's cumbersome and long-winded. As we saw – again – with Rorty, the same does not seem to be true with the mental and the physical. There seems to be no prospect of reducing the mental to the physical, even in a long-winded way.

Even if you could effect this reduction, a third disanalogy would still hold. Chemistry is explained by physics in a very obvious and straightforward manner – namely, as just observed, by the reduction of chemistry to physics. By contrast, the mental is not explained by the physical in any very obvious and straight-forward manner – and in particular not, so far as we can tell, by the reduction of the mental to the physical. (A parallel remark applies in discussions of the objectivity of ethics, another place where supervenience is often appealed to (**4.3-4.5**). Just to say that the moral supervenes on the physical is not to explain anything about the nature of the moral.)

In the light of these three disanalogies, we should say this. Even if the mental does supervene on the physical, nothing is *explained* by this supervenience. Perhaps, in fact, nothing *could* be explained by supervenience. Indeed, that pessimistic suggestion has already been made by the man who invented the term 'supervenience', Donald Davidson:

> There are no strict psychophysical laws [i.e. laws linking the mental with the physical] because of the disparate commit-ments of the mental and physical schemes. It is a feature of physical reality that physical change can be explained by laws that connect it with other changes and conditions physically described. It is a feature of the mental that the attribution of mental phenomena must be responsible to the background of reasons, beliefs, and intentions of the individual. There cannot be tight connections between the realms if each is to retain allegiance to its proper source of evidence.[37]

6.4.4 Dual-aspect theory   When Davidson speaks here of 'physical *description*' and of the '*attribution* of mental phenomena', he gives us the key to an understanding of his own account of the relation between the mental and the physical. For Davidson, talk about minds and talk about physical bodies are two different sorts of talk with one sort of subject-matter:

If one event causes another, there is a strict law which those events instantiate *when properly described* [viz., physically]...Even if someone knew the entire physical history of the world, and every mental event were identical with a physical, it would not follow that he could predict or explain a single mental event (*so described*, of course)...When we *portray* events as perceivings, rememberings, decisions and actions, we necessarily locate them amid physical happenings...but so long as we do not change the *idiom* that same *mode of portrayal* insulates mental events from the strict laws that can in principle be called upon to explain and predict physical phenomena.[38]

As the italicized phrases in the last quotation show, Davidson sees talk about minds as an 'idiom', a 'mode of portrayal'. As a matter of science, there are series of physical events, related by strict scientific laws. But it is also possible to interpret at least some of these series of physical events as *mental* events (e.g. 'perceivings, rememberings, decisions and actions'). When we do that, we get a quite different picture of reality:

The explanations of mental events in which we are typically interested relate them to other mental events and conditions. We explain a man's free actions, for example, by appeal to his desires, habits, knowledge and perceptions. Such accounts of intentional behaviour operate in a conceptual framework removed from the direct reach of physical law by describing both cause and effect, reason and action, as aspects of a portrait of a human agent.[39]

When we consider events involving intelligent agents, it can happen that the very same series of events can be seen or interpreted in two very different ways: as a series of *physical* events, happening according to strict and deterministic physical laws, and forming a proper part of the subject-matter of natural science; or as a series of *mental* events, happening according to the norms of intentional psychology (another name for folk psychology, **6.3.4**). For Davidson, then, mental talk and physical talk are different ways of talking about the same thing. To put it another way, Davidson's account of the relation between the mental and the physical is a form of dual-aspect theory.

The *locus classicus* for this sort of view is the *Ethics* of Spinoza (1632–77):

> *The order and connection of ideas is the same as the order and connection of things*...substance thinking and substance extended are one and the same substance, comprehended now through one attribute, now through the other...Thus, whether we conceive nature under the attribute of extension, or under the attribute of thought, or under any other attribute, we shall find the same order, or one and the same chain of causes – that is, the same things following in either case.[40]

Another version of dual-aspect theory that we've already reviewed (and found wanting) is Richard Rorty's view that 'neuronal states' and 'mental states' are names from two vocabularies for talking about the same items. A fourth version is Bertrand Russell's *neutral monism*, a theory which Russell illustrates

> by comparison with a postal directory, in which the same names come twice over, once in alphabetical and once in geographical order; we may compare the alphabetical order to the mental, and the geographical order to the physical...Just as every man in the directory has two kinds of

neighbours, namely alphabetical neighbours and geographical neighbours, so every object will lie at the intersection of two causal series with different laws, namely the mental series and the physical series.[41]

A fifth version of dual-aspect theory is found in Sir Peter Strawson's *Individuals*:

A necessary condition of states of consciousness being ascribed at all is that they should be ascribed to the *very same things* as…corporeal characteristics…The concept of a person is logically prior to that of an individual consciousness…The concept of a person is to be understood as the concept of a type of entity such that *both* predicates ascribing states of consciousness *and* predicates ascribing [physical] characteristics are *equally* applicable to an individual entity of that type.[42]

For Davidson, events are the common currency, and our choice to describe them as mental or physical is what marks the mental–physical divide. For Spinoza, the common currency is 'substance', which, again, we can as we like talk about as mental or physical. For Rorty, the common currency is made up of the items that can be called either 'neuronal states' or 'mental states' (though the former name is better). For Russell, the common currency is the items, whatever they are, that appear in both the mental directory and the physical directory, and the mental–physical divide is the distinction between the directories. And for Strawson, the common currency is the persons to whom we apply predicates of both the mental and the physical kinds. These five theories have their differences, but they are all recognizably of a single sort. Moreover, there are two important problems that all of them face.

The first problem for dual-aspect theories is a problem that supervenience theories also face. It is a lack of explanatory power. Suppose Strawson is right that we have two sorts of predicates, mental and physical, that we apply to persons. Or suppose Davidson is right that we can, at our discretion, choose whether to describe any particular event as a mental or a physical event. Or again, suppose Spinoza or Russell is right, and that there is a single basic reality with two sorts of attributes, physical and mental. In all these cases, we are left with a feeling that the dual-aspect theorist has simply helped himself to the categories of the mental and the physical, and has not said enough to explain how, and why, they are related.

In particular, the dual-aspect theorist tends to fail spectacularly on a question that, whatever its other faults, eliminativism and reductive materialism at least try to answer. This is the question why, given that there is a physical world, there is also a mental world. Why, if you set up a physical world like ours, do you also get in that world creatures like us, who have minds? In other words, dual-aspect theory tends not to answer very well the question of consciousness. But if David Chalmers was right (**6.1**), this is the biggest question of all in the philosophy of mind.

Another example of a theory that fails to explain this is panpsychism. Panpsychism, the classic exposition of which is Leibniz's (1646–1716) *Monadology*, is a philosophical view which can be argued for like this: (1) since there is consciousness in the complex parts of the world, and (2) since the complex is only a sum of simple parts, it follows (3) that there must also be consciousness in the simple parts of the world. In other words, panpsychism responds to the difficult question 'But how does *consciousness* get into the picture?' by helping itself to consciousness from the start. This is not explanatory; though perhaps a panpsychist would say that it is the best we can do.

The second problem for dual-aspect theories is a problem that every theory of mind and body has to face up to – but which dual-aspect theories bring out with peculiar clarity. This is the problem of free will, which I shall briefly discuss in **6.5**.

6.5 **Free will**

To see the problem, recall Donald Davidson's words, quoted above. Our explanations of 'a man's free actions', says Davidson, 'operate in a conceptual framework removed from the direct reach of physical law.'[39] What does Davidson mean here by 'direct'? He means, of course, that physical law does not cover a man's free actions as so described. To talk about someone's free actions is to talk about events in a vocabulary that does not refer to the operation of scientific laws, and so is not a deterministic vocabulary. Does that mean that 'a man's free actions' are not determined at all by scientific laws? No: it simply means that to see how they are determined by scientific laws, you need to redescribe those actions as physical events. Talking about mental events is, for Davidson, just a roundabout and baroque way of talking about physical events; and there is no reason that Davidson can see to doubt that physical events are causally determined. (Others have seen reason to doubt this, but I won't pursue the point here.[43]) It follows that mental events are causally determined too, albeit 'indirectly', and that our 'portrait' of ourselves as free human agents is, in the end, no more than a product of our mental way of talking.

Parallel points follow for Strawson, Russell and Spinoza. Spinoza is of course notoriously forthright on free will: 'In nature there is nothing contingent, but all things have been determined from the necessity of the divine nature to exist and produce an effect in a certain way.'[44] Strawson is more circumspect than Spinoza. He speaks of a contrast between 'participant' or 'reactive' attitudes and other attitudes, where the participant attitudes are the ones that involve us in imputing free will to others and ourselves. Strawson insists that it simply isn't possible for us to drop our participant attitudes – any more than it is possible for us to drop our non-participant attitudes: 'it is *useless* to ask whether it would not be rational for us to do what it is not in our nature to (be able to) do.'[45] That we have participant attitudes to whatever we are treating as persons, and non-participant attitudes to whatever we are treating as non-persons, is simply, for Strawson, a datum of 'descriptive metaphysics', a brute fact about the way we see the world. In this way Strawson's dichotomy of participant and non-participant attitudes is, of course, very like his dichotomy of mental and physical predicates. It is also, we may be tempted to add, just as explanatorily unsatisfying as that dichotomy. Just as the dichotomy between mental and physical predicates tends to leave us haunted by the feeling that Strawson is *really* a physicalist of sorts, so likewise the participant/non-participant dichotomy leaves us haunted by the feeling that Strawson is *really* a determinist of sorts. (Notice, for instance, that Strawson's usual word for the opposite type of attitude to 'participant' attitudes is not 'non-participant': it is 'objective'.)

To repeat, the problem of free will is not a problem only for dual-aspect theories of the mind; although, as I hope I've now shown, it is a problem that dual-aspect theories bring out with particular clarity. In fact, of course, every theory of the mind has to face up to the problem of free will. That problem is another manifestation of the clash that I have been exploring in this chapter, the clash between the scientific and the personal perspectives that arises when we try to establish the place of mind in a mindless world. Indeed, perhaps the clash about free will is the most worrying clash of all. Science tells us, apparently, that the world runs on deterministic lines; but it is hard to know how to find 'elbow room' for human agency if determinism is true. Here again the scientific perspective and the personal perspective seem to clash irreconcilably. Just as they clash, as the last chapter showed, when we try to make sense of the notion of a person; and just as they clash, as this chapter has shown, when we try to make sense of the more basic idea that there *is* a personal perspective grounded in consciousness.

The aspects of the problem of the inescapable self that I've examined in this chapter have much in common with the aspects examined in previous chapters. In particular, this chapter has raised questions that seem to leave us in an almost insoluble philosophical dilemma: it has presented us with a choice between alternative views, where both the alternative views are, for one reason or another, almost impossibly unattractive. In chapter 7, I shall complete the story that this book tells, by saying what I think we ought to do about these intellectual dilemmas.

1 Chalmers 1996: 4–5.

2 Fodor 1992.

3 Prior 1976: 78–84.

4 Nagel 1979.

5 Nagel 1979: 172.

6 Jackson 1998: 291, where he summarizes his argument from Jackson 1982.

7 Jackson himself has now rejected the Knowledge Argument. Jackson 2003's position is that Mary's 'new knowledge' is only genuine new knowledge if its object (the redness) is real; and that object is only real if it is physical; so either what Mary 'learns' is not incompatible with physicalism, or else she doesn't learn anything. This argument looks question-begging to me, since it just *assumes* that being real means being physical. For a little more on the Knowledge Argument, see **6.4.2**.

8 Nagel 1979, McGinn 1999.

9 Scheffler 1967: 1.

10 Williams 1978: 64–5.

11 Wittgenstein, *Philosophical Investigations* I, 308.

12 Skinner 1971, Ryle 1949.

13 Watson 1913: 158.

14 Ryle 1949: 57.

15 e.g. Gertler 2003.

16 Geach 1957, Chisholm 1957.

17 Davidson 1980: 217.

18 Dennett 1991: 406. Epiphenomenalism is the view that mental events are a separate category of events, which are caused by physical events in the brain but have no effects upon any physical events; see Robinson 2003.

19 Dennett 1991: 410.

20 Descartes, *Discourse* 5, CSM I: 139–40.

21 Turing 1950.

22 Searle 1991: 510.

23 Wittgenstein, *Philosophical Investigations* I, 152, 154.

24 Searle 1991: 516.

25 Churchland 1991: 605.

26 Churchland 1979: 29–30.

27 Churchland 1991: 611.

28 Churchland 1991: 604.

29 Wittgenstein, *Philosophical Investigations* I, 19.

30 One exponent of simulation theory is Goldman 1992.

31 For this robust response, see Kitcher 1984.

32 Rorty 1979, ch. 2.

33 The qualification is necessary because some mental states, e.g. pain, look like they *can* be identified without reference to any particular external context. However, most mental states, e.g. seeing a tree or thinking 'That elephant is not a mastodon', evidently do require an external context.

34 Lewis 1990: 514–15, quoting Nemirow 1980: 475–6.

35 Ryle 1949, ch. 2.

36 At least, it does if scepticism is false. If scepticism is true, then quite possibly there is no Australia, and what gives my thoughts 'about Australia' their content is something else in my environment, e.g., perhaps, a mad scientist who is sticking a probe in my brain, or else something in my subconscious that makes me dream 'of Australia'. Even then, it will still be true that the mental is the environmental, even though I may be radically mistaken about what my environment is like.

37 Davidson 1980: 222.

38 Davidson 1980: 224–5.

39 Davidson 1980: 225.

40 Spinoza, *Ethics*, II.vii.

41 Russell 1956: 139.

42 Strawson 1959: 102–4.

43 e.g. Anscombe 1975.

44 Spinoza, *Ethics*, I.xxix.

45 Strawson 1982: 74.

7

Ethics as First Philosophy

7.1 **Intellectual dilemmas**

In this book we've seen a series of intellectual dilemmas:

1. Scepticism about the external world (chapters 1 and 2)
2. Scepticism about altruism (chapter 3)
3. Scepticism about objective moral reasons (chapter 4)
4. Scepticism about the existence of the self and the nature of personal identity (chapter 5)
5. Scepticism about the place of consciousness in a naturalistically understood world (**6.1** to **6.4**)
6. Scepticism about free will (**6.5**)

As I stressed at the beginning of this book (**0.2**), the interrelations between these problems are not the tight logical relations of identity or entailment. Nonetheless, the problems naturally go together psychologically, and have gone together historically. Moreover, each of these intellectual dilemmas has broadly the same structure. In each case, there is a tension between two conflicting philosophical positions which resists resolution. Each position seems well supported, maybe close to irresistible. And yet it looks incoherent, or at the very least highly paradoxical, to hold both of the conflicting positions.

My first two chapters showed how the problem of scepticism about the external world emerges from Descartes's writings, and resists not only his attempts to solve it but the attempts of everyone since as well. Because there is, apparently, no good way of refuting the basic sceptical argument (**2.2**), I find myself facing an intellectual dilemma. I find myself naturally impelled, on the basis of (to put it mildly) abundant evidence, to believe that there is a world outside my own head. Yet I also find that I can't rule out a wide variety of sceptical nightmare scenarios, such as the scenario that we are brains in a vat, or that we are all victims of a Cartesian deceiving demon. Since I can't rule out these possibilities, I can't know that external-world scepticism is false. Hence the intellectual dilemma.

As chapter 3 showed, the self can seem inescapable in ethics as much as in epistemology. It seems that you have to take the self to be the starting-point of ethics, just as the self has to be the starting-point of epistemology. (Where else could you start from, without begging the sceptical questions?) But if your starting-point is the motivations and the inclinations of the self, then it becomes deeply puzzling how anyone can be motivated by anything beyond his own self-interest. Ideally, I suggested in chapter 3, we should be able to know about the existence of individual values out there in the world – individual human beings prominent among these values, with other values including things like natural beauty, the goodness of friendship, pleasure, knowledge, and so forth. If we could know that all of this was 'out there', then it would provide an objective basis for our motivations, and for our justifications too, and so would provide a solid answer to the question of altruism. But how can I know there are objective goods 'out there', if, as the first two chapters suggested, I already have the epistemological problem, and don't even know that there *is* an 'out there'?

Besides that problem, there is also a special problem about the idea of objective goods in a naturalistic world. This problem motivates a third form of sceptical doubt. It's natural for us to believe that there are such goods, out there in the external world.

Indeed, it is possible to argue – perhaps Kant means to argue – that ethical objectivism is a presupposition for action, even in people who officially buy into subjectivism of some sort. Yet it is very hard to see how objective goods, or objective reasons, can be part of the world that value-neutral physical science describes. There are light-meters for registering qualities of light, thermometers for registering qualities of heat, pressure-gauges for registering qualities of pressure. Could there be an ethicometer, a device for measuring *moral* qualities? The natural reply is 'Of course not'. And yet we also have a natural belief in objectively existing moral qualities. The tension between these two natural beliefs makes for a third intellectual dilemma.

We face a fourth intellectual dilemma about personal identity. The dilemma here is partly about squaring the idea of a self in the sense of a subject of consciousness, with the idea of a person in the sense of a biological human animal living out a number of cultural and social roles. Ideally, I would like to be able to say that I am not only a point of view *on* the world, but also a human animal living *in* the world. Such a combination would solve the scientific/humane conflict, insofar as it arises regarding personal identity. But this view of myself is not easily available, given the problem of the inescapable self. Because we don't know that there is an external world, we don't even know that there are any human animals, nor how selves relate to them if there are.

There is also – to move on to our fifth intellectual dilemma – a problem about the place of consciousness in the natural world. As a result, we don't know how to make sense of the fact that there are selves at all. We have no clear understanding of how it can be that there are in the universe such things as minds. Consciousness, the existence of subjects or points of view, seems from the scientific perspective like an ontological extravagance. As Dennett and others have often pointed out, we could run the whole system *without* that epiphenomenon. And yet, as Chalmers and others have responded, there it is. Consciousness is scientifically intractable – yet subjectively undeniable. That sentence sums up the fifth intellectual dilemma.

Again, persons are not only points of view; they are also *agents*. The fact of agency is naturalistically mysterious too: how can it be that any such thing as agency shows up in the world of causes and effects? This isn't just a problem about free will. Never mind *free* agency; how come there is even *agency*? An agent can be defined as any conscious subject who acts *for the sake of a perceived good*. This definition raises one question about how motivations 'for the sake of a perceived good' can exist at all in a naturalistic world. And it raises another question about how this sort of motivation can be *free* – that is to say, how this kind of motivation can exist in its own right and unreduced to the usual cause–effect relations of the world. Everyone knows how strong our natural inclination is to think that we are agents who have free will. (In Dr Johnson's words: 'Sir, our will is free, and there's an end on't.') These puzzles about how there could possibly be either agency or free agency clash with our natural inclination to believe in these phenomena to create a sixth intellectual dilemma.

No doubt these six are not the only intellectual dilemmas we face. But they are obviously among the most important ones that we can encounter. In the earlier chapters of this book, I have shown how these intellectual dilemmas emerged in Western philosophy, and how a variety of philosophers have sought to respond to them. In this, the last chapter, I shall try to give the reader some idea of my own responses to them. Of course, anything that I say here about these intellectual dilemmas is bound to be brief and impressionistic; and of course, it would be ridiculously presumptuous for me to think that I could, definitively, *solve* them here. Nonetheless, I hope that what I say will be enough at least to give the reader some idea of how we might learn to live with these deep and complex problems.

7.2 **One response to intellectual dilemmas: the no-nonsense response**

One very simple response is what I shall call the no-nonsense response. This is the familiar down-to-earth, man-in-the-street reaction that Dr Johnson perhaps exemplifies: the response that says simply 'So much the worse for philosophy. If it leads you into scepticism, or into these intellectual dilemmas, then philosophy is silly. No ordinary person takes these questions seriously anyway.'

This dismissive response may be tempting when we get impatient with the sheer difficulty of doing philosophy, or discouraged by the task of tracing a way through its labyrinthine complexities. Nonetheless, it is an inadequate response. Right at the beginning (**0.3**) I commented that, in fact, 'ordinary people' quite often do take sceptical questions seriously. And even when they don't, we still have to ask whether they are right not to take sceptical questions seriously. As I've argued, the sceptical dilemmas I have discussed are not silly or trivial problems at all – even if some people think they are. On the contrary, they are the stuff of nightmare. They are a good deal more serious, more rationally troubling, than some non-philosophers (and some philosophers too) like to admit.

Typical sceptical arguments, like the basic sceptical argument of **2.2**, are genuinely worrying. It is implausible to think that these arguments involve some hidden logical blunder which everyone (or nearly everyone) has been missing all along. Consider what Sir Peter Strawson suggests:

> with many sceptical problems, their statement involves the pretended acceptance of a conceptual scheme and at the same time the silent repudiation of one of the conditions of its existence. That is why they are, in the terms in which they are stated, insoluble.[1]

Here Strawson is thinking particularly of scepticism about other minds. What blunder or self-contradiction is involved in this form of scepticism? According to Strawson, it is this: I can't talk about my own mind unless I have already learned to talk about other minds. Therefore, I can't be in a position to ask the sceptical question 'Are there any other minds beside my own?' until I am already in a position to answer 'Yes' to that question. This means that the sceptical question is misguided.

Maybe Strawson is right that I can't talk about my own mind unless I have already learned to talk about other minds. However, the fact that I can *talk* about other minds hardly proves that there *are* other minds. A Cartesian could agree with Strawson that he first learned the use of mental and psychological terms from his apparent encounters with other minds. He could still go on to ask: 'These apparent other minds: are they *real*?' This question involves no blunder.

One moral is that Strawson's attempt to refute scepticism about other minds fails in the same way as Grayling's (**2.3.4**). Another, more general, moral is that it is typically not possible to show that scepticism rests on some simple mistake that everyone has somehow failed to spot.

7.3 **Another response: Wittgenstein and quietism**

The no-nonsense response to our intellectual dilemmas is wrong; so is the sort of response that assumes that scepticism involves some foolish blunder that we have overlooked. Another possible response claims that our intellectual dilemmas are not so much to be solved as dissolved. Since they are based upon irrational uses of our rationality, we can escape them by seeing and abandoning the misuses of rationality that set them up. The main proponent of this view, which I shall call quietism, is Ludwig Wittgenstein. I shall argue that the quietist response does little better than the no-nonsense response.

In this book we have already seen one reason why Wittgenstein is such an important philosopher. This is because of his contributions to a number of central philosophical debates, especially those about scepticism and the nature of mind.[2] There is another reason for Wittgenstein's importance – a surprising one, when you compare it with the first reason. This is his rejection of the whole idea of philosophical debate:

> the clarity that we are aiming at is indeed *complete* clarity. But this simply means that the philosophical problems should *completely* disappear.
>
> The real discovery is the one that makes me capable of stopping doing philosophy when I want to. – The one that gives philosophy peace, so that it is no longer tormented by questions which bring *itself* in question. – Instead, we now demonstrate a method, by examples; and the series of examples can be broken off.[3]

Some hints about the shape of Wittgenstein's argument here are already visible from my discussion of semantic contextualism in **2.6.1**. As I said there, Wittgenstein thinks that all meaning arises in the context of some particular 'language game' – some particular sort of human linguistic institution. But crazy sceptical doubts lack the context of a language game. Therefore, they don't make sense. To quote a passage of Marx that Wittgenstein would surely have approved of: 'All mysteries which lead theory to mysticism find their rational solution in human practice and in the comprehension of this practice.'[4]

As I pointed out in **2.6.1**, the trouble with this argument is that sceptical questions like 'Am I dreaming?' certainly *seem* to make sense. If in fact they don't make sense, it is a puzzling question why they seem to. If, on the other hand, these questions do make sense, either Wittgenstein is wrong that nothing can make sense outside the context of a language game; or else he is wrong to think that sceptical questions can't themselves form a language game.

Why, anyway, did Wittgenstein think that we can only make sense within a language game? The answer brings us on to his quietism: his insistence that 'every sentence in our language "is in order as it is"'.[5] 'What we do', he tells us in the royal plural, 'is to bring words back from their metaphysical to their everyday use', which 'philosophy may in no way interfere with', but may, 'in the end, only describe'.[6] Philosophy goes wrong, Wittgenstein thinks, because it *perverts* the ordinary uses of words: our 'forms of expression prevent us in all sorts of ways from seeing that nothing out of the ordinary is involved, by sending us in pursuit of chimeras'.[7] Philosophy is an irrational use of our rationality because our rationality is not *designed* for dealing with metaphysical problems, but only with everyday ones.

On the view of philosophy that (for instance) Plato, Aristotle, Aquinas, Descartes, Leibniz, Spinoza, Locke, Hegel, Mill and Russell accepted, there is a substantive body of deep and important philosophical truths, systematically connected up with each other into the shape of a single theory, and awaiting our discovery as the 'truth about reality'. Wittgenstein absolutely rejects this conception of philosophy. As he sees it, there is no such body of truths for us to discover, apart from commonplaces about the way our language works: 'If one tried to advance *theses* in philosophy, it would never be possible to debate them, because everyone would agree to them.'[8] For Wittgenstein rather as for T. S. Eliot, all there is for us to discover is where we already are: 'the end of all our exploring/ Will be to arrive where we started/ And know the place for the first time'.[9]

There is no hidden metaphysics awaiting revelation. Rather, 'nothing is hidden', or even if it is, 'what is hidden…is of no interest to us'.[10] The real source of the motley ragbag of linguistic illusions that we call 'philosophical problems' is simply the perverse and deceptive ways in which we arrange the perfectly common-place materials in front of us. In his *Remarks on the Foundations of Mathematics*,[11] Wittgenstein compares the game of thumb-catching, in which a person puts his left hand around his right thumb, and then tries to catch hold of his left thumb with his right hand. If someone expressed amazement that he had never succeeded in *winning* at thumb-catching, this would be a comical misunder-standing. Rather like Peter Strawson (**7.2**), Wittgenstein thinks that it is no better to complain that no one has ever succeeded in answering the sceptic. That complaint, according to him, involves misunderstandings that are as unfounded as the thumb-catcher's – misunderstandings that arise when 'language goes on holiday'.[12]

> Our investigation is therefore a grammatical one. Such an investigation sheds light on our problem by clearing misun-derstandings away. Misunderstandings concerning the use of words, caused, among other things, by certain [misleading] analogies between the forms of expression in different regions of language…[13]

This is why Wittgenstein says that 'the work of the philosopher consists in assembling reminders for a particular purpose'.[14] The reminders he means are reminders of what the structure of our language games already is, and of how that structure can create confusion when we mix up one language game with another. As, for example, when G. E. Moore tries to refute the sceptic simply by pointing to his own hand and saying 'This is here':[15]

> If…someone says that the sentence 'This is here' (saying which he points to an object in front of him) makes sense to him then he should ask himself in what special circumstances this sentence is actually used. There it does make sense.[16]

The philosopher is not an explorer or discoverer of dazzling new intellectual worlds, like those discovered by the mathematician or the physicist. Rather, the philosopher is a *therapist*, uncovering and dismantling the simple but crucial confusions that prevent us from getting free from the philosophical problems that 'torment' us. ('Torment', incidentally, is a word that Wittgenstein uses more than once to describe the experience of doing philosophy. The verb strikes me as a revealing one, for reasons we'll see in a minute.)

There is not a philosophical method, though there are indeed methods, like different therapies.

The philosopher treats a question; like an illness.

What is your aim in philosophy? – To show the fly the way out of the fly-bottle.[17]

Something like the same idea – that the point of doing philosophy is to become able to *stop* doing it – is found in David Hume:

The only method of freeing learning, at once, from these abstruse questions, is to enquire seriously into the nature of human understanding, and show, from an exact analysis of its powers and capacity, that it is by no means fitted for such remote and abstruse subjects. We must submit to this fatigue, in order to live at ease ever after.[18]

When Wittgenstein first began to expound his therapeutic conception of philosophy in lectures in Cambridge in the 1930s, his approach attracted whole schools of enthusiastic disciples. It still does today. Here, for example, is Stanley Cavell, trying to put his finger on the source of the neurosis – as Wittgensteinians call it – that leads us to ask sceptical questions of the sort I raised in chapters 1 and 2. 'Whence', Cavell asks,

> comes this sense of something amiss about the simplest claim to knowledge under optimal conditions, where there is no practical problem moving us? The answer I have has already been suggested: the philosopher *begins* his investigation with the *sense* that, as I am expressing it, something is, or may be amiss with knowledge as a whole.[19]

And where would this wider sense of amissness arise from? Cavell tells the story of an occasion when he himself felt that sense:

> I was left a telephone message which consisted of the name of an old friend, the name of the hotel he was stopping at, a telephone number, and the request to ring him at a certain hour…The telephone number was *obviously* the number of his hotel (it was written just under the name of the hotel)…so I rang the number without further thought. 'Good morning' came a secretary's morning voice at the other end; and it continued with what I took to be the initials of some kind of firm…I apologised for having dialled the wrong number [and] hung up…Only [after some time] did it occur to me – with a thrill of 'astonishment' – that the number on my slip [might] not be (= not have been meant as?) the number of the hotel. So I called the number again, and…in five seconds my friend's familiar voice was in my ear.[20]

Cavell's comment on his story is this:

The experience does, I find, resemble the experience and the conclusion of traditional epistemology. There is an initial threatening sense or fact of something amiss, something which *must* be accounted for; the *going over* of a situation to see where an unnoticed inference or assumption may have been made; the sense that something in this one instance contains a moral about knowledge as a whole.[21]

Why have people pursued the programme of 'traditional episte-mology' – that is, the programme of trying to answer sceptical questions like 'How do we know we're not just brains in vats?' Cavell roots the motivation of such questions in particular kinds of everyday experience of deception. As, of course, does Descartes himself: 'From time to time I have found that the senses deceive.'[22] The difference is that Descartes concentrates on the *reasoning* that such experiences prompt; whereas Cavell concentrates on the *trauma* that they involve.

Indeed, if we are going to call Wittgenstein's conception of philosophy a *therapeutic* one, we might as well call Cavell's conception a *psychiatric* one. Apparently Cavell does not see the asking of sceptical questions mainly as an exercise of rationality – not even as an irrational exercise of rationality. Rather, he sees the asking of such questions as a symptom of a mental or emotional disorder. The sceptical mood, for Cavell, is just that – a mood.

True, Cavell goes on to suggest that something beyond the mild trauma of his experience with the phone number is needed to get us into a *fully* sceptical mood. For all that, a mood prompted by an experience is still what we are talking about:

For [radical or metaphysical scepticism], an experience of a different order is needed, an experience that philosophers have characterised, more or less, as being one of realising that our experiences may not be *of* the world I take them to be of at all, or that I can only know how objects appear (to us) to be, never how they are in themselves. I can here only attest to my having had such experiences and, though struggling against them intellectually, have had to wait for them to dissipate in their own time.[23]

Here again the talk is not of sceptical arguments, but of a sceptical mood or experience, to which the best response is the kind you might give to a headache: 'Wait for it to dissipate in its own time.'

Why do we take sceptical arguments seriously? The simplest and most obvious explanation is 'Because they look like *good* arguments.' Cavell and Wittgenstein reject this simple explanation in favour of a psychiatric diagnosis. So, only a little more circumspectly, does John McDowell:

If I am right about the character of the philosophical anxieties I am to deal with…engaging in 'constructive philosophy' is not the way to approach them…we need to exorcise the problems rather than set about answering them.[24]

In all three of these philosophers – and plenty of others too – the idea is that the asking of sceptical or metaphysical questions involves some kind of confusion on our part, or betrays some sort of trauma that we have suffered. In a word, their idea is that the urge to do philosophy involves something *pathological*.

At least in the way that Wittgenstein develops it, this striking idea is largely original to Wittgenstein. However, another form of the idea that there is something pathological about philosophers is developed by Nietzsche. In his famous discussion of 'The Problem of Socrates' in the second section of his *Twilight of the Idols*, Nietzsche describes philosophical questioning as a symptom of an unhealthy or decaying culture. A strong, proud, aristocratic and self-confident society like Periclean Athens will simply not allow itself to be poisoned by doubts. When someone like Socrates (or Descartes) comes along and succeeds in making his society take his doubts seriously, instead of just laughing at them or treating them with contempt, this is a victory for the rabble (*Pöbel*): it is a corruption and degradation of that society. For Nietzsche, philosophers are pathological specimens because they are cultural degenerates.

Is it right to think that philosophy is pathological, whether for Nietzsche's or for Wittgenstein's reasons?

Here we can point out that most philosophers have been, in all other respects aside from their philosophizing, anything but sick in the head. The abundant mental energy, creativity, liveliness and keenness of mind that we see in the lives of philosophers such as Socrates, or Aristotle, or Aquinas, or Locke, or Hobbes, or Hume, or Kant, or Hegel, or Mill, or indeed Descartes himself, is hardly the sort of evidence that would support a medical diagnosis of mental illness.

On the other hand, there are of course exceptions – philosophers who seem to have had at least some of the symptoms of mental illness. Nietzsche is one, and Wittgenstein, it seems to me, is another. Dare we suggest, then, that there is something telling about the fact that the two keenest advocates of the idea that philosophy is pathological were themselves emotionally and mentally disturbed to some degree?[25]

Nietzsche's unfortunate ending in hopeless insanity is well known, and I shall say nothing about it here.[26] The pathological features of Wittgenstein's psychology are less extreme, and certainly don't add up to anything as severe as insanity. But they are there all right, as a little biography – following the work of Ray Monk – will quickly show.

I've already commented on the depth of personal devotion that Wittgenstein commanded from others. Almost everyone who met Wittgenstein was in awe of him ever after: his personality –

tortured and confused though it was in some ways – seems to have combined dazzling intellectual brilliance and austere moral rectitude in a quite exceptional way. One of his most devout pupils (or followers) was Francis Skinner, who in 1930 'was recognised as one of the most promising mathematicians of his year' at Cambridge University.[27] Wittgenstein returned Skinner's devotion and in some sense, possibly though not certainly a sexual one, they became lovers. However, the distribution of power in their relationship was anything but balanced:

> In his devotion to Wittgenstein (which he maintained for the rest of his tragically short life), Skinner surrendered his own will almost entirely. Everything else took second place…[When his sister and mother] came to Trinity to meet Francis, they would be met by him rushing down the stairs and hushing them with 'I'm busy. I've got Dr Wittgenstein here. We're working. Come back later.'[28]

Skinner completed his undergraduate degree in mathematics with first-class honours. His college, Trinity, then awarded him a three-year graduate scholarship to do further mathematical work. In fact, Skinner spent this time (and money) not on his own mathematics, but on assisting Wittgenstein's philosophical work. Moreover, at the end of his graduate scholarship, Skinner 'abandoned academic life altogether for a job that Wittgenstein considered more suitable for him':[29]

> Wittgenstein discouraged Francis from going on with academic work. 'He would never be happy in academic life', he decided, and Francis, as always, accepted his decision.[30]

So what else should Skinner do? His health was poor, as were his parents, which ruled out medicine, Wittgenstein's first preference for Skinner. 'Wittgenstein's (and therefore Skinner's) second choice of career after medicine was that of a mechanic':[31]

> And so in the summer of 1936 Francis was taken on as a two-year apprentice mechanic at the Cambridge Instrument Company. For most of the time he was employed in making mainscrews, a repetitive and tiring task that he neither enjoyed nor found at all interesting; it was simply a drudge which he put up with for Wittgenstein's sake…What he wanted more than anything else was to live and work together with Wittgenstein, and this he had been denied by Wittgenstein himself.

Skinner's time at the factory was, pretty plainly, a miserable period of his life.[32] As for Wittgenstein, soon after he had talked Skinner into taking a boring and menial job out of devotion to him, he abruptly left for Norway – partly, it appears, because he and Skinner had quarrelled. Skinner was to see a good deal less of Wittgenstein thereafter, and their relations seem to have become much less intimate. One reason for this estrangement was possibly that, while Skinner was still working at the factory, Wittgenstein had become close to another young man, Keith Kirk, whom Skinner had introduced to him. Wittgenstein never entirely abandoned Skinner in favour of Kirk; yet the evidence of Wittgenstein's diary is that Kirk came to occupy a place in Wittgenstein's affections somewhat similar to that previously held by Skinner.[33]

But Skinner had already chosen Wittgenstein over his family. His loyal acceptance of Wittgenstein's career advice had seriously alienated his parents, who had had much higher hopes for him. Skinner was thus left very isolated. He also found, at the end of his time in the Cambridge Instruments Factory in late 1939, that he no longer had much capacity left for serious mathematical research. At the time of his death from polio a year or two later, in 1941, Skinner seems to have been a broken man.

Given Wittgenstein's behaviour, it is hard to resist asking who broke him: a question which Wittgenstein himself was tortured by for the rest of his life. But I am not telling this sorry tale to raise the question of blame. Rather, I am telling it to bring out a parallel between Wittgenstein's personal life – specifically, his dealings with Skinner – and his philosophy.

In philosophy Wittgenstein tells us, above all, not to presume on our language's resources. Language, he thinks, is not a single universal tool, even though it often looks like one (remember the analogies that Wittgenstein calls 'misleading'). Instead, language is a ragbag of different tools, each of which can only be used for the specific purpose it was made for. To use the tools of language outside the contexts that they belong in is to misuse those tools, and hence to say *nothing* (or at least, far less than you think you are saying). Therefore, says Wittgenstein, the philosopher should give up his pretentious and misguided attempts to find novel uses for the tools of language. He should remember, in sober humility, the original and proper use of each of those tools, however banal and mundane it may seem to his overblown imagination. In short, he should re-immerse himself in the commonplace, and give up trying or pretending to say anything special.

Compare Wittgenstein's advice to Skinner – and to other young men he knew, such as Maurice Drury and Norman Malcolm. The advice was that he should immerse himself in the commonplace detail of a menial job. He should turn aside from the philosopher's overambitious attempt to find analytical tools that make sense of everything, and attend instead – not metaphorically but literally – to just one particular set of tools.

It is worth quoting Marx again: Wittgenstein's view of philosophy says, in effect, that the rational solution to 'all mysteries which lead to mysticism' is found 'in human practice and in the comprehension of this practice'.[4] At the personal and practical level, this view cashed out as Wittgenstein's choosing for Skinner the particular, and desperately unambitious, human practice of making screws, rather than allowing him to indulge his ambition to delve further into the mysteries of mathematics and philosophy.

I believe that Wittgenstein's attitude to the resources of language is as much a waste of those resources as his career choice for Skinner was a waste of Skinner. Francis Skinner, remember, could almost certainly have had a brilliant career as a professional mathematician or philosopher. His family knew this, and were outraged that he was denied the chance by Wittgenstein's interventions. A misguided asceticism on Wittgenstein's part, a false intellectual humility, and a naïve acceptance of a William Morris view of the dignity of manual or menial labour had disastrous consequences for Skinner's life. Arguably they had a detrimental effect on Wittgenstein's own life also, since he himself abandoned philosophy at one point and spent several years as a primary-school teacher in his native Austria. This job he did very conscientiously and very badly.[34] He does not seem to have enjoyed it much either, since he admitted that, at close quarters, he found the working classes 'odious', 'base' and barely human.[35]

Wittgenstein's career advice might have been equally calamitous for others too, had they followed it (as Norman Malcolm did not), or had they not been lucky enough to be pushed by Wittgenstein into a job that turned out to suit them well (as happened to Maurice Drury, whom Wittgenstein talked into a medical career). By refusing to allow that Skinner's academic abilities might give his life a kind of worthwhileness that a manual worker in a screw factory could never attain, Wittgenstein – for all his earnest idealism and good intentions – harmed Skinner profoundly. If we allow Wittgenstein to convince us that the expressive resources of our language are completely determined and completely exhausted by the language games in which they originate, there is a danger that he will be just as bad for us philosophically as he was for Skinner personally.

The error at the root of Wittgenstein's loathing of academic life, and his uncritical idealization of manual labour, is perhaps too distant, too obscure, and too psychologically multiform to be cleanly extracted. The error at the root of his philosophical quietism is easier to identify. It is the genetic fallacy – the mistake of thinking that where something comes from is what it is – applied to language and its uses. That this is a mistaken view of language is obvious: the possible uses of any given piece of language are indefinitely flexible, and constantly revisable. Linguistic possibility is not exhausted by linguistic origin, any more than the talents and abilities that a young mathematician may have developed at thirty-two are exhausted by a list of the mathematical talents and abilities that he had when he was sixteen. Since linguistic possibilities are not restricted in this way, one of the later Wittgenstein's most basic ideas – that no linguistic usage can make sense outside the language game in which it originated – is just plain wrong. And with the exposure of that mistake goes the justification for Wittgenstein's quietism – his refusal to pursue philosophical, metaphysical and sceptical questions of the sort that philosophers had pursued from Socrates to Bertrand Russell.

Russell, incidentally, was one of the earliest and the most acerbic critics of Wittgenstein's quietist turn:

The earlier Wittgenstein, whom I knew intimately, was a man addicted to passionately intense thinking, profoundly aware of difficult problems of which I, like him, felt the importance, and possessed (or so I thought) of true philosophical genius. The later Wittgenstein, on the contrary, seems to have grown tired of serious thinking and to have invented a doctrine which would make such an activity unnecessary.[36]

7.4 **Hume: naturalist or sceptic?**

Another important response to intellectual dilemmas is offered by David Hume. In academic philosophy there has been much debate about whether Hume's basic outlook in philosophy is scepticism or 'naturalism', a word which I'll use in this context (and this context alone: contrast **2.6.4**, **4.3** and **6.2**) to mean something like an early form of 'naturalized epistemology' (**2.6.4**) – an early form of the view that all philosophers can do is map how we do in fact acquire beliefs, without worrying too much about what beliefs we ought to acquire. As a result, Hume scholars have been rather too eager to draw up battle lines over the following choice: is Hume's most basic message the normative claim that we can have no rational justification for our anti-sceptical beliefs; or is his, rather, a descriptive philosophical project, the project of describing how, as natural animals living in a natural world, we do in fact – by way of custom, habit and nature – come to have the beliefs we do?

If this is the right question to ask about Hume, then surely the answer to it is 'Both'. As I said in **2.6.4**, naturalized epistemology is perfectly consistent with scepticism. That is one of the reasons why naturalized epistemology is so unsatisfactory when it is presented as an answer to the sceptic. The idea that Hume must be *either* a sceptic *or* a naturalized epistemologist seems similarly questionable, since it can quickly be shown that he is a sceptic *and* a naturalist.

Hume's scepticism is obvious when he writes as follows:

This sceptical doubt, both with respect to reason and the senses, is a malady, which can never be radically cur'd, but must return upon us every moment, however we may chace it away, and sometimes may seem entirely free from it. 'Tis impossible upon any system to defend either our under-standing or senses; and we but expose them farther when we endeavour to justify them in that manner. As the sceptical doubt arises naturally from a profound and intense reflection on those subjects, it always encreases, the farther we carry our reflections, whether in opposition or conformity to it.[37]

And Hume's naturalism is obvious in the very next sentence:

Carelessness and in-attention alone can afford us any remedy. For this reason I rely entirely upon them; and take it for granted, whatever may be the reader's opinion at this present moment, that an hour hence he will be persuaded there is both an external and internal world.

Hume does not *choose* between the sceptical view that we can have no guarantee of the reality of anything outside our own heads, and the naturalist view that it is only 'nature' and 'custom' that make us believe in an external reality. He takes both views, using the scepticism to support the naturalism, and the naturalism to support the scepticism. Philosophical reason, he blandly tells us, is quite unable to dispel the 'clouds' of sceptical worry. But it doesn't need to, because

nature herself suffices to that purpose, and cures me of this philosophical melancholy and delirium, either by relaxing this bent of mind, or by some avocation, and lively impression of my senses, which obliterate all these chimeras. I dine, I play a game of backgammon, I converse, and am merry with my friends; and when after three or four hours' amusement, I wou'd return to these speculations, they appear so cold, and strain'd, and ridiculous, that I cannot find in my heart to enter into them any farther.[38]

Ever since ancient times, critics of scepticism have asked whether sceptical views about (say) the existence of an external world are consistent with a normal life in which we withdraw money from banks, or embrace other people, or – to take Hume's examples – dine, socialize or play backgammon. Hume would answer that there is no conflict here, because, in practice, the sceptic cannot help ignoring his scepticism:

> the sceptic still continues to reason and believe, even tho' he asserts, that he cannot defend his reason by reason...Nature has not left this to his choice, and has doubtless, esteem'd it an affair of too great importance to be trusted to our uncertain reasonings and speculations. We may well ask, *What causes induce us to believe in the existence of body?* but 'tis in vain to ask, *Whether there be body or not?* That is a point, which we must take for granted in all our reasonings.[39]

Scepticism, says Hume, is true; but in practice we can't help disbelieving it. The real truth is something that our human natures simply cannot take on board. Scepticism is true; yet the whole way we live – and we can't help living this way – is premissed on the falsehood of scepticism. So for Hume the solution to our intellectual dilemmas is that there is *no* rational solution. But fortunately, this doesn't matter, because, as Hume famously puts it, 'reason alone can never be a motive to any action of the will'.[40] Since human reason is causally inert, it will make no difference to our behaviour and practice even if we do work out that philosophical scepticism is true as a matter of theory.

In one way, I disagree profoundly with Hume's conclusion here; in another way, I think it is closer to the truth about how we ought to deal with our intellectual dilemmas than any of the other alternatives that I have canvassed so far. It is time for me to explain what I mean by saying this, and to reveal – at last – my own responses to the intellectual dilemmas that I have described in this book. I shall begin to do that in **7.5**.

7.5 **Four ways of doing ethics – and four ways of doing epistemology**

As I've pointed out before, epistemology can be normative or descriptive. In descriptive epistemology we look for a description of how we in fact acquire beliefs; in normative epistemology we look for standards or norms governing how we ought to acquire beliefs. It is important not to confuse these activities – as happens in naturalized epistemology (**2.6.4**). Descriptive and normative epistemology are both philosophically worthwhile in their different ways. However, descriptive epistemology on its own is liable to degenerate into an uncritical record of psychological events. Philosophically speaking, normative epistemology is where the real action and the real excitement is.

Now the available positions in normative epistemology closely mirror those available in normative ethics. Our attention has usefully been drawn to this point in the writings of a number of recent philosophers.[41] However, the point itself is anything but new: an explicit parallel between ethical and epistemic virtues is already set up by Aristotle in the *Nicomachean Ethics*.[42]

On the ethics side of the parallel, wc have – as Rosalind Hursthouse describes them – these three positions:[43]

Consequentialism: an action is right if and only if it brings about the best consequences.

Deontology: an action is right if and only if it is done in accordance with the moral rules.

Virtue ethics: an action is right if and only if it is what a virtuous agent would characteristically do in the circumstances.

Obviously all three positions need some further filling out. How does consequentialism measure the goodness of consequences?

(Pleasure is one measure, welfare a second, the satisfaction of preferences a third.) What are the moral rules to which deontology appeals? (They might, for instance, be about intentions, or be drawn from a list of duties known by revelation or moral perception – or both.) And just what is a 'virtuous agent'? (Aristotle has one list of virtues, Confucius another, Nietzsche a third; the virtues that Jesus lists in the Sermon on the Mount are different again.)

Still, despite the schematic nature of the contrast I've just drawn, the point of each of these positions should be clear enough. Consequentialism tells us to do *whatever* brings about the best consequences. Deontology directly contradicts this, by telling us not to do anything that breaks the moral rules, *even if* doing that brings about the best consequences. And virtue ethics aims to transcend the opposition of consequentialism and deontology, by switching the focus of analysis from *actions* to *agents*. The idea in virtue ethics is that the definitions offered by consequentialism and deontology are at best misleading, because they draw our attention to actions when it is agents that have the analytical priority. Often virtue ethicists will go further, and say that those definitions are not just misleading but actually false. Sometimes there is right action which is neither in accordance with the moral rules nor productive of the best consequences. And this, it is claimed, is a fact that only virtue ethics can reflect.

So much for ethics. How does the epistemological side of the parallel shape up? It takes as central the notion of a belief-acquiring mechanism, a possible way of coming to have beliefs: an *epistemic route*, as I shall call it. We can say that epistemic routes are to normative epistemology as action types are to normative ethics. And then the analogy looks like this:

Epistemic consequentialism: an epistemic route is to be followed if and only if it brings about true belief (or knowledge).

Epistemic deontology: an epistemic route is to be followed if and only if it can be followed without breaking the epistemic rules.

Virtue epistemology: an epistemic route is to be followed if and only if it is the route (or a route) that an intellectually virtuous agent would characteristically follow in the circumstances.

Once again, all three of these statements are obviously no more than frameworks to be filled in. The epistemic consequentialist needs to choose between the alternatives true belief and knowledge. (Some epistemic routes, such as guessing, might sometimes work as ways to true belief, but true beliefs obtained by guesswork are surely not knowledge; so the epistemic consequentialist had better decide whether he cares about knowledge too, or only about true belief.) The epistemic deontologist needs to tell us what the epistemic rules are to which he appeals. (There might, for instance, be rules against using guesswork, or astrology, or other disreputable epistemic routes, even when these routes work: contrast my discussion of reliablism in **2.5.4**.)

As for the appeal to virtue: just as in the ethical case, we need to know (1) what does an 'epistemically virtuous agent' look like? And (2) what are the epistemic virtues? A typical answer to (1) is John Greco's:[44] an epistemically virtuous agent is one who has stable, effective, and causally explicable dispositions to acquire knowledge. A typical answer to (2) is James Montmarquet's:[45] the epistemic virtues at least include 'virtues of impartiality' such as openness to others' insights and readiness to admit one's own fallibility, 'virtues of intellectual sobriety' such as caution and an unwillingness to jump to conclusions, and 'virtues of intellectual courage' such as persistence in inquiry and willingness to question taboos.

All very interesting. But I haven't put up these alternatives in epistemology because I want to take any of them. I have displayed them because I want to point to a fourth alternative in epistemology, which runs parallel to a fourth alternative that, in other writings, I have already taken in ethics.[46]

This fourth alternative in ethics is the replacement of *virtue* theory by *value* theory. To take this alternative is to argue that, while normative ethics certainly is about virtues, it's not centrally about virtues. The analytical heart of normative ethics cannot be a list of virtues, as the virtue ethicist thinks. For our virtues express our *response* to value, and so presuppose value itself as something else that we must also analyse, if we want to analyse ethics by way of the virtues.

Nor, for the same reason, can any list of rules be the analytical heart of normative ethics, as the deontologist thinks. Our rules too express our *response* to value, and so presuppose value itself as something else that we must also analyse, if we want to analyse ethics by way of a list of rules.

So the utilitarians and consequentialists are right to make the theory of value central to ethics. They are right to think that the analytical heart of normative ethics is a list of values or goods, 'out there in the world', of just the sort that is wide open to ethical scepticism (**4.1**).

However, writers in the utilitarian or consequentialist tradition have misunderstood the nature of our response to the various goods on the list. Almost without exception, they have assumed that the only rational response to value is to *promote* or *maximize* it. This response might make sense if we found ourselves confronted by a single measurable value. But, of course, we don't. The values we encounter in the world (or seem to encounter) are irreducibly and incomparably various; and they are, with a few unimportant exceptions, not measurable at all. Thus, although *some* of the relations between the values we encounter are determinate, there is no way of finding a 'common currency' between them all, of the sort that might ground a complete story about how to trade off any one of them against any of the others, and so might provide a meaning for the consequentialists' injunction to promote or maximize the good. In the absence of that common currency, the idea of maximizing the good doesn't even make sense.

If we can't maximize value, how should we respond to it (or rather, to them − values, plural)? If maximization is impossible, you might think that the only alternative is anarchy: any response to the goods is as practically rational as any other. But this is not so. Even in the absence of maximizing practical rationality, there is still a real distinction to be made between the practically rational and the practically irrational. For one thing, since each good is a *good*, it will always be practically irrational to treat *nothing* as a good: practical rationality at least requires some response to some good. For another, since the value of each good cannot be expressed in a common currency which compares the value of every good with every other, it will always be practically irrational to destroy any one good in the interests of any other good: practical rationality always requires at least *some* response to *every* good.

The upshot is that we can give a general formula which captures, at least schematically, what is involved in a practically rational response to an irreducible variety of incomparable goods. This general formula is what I have elsewhere called the 'Threefold Schema'.[47] This says that each of the different goods exacts from us, as required by practical rationality, a minimum level of response. Above that minimum level, *it's up to us* how we respond to the variety of goods. As a matter of how we structure the stories of our own lives, we may choose to highlight or foreground one good, and do relatively little about some other good. Wherever the demands of the various goods confronting us are not so stringent as to leave us with only one morally acceptable option, we have freedom to choose which goods we will pursue, provided we always give each of the goods we recognize at least the minimum level of response (as it might be called, the *honouring* or *respecting* level of response), and do not allow ourselves to go below that level relative to any of the goods in question (by *violating* it). In short, what practical rationality tells us to do, confronted by a variety of different goods, is this: pursue any good or goods, provided you respect every good and violate none.

So this is a fourth way in normative ethics, which I recommend to the reader as an alternative to all three of the other options more standardly found on the menu (consequentialism, deontology and virtue ethics). If we pursue the ethical–epistemic parallel that I have set up, we ought to find that there is a fourth way in normative epistemology too, the structure of which is analogous to the structure of my fourth way in ethics. What is this fourth epistemic way?

To set up the analogy, I need to begin with another equivalence. I said above that epistemic routes are to normative epistemology as action types are to normative ethics. I now need to add that evidence is to normative epistemology as values are to normative ethics.

With that equivalence in place, we may begin with the point that, while normative epistemology certainly is about epistemic virtues, it's not *centrally* about epistemic virtues. The analytical heart of normative epistemology cannot be a list of epistemic virtues. For our epistemic virtues express our *response* to the evidence that confronts us, and so presuppose evidence itself as something else that we must also analyse, if we want to understand epistemology by way of the epistemic virtues.

Nor, for the same reason, can any list of rules be the analytical heart of normative epistemology, as the epistemic deontologist thinks. Our epistemic rules too express our *response* to the evidence that confronts us, and so presuppose evidence itself as something else that we must also analyse, if we want to understand epistemology by way of the epistemic virtues.

So the epistemic consequentialists are right to make the notion of evidence central to epistemology. That is, they are right to think that the analytical heart of normative epistemology is a list of the kinds of evidence, and of the relative value of those kinds of evidence.

However, if intellectual dilemmas are genuinely possible, then epistemic consequentialism misunderstands how we should respond to the various sorts of evidence that can confront us. For epistemic consequentialists assume – and in epistemology as in ethics, they are not the only epistemologists who assume this – that the only rational response to the evidence is a maximizing one. This is to adopt whatever belief the evidence makes most rational.[48]

This maximizing response to the evidence makes sense wherever we find ourselves confronted by a single kind of evidence, or by a variety of different kinds of evidence whose relative weight and importance is easily comparable. For in that sort of case, the definite description 'the most rational belief given the evidence' will fit some one thing; it will have something to refer to. But if there are genuine intellectual dilemmas, then there can be cases where no such comparability is available, and hence where there is no such thing as '*the* most rational belief given the evidence'.

Perhaps, for example, we face a genuine intellectual dilemma about consciousness. Maybe the problem about consciousness is precisely that, when we try to decide what we think about it, we face a choice between two incomparable sorts of evidence: the evidence of introspection, which makes the existence of consciousness utterly non-negotiable; and the evidence of science, which suggests that we can do everything we need to do from a naturalistic perspective without ever invoking consciousness. If this is a real intellectual dilemma; and if the source of the dilemma is the incomparability of the two sorts of evidence that the two sides of the dilemma appeal to; then that will show that there are genuine cases where the maximizing response to the evidence in front of us is an impossibility. And so it will show that epistemic consequentialism's injunction to adopt the most rational belief, given the evidence, cannot be applied in every case.

Cue the fourth alternative for normative epistemology. This will say that the kinds of evidence that we encounter are indeed irreducibly and incomparably various – as the occurrence of genuine intellectual dilemmas shows. Hence the idea of a maximizing response to the evidence doesn't always make sense. But that doesn't mean that the only other alternative facing us in intellectual dilemmas is an epistemic anarchy in which any belief is as epistemically rational as any other. Even in the absence of a single 'most rational belief to adopt given the evidence', there is still a distinction to be made between the epistemically rational and irrational. The basis of this distinction will be a distinction, objectively, between the *true* and the *plausible*, and subjectively, between the *to-be-believed* and the *permissibly believed*. (The parallel distinctions in ethics are the distinctions, objectively, between the right and the good, and subjectively, between the to-be-done and the permissible.)

In intellectual dilemmas, then, we will find that more than one conflicting belief is plausible; and that will give us grounds for thinking that there is more than one of these conflicting beliefs such that we have epistemic permission to hold it. We will not fail in our epistemic obligations in an intellectual dilemma if we at least recognize that all the beliefs involved are at least plausible. (This is the analogue of respecting all of a variety of goods in the ethical case.) And we will be epistemically permitted, in an intellectual dilemma, to make a free choice between the different alternatives on offer. (This is the analogue of pursuing any good you like in the ethical case.) And now my analogy between ethics and epistemology is fully spelled out, so that we have a full picture of what it would mean to take the fourth alternative in epistemology, in parallel with the fourth alternative in ethics.

7.6 Two simple questions

At this point, however, we need to stop and ask two simple questions about the proposal offered in **7.5**. First question: who says there are any insoluble intellectual dilemmas? Second question: am I really, seriously, advocating the suggestion that when faced with an intellectual dilemma, we can believe either one side or the other of that dilemma (or, presumably, neither side) – just as we like?

These questions begin to show the *dis*analogies between the ethical and epistemic cases. So with the first question: it is – or so I have argued elsewhere[49] – beyond doubt that there is an irreducible plurality of different kinds of *value*. But it is not, I suspect, beyond doubt that there is an irreducible plurality of different kinds of *evidence*. Maybe we only think that there are different kinds of evidence involved in, say, the apparent conflict between naturalistic science and the personal perspective, because we don't yet fully understand the nature of that conflict, or of the kinds of evidence involved. And maybe, once we do understand properly what is going on in that apparent conflict, we will see that there isn't really an intellectual dilemma there at all. Notwithstanding the case for the existence of genuine intellectual dilemmas that I've developed in this book, the evidence that there are real and insoluble conflicts between different sorts of incomparable evidence remains much thinner than the evidence for the existence of genuine practical dilemmas – real conflicts between two different sorts of incomparable value. In the epistemic case, it's much more likely than in the ethical case that further research may yet show that all the apparent dilemmas are actually unreal. Furthermore, intellectual dilemmas are rarer than moral ones: the maximizing strategy of believing 'the most epistemically rational belief given the evidence that confronts me' looks like succeeding in a much wider variety of cases than the corresponding strategy of performing 'the most practically rational action, given the values that confront me'.[50] Incomparable values are all over the place; incomparable forms of evidence are not.

In the light of this, no doubt a little caution is in order. In this book I have looked at six different areas where there might be genuine intellectual dilemmas. But perhaps it is rash to assume that all of these apparent intellectual dilemmas are real, without at least airing the possibility that further research might unmask one or more of them as only apparent.

To air this possibility is, of course, all I can hope to do here. Each one of these six issues deserves, and has received, not just a book but a whole library of books to itself. However, I have promised to give the reader some idea of my own responses to these problems; so at the risk of being utterly superficial, not to say highly controversial, let me now offer a lightning review of our six dilemmas. I will show that there is reason to think that at least two of them are indeed no more than apparent dilemmas. Hence, of course, my second question ('In an intellectual dilemma, is it up to us which side we believe?') only arises for the remaining dilemmas. We can postpone that question until **7.8**, where we will turn to the dilemmas that really are intractable.

The two soluble, and hence only apparent, dilemmas are those concerning altruism, as discussed in chapter 3, and ethical objectivity, as discussed in chapter 4. To show why both are only apparent dilemmas, I shall begin with the problem of ethical objectivity. Against this I shall deploy what I call the 'Truth Argument'.

7.7 **The Truth Argument**

In simple terms, the Truth Argument says this: naturalism denies the existence of norms while itself purporting to be true. But to be true is a matter of satisfying the norm of truth – one of the most important (and mysterious) norms of all. Hence naturalism is self-refuting.

I believe that the Truth Argument is sound. But it is not a simple or easy task to identify the best fully developed version of the argument. To fulfil that task properly would be a book-length project. All I want to do here is sketch how it might be supported, and point out why it matters in the present context.

First, why does the Truth Argument matter? The answer is, of course, that if the Truth Argument is sound, then it blows out of the water any and every version of the 'argument from queerness' for moral subjectivism (**4.3**). I spent much of chapter 4 worrying about post-Cartesian science's commitment to value-neutrality, and the way this tends either to exclude all value from the world, or else to categorize it, in Mackie's word, as 'queer' – metaphysically odd or suspect. If the Truth Argument is correct, the whole of this popular picture of the nature and purpose of science is simply a huge mistake. Science is in no position to stigmatize the existence of moral properties (or moral reasons) as somehow metaphysically dubious, just because they are normative entities. For science itself is already committed to the existence of normative entities, just as soon as it aims at the norm of *truth*.[51] It isn't that there is a 'fact–value gap', with hard-nosed, non-evaluative science hunting for good solid incontestable facts on one side of it, and airy-fairy ethics, aesthetics and normative epistemology on the other side of it, hunting for dubious entities called 'values'. If we correctly understand the norm of truth, we'll see that even talk about facts is, in an important sense, already normatively loaded.

If the Truth Argument is right, the post-Cartesian commitments to the sole reality and the value-neutrality of science are simply inconsistent. So there is no dilemmatic clash between the alleged value-neutrality of science and the intuition that there exist objective moral properties. The value-neutrality side of this clash is unsustainable, because the existence of science itself shows the possibility of a norm of truth, and that possibility in turn shows something more general: the possibility of the existence of *other* norms, such as moral norms. Thus chapter 4's alleged intellectual dilemma about ethical objectivity dissolves.

Notice, by the way, that this dilemma dissolves whether or not chapter 2's alleged dilemma about external-world scepticism dissolves as well. The existence of the norm of truth does not depend on the existence of the external world. The norm of truth applies even to brains in vats and selves caught in Cartesian predicaments, as also do some other interesting norms, such as the norms of rationality and meaning, which I won't say much about here.

As chapter 4's alleged intellectual dilemma about ethical objectivity dissolves, so likewise does chapter 3's alleged intellectual dilemma about altruism. If truth is the norm (or one of the norms) that science aims at, then we can see how it is possible to take this norm as your objective. But this norm of truth has nothing inherently to do with the egoist's self-interest. So the possibility of aiming at this norm shows something more general: the possibility of aiming at *some* norms that have nothing to do with one's own self-interest. And once that possibility becomes real, the arguments for egoism collapse. For they all depended on finding something impossible in seeking *any* end outside yourself. But truth is an end outside ourselves, and (apparently) we all aim at it. Hence there is no general reason for thinking that it's impossible for me to be motivated by any end beyond myself.

7.8 Three more intellectual dilemmas

If the suggestions I offer in **7.7** are along the right lines, they show that, for two of our six intellectual dilemmas, the second question that I raised at the beginning of **7.6** does not even arise. In the case of the supposed dilemmas about objectivity and altruism, we do not get as far as asking what to do about the intellectual dilemma that we find ourselves in. This is for the simple reason that we don't find ourselves in an intellectual dilemma in these cases, because one of the two conflicting bodies of evidence does not, in fact, constitute plausible evidence after all.

What – to continue our swift review – about the other four intellectual dilemmas? Are these genuine, or only apparent?

In the case of scepticism about the self or the person (chapter 5), I suspect the truth is twofold. First, there is no genuine intellectual dilemma about the existence of anything like the unchanging, enduring soul-substance that Descartes and Plato believed in. About this, the sceptics are just right: nothing of the sort exists, and there is no reason to think it does.

Second, if there is an intellectual dilemma about the relation between the point of view – the subjective self – and the human animal, then it is the very same intellectual dilemma as the one about the existence or otherwise of the external world. The problem how I – my point of view – relate to my body just is the problem how my point of view relates to the world. So I'll discuss this problem under the heading of external-world scepticism, below.

As for the first of the two dilemmas described in chapter 6: there surely would be a genuine intellectual dilemma about the relation between the first-person perspective and the scientific perspective, if it was part of the ambition of science to reconstruct the entire world *without* the first-person perspective. For this activity of reconstruction would necessarily be one that some particular agent engaged in, and so one that some particular point of view engaged in. For such a point of view to aim at undermining itself does indeed look incoherent – as incoherent as the ambitions of naturalism were shown to be by the Truth

Argument, in the case of ethical objectivity. However, as I pointed out in **6.3.4**, it isn't clear that even the eliminativist is seriously proposing that the first-person perspective should be *abolished* rather than upgraded to accord with science. If not, what we are left with is less a strict dilemma than a tension between the ambitions of science and the personal perspective. For this aspiration to make the first-person perspective 'accord with science' is a very long way from being achieved.

Similarly with chapter 6's other intellectual dilemma, about free will and agency. Here too it seems to be the ambition of science to describe the entire world without including agency, or free agency, as one of the phenomena found in the world. Since this activity of agent-free description is necessarily one that some particular agent engages in, it may be possible to show that this ambition too is incoherent. However, that also is only a suggestion that will need to be cashed out properly, if we are to avoid concluding that the problem of free will and agency presents us with a genuine intellectual dilemma (or perhaps with more than one dilemma).

This very quick and superficial survey leaves only one intellectual dilemma undiscussed: chapters 1 and 2's dilemma about external-world scepticism. What I want to say about this, my first and last dilemma, I can say only briefly here. But it deserves to be said in a separate section: the next, and the last of this book.

7.9 External-world scepticism and the unity of epistemic and ethical virtue

My response to the other dilemmas has been to suggest, very quickly, some reasons for thinking that there may be ways of solving (or resolving or dissolving) them. My response to the problem about external-world scepticism is rather less optimistic. Whether or not I was right to suggest that there might, in the end, be ways out of our other dilemmas, I see good reasons for doubting that the problem of external-world scepticism could ever be solved. If anything is a genuine intellectual dilemma, this is.

The dilemma is that we usually feel, in practice, perfectly sure of the reality of the external world; and yet this sense of decisive certainty is completely unsupported by decisive rational evidence for the existence of the external world. We have a body of broadly sensory evidence that it is certain that there is an external world, and a body of broadly rational evidence that it is anything but certain. Both of these bodies of evidence are highly plausible; but it isn't in the least clear which of them is to be believed; and the two bodies of evidence seem to be of such different sorts that it is very unclear how, if at all, they may be compared. Nor is there much sign, as there might be (say) with the problem of consciousness in the philosophy of mind, that there are any new 'killer arguments' out there, which could resolve the issue one way or the other, and show that this intellectual dilemma is only apparent. The problem about external-world scepticism looks like a genuine intellectual dilemma if anything does. It is, perhaps, the paradigm case of an intellectual dilemma.

Here if anywhere, then, we come back to the second question that I raised at the beginning of **7.6**: the question whether we really have equally good reason, when faced with an intellectual dilemma, to believe either or neither side of that dilemma – just as, by my parallel argument in ethics, we have equally good reason to choose to do whatever we like when we are confronted by a variety of different goods, provided we violate none of those goods.

My answer to this question is 'Yes and No'. 'Yes', because we have equally good *epistemic* reason to believe either or neither side of any intellectual dilemma. But also 'No', because we don't have equally good *moral* reason to believe either or neither side: not, at least, in the case of the problem of the external world. I want to close by suggesting that our reason for believing in the external world is, ultimately, an ethical one. My argument for this claim should help to explain why I have called this final section 'the unity of epistemic and ethical virtue'.

I say that we have no decisive *epistemic* reason to believe that radical scepticism is false, and that there really is an external world; but we do have a decisive *ethical* reason to believe in the external world. By 'ethical reason' I don't mean a reason drawn from welfare – for example, the 'pragmatist' argument that runs 'We should believe what makes things go well for us; things will go better for us if we believe in the external world; therefore we should believe in the external world.' Nor do I mean a reason drawn from evolutionary thinking, for example the reason that belief in the external world will increase our fitness for survival. For whether believing in the external world does make things go better for us, or increase our evolutionary fitness, depends on the way the world is. There are imaginable circumstances in which our well-being, or our evolutionary fitness, would not be increased by believing in the external world. (There are also imaginable circumstances in which our well-being, or our evolutionary fitness, would be increased by not believing in the external world.) And we cannot be sure that we ourselves are not in such circumstances, without already being sure that scepticism is false.

Rather, what I have in mind when I say that we have a decisive ethical reason to believe in the external world is a line of thought suggested by Iris Murdoch in her book *The Sovereignty of Good*. Murdoch's central claim here is that 'Attention, a just and loving gaze directed upon an individual reality, is the characteristic and proper mark of the active moral agent' – and, as she constantly stresses, of the active artist too.[52] The moral life, exactly like the artist's life, is a constant struggle to escape from 'the fat relentless ego',[53] and to realize the *otherness* of people (and realities more generally) other than myself:

Realism, whether of artist or of agent, [is] a moral achievement...The more the separateness and differentness of other people is realised, and the fact seen that another man has needs and wishes as demanding as one's own, the harder it becomes to treat a person as a thing...[54]

The only way for us to make this escape is by making the constantly necessary effort to turn our attention away from ourselves, and outwards towards the world. Both in the artist's activity and in the moral life, this redirecting and refocusing of our attention, which at best is 'unsentimental, detached, unselfish and objective', is no more and no less than love:

> If, still led by the clue of art, we ask further questions about the faculty which is supposed to relate us to what is real and thus bring us to what is good, the idea of compassion or love will be naturally suggested. It is not simply that suppression of self is required before accurate vision is obtained. The great artist sees his objects (and this is true whether they are sad, absurd, repulsive or even evil) in a light of justice and mercy. The direction of attention is, contrary to nature, outward, away from self which reduces all to a false unity, towards the great surprising variety of the world, and the ability so to direct attention is love.[64]

According to Murdoch, our alternatives in the moral life lie in the range between two stark opposites. We can remain self-absorbed, caught up in our own self-absorbed and shabby fantasies – the way of selfishness and illusion. Or we can turn outwards towards the world beyond ourselves – the way of love.

> Morality, goodness, is a form of realism. The idea of a really good man living in a private dream world seems

unacceptable…The chief enemy of excellence in morality (and also in art) is personal fantasy: the tissue of self-aggrandising and consoling wishes and dreams which prevents one from seeing what is there outside one…

'Good', 'real', 'love': these words are closely connected.[55]

Now to attend to other people and other things in this way is, necessarily, to treat them *as real*. There can be no just and loving attention – not even to a fictional character whom I am in the process of creating as I write about him – which does not take the reality of its object as a given. The objects of my just and loving attention are external to my wishes and fantasies. They have a life or lives of their own, which I can only discover, not invent. I discover this life by deploying my attention to understanding the nature of whatever it is that I am engaging with – whether that is the nature of another real person or the nature of a fictional person. (It is of course part of the work of truthful attention to see the difference between real persons and fictional ones.)

It is an essential part of the central activity of the moral life to see the *targets* of the moral life – other people and other things – as having a reality of their own: in other words, as being inhabitants of the external world. Thus anyone who tries seriously to engage in the moral life is already committed to thinking of the world to which he is trying to direct his just and loving attention as a *real* world, not just as some sort of illusion. And that is why we have a moral reason to resolve the intellectual dilemma between external-world scepticism and realism in favour of realism: not because realism has welfare pay-offs for us, but because realism is already presupposed in all our moral activity anyway. In a sense, then, Hume was exactly wrong about the key to freedom from scepticism about the external world; the key is not 'carelessness and inattention', but, precisely, *attention*.

'But the attention Murdoch speaks of is not only loving but also *truthful* attention. What, then, if the sceptic has the truth: that there is nothing out there beyond the self to attend to or to love; or that if there is, it is only a series of illusions?'

We cannot, of course, *disprove* the possibility of scepticism. If we could, we would not have been in an intellectual dilemma in the first place. But from the fact that we are in an intellectual dilemma, it also follows, familiarly enough, that we can't prove scepticism either. Not, at any rate, at present. If it ever did turn out that there was decisive evidence in favour of (say) the Cartesian Demon hypothesis, then the 'loving' and 'truthful' elements in 'loving truthful attention' would indeed collide and implode in the catastrophic way that this question suggests; and the moral life would then be left with little or nothing to be about. In one way this is not much of a threat, since decisive evidence for the Cartesian Demon hypothesis seems about as likely as decisive evidence against it. In another way it helps to highlight an important fact about our engagement with the world – the fact that it is always a *risky* venture.

'But isn't it a bit precious, or high-faluting, to treat loving truthful attention as the solution to epistemological scepticism? Do we really want to end up talking about discovering the reality of bus tickets or parked cars by directing our loving truthful attention onto them, or taking the risk of supposing that they're real?'

This question presupposes a false division of our engagement with the world into discrete sections, about each of which the same question – 'Does *this* involve loving truthful attention?' – can sensibly be asked. Compare a common tactic which is supposed (wrongly) to show that there can be actions that are voluntary, but not deliberate: you divide up a continuum or stream of activity into discrete parts, say drummings of fingers or scratchings of ears, and ask whether each of these involves a separate act of deliberation or intention. In both cases, the right answer is that our engagement with the world is not so divisible. It is more like a continuous stream of activity than a series of punctual deeds. And concerning the overall stream of activity that constitutes our engagement with the world, I see no reason to think that it might be strained or odd to regard that, overall, as a mode of loving truthful attention, even if small detailed parts of our engagement are less easily seen in that way.

The question also reflects a deep and important prejudice, one which I myself shared when I began writing this book. The prejudice is that the answer to the problem of epistemological scepticism *has* to be scientific, mechanized, value-neutral, hygienically rational, if it is to work or be fit for exhibition at all. This prejudice is at home in an intellectual climate where (as we've seen) the value-neutrality of science is set up as an ideal. For all that, it is a mistake.

It isn't really so hard to see reasons to think that the problem of external-world scepticism was always, in a way, a moral problem, and that the solution to it had better therefore be moral too. As Murdoch puts it above, 'the idea of a really good man living in a private dream world seems unacceptable'. Plenty of real-life stories spell this out. As a matter of common experience, the distinguishing mark of bad people turns out, again and again, to be their incapacity to realize or appreciate the reality of other people. In T. S. Eliot's words:

> Hell is oneself,
> Hell is alone, the other figures in it
> Merely projections. There is nothing to escape from
> And nothing to escape to. One is always alone.[56]

Descartes's problem of external-world scepticism creates a genuine intellectual dilemma. It poses an epistemic question to which we have no satisfactory epistemic answer. But there is a *moral* answer: to realize the world by attending to it. In the end, this is not a matter of certainty or deduction, but of trust.

This, then, is my moral answer to external-world scepticism. If it sounds like an assertion of the pre-eminence of faith over knowledge, so be it. Contemporary philosophical fashion is not, of course, entirely in favour of that sort of assertion. But I am not the only person to point, recently, to the fundamental place of trust and risk in our intellectual lives. In the words of Crispin Wright:

> at the foundation of all our cognitive procedures lie things we merely implicitly trust and take for granted…[my strategy of response to scepticism] concedes the basic point of the sceptical arguments to which it reacts, namely that we do indeed have no claim to know, in any sense involving possession of evidence for their likely truth, that certain cornerstones of what we take to be procedures yielding knowledge and justified belief hold good…there is no disguising the fact that the exercise comes as one of damage limitation. That will disappoint those who hanker after a demonstration that there was all along, actually, no damage to limit – that the sceptical arguments involve mistakes. Good luck to all philosophers who quest for such a demonstration.[57]

Most contemporary philosophers are less willing than Wright or myself to take trust, or risk, or an attentive attitude, or something similar, as basic to epistemology. The commonest response to scepticism today, I suspect, is still to treat it either as a solved problem, or simply as an old-fashioned one – but either way as not one worth worrying about. It is no accident that this return to philosophical dogmatism (**2.3.6**) has been accompanied, historically, by a decline in Christian (especially Protestant) belief. The parallel between Descartes and Luther (**1.3**) goes deep. Perhaps Descartes would have done better to try a more thoroughly Lutheran route than he actually took, laying a greater emphasis on the need to find reasons for a sort of intellectual faith where knowledge runs out, and for taking risks where we cannot ever be sure.

Of course, my 'moral answer' is not only an assertion of the pre-eminence of faith over knowledge. It is also – like the title of this section – an assertion of the pre-eminence of ethics over the rest of philosophy. The unity of the epistemic and the ethical virtues is strikingly revealed by the fact that we have to appeal to an *ethical* reason to settle the thoroughly epistemological question whether there is an external world; in a different way, it is also revealed by the Truth Argument (**7.7**). Value always lies at the very foundations of our knowledge, our science and our certainty. In the end, indeed, it is only by appealing to value that we can hope to escape from the otherwise inescapable self.

1 Strawson 1959: 106.

2 See **2.3.2**, **2.3.6**, **2.6.1**, **5.5**, **6.3.1**. Wittgenstein is also a central figure in 20th-century debates about meaning and metaphysics, but I have no space to cover these topics here.

3 Wittgenstein, *Philosophical Investigations* I, 133.

4 Marx, *Eighth Thesis on Feuerbach*.

5 Wittgenstein, *Philosophical Investigations* I, 98.

6 *PI* I, 116; I, 124.

7 *PI* I, 94.

8 *PI* I, 128.

9 T. S. Eliot, *Four Quartets*, 'Little Gidding' V.

10 Wittgenstein, *Philosophical Investigations* I, 435; I, 126.

11 Wittgenstein, *Remarks on the Foundations of Mathematics*, Part I, App. III, paras. 12 –13.

12 Wittgenstein, *Philosophical Investigations* I, 38.

13 *PI* I, 90.

14 *PI* I, 127.

15 G. E. Moore 1939 (see also **2.5**).

16 Wittgenstein, *Philosophical Investigations* I, 117.

17 *PI* I, 133; I, 255; I, 309.

18 Hume 1974: 12.

19 Cavell 1999: 139–40.

20 Cavell 1999: 140–1.

21 Cavell 1999: 141.

22 Descartes, Meditation 1, CSM II: 12.

23 Cavell 1999: 143.

24 McDowell 1994: xxiv.

25 There are other arresting parallels between Nietzsche and the later Wittgenstein. One is the simple matter of prose style: Nietzsche and Wittgenstein are two of the greatest masters of the German aphorism. A second is the crucial philosophical importance that both attach to prose style: compare the section headed 'Why I write such good books' in Nietzsche's *Ecce Homo*, and the Preface to Wittgenstein's *Philosophical Investigations*.

26 See e.g. Hollingdale 2001 or Safranski 2003.

27 Monk 1990: 331.

28 Monk 1990: 333.

29 Monk 1990: 334.

30 Monk 1990: 359.

31 Monk 1990: 360.

32 Monk 1990: 361–2.

33 Monk 1990: 426–7.

34 Monk 1990: 232–3.

35 Monk 1990: 212.

36 Russell 1959: 216–17.

37 Hume 1969: 267.

38 Hume 1969: 316.

39 Hume 1969: 238.

40 Hume, *Treatise of Human Nature* 2.3.3; Hume 1969: 460.

41 e.g. Percival 2002; for a survey of recent work, see Greco 2001.

42 Aristotle, *Nicomachean Ethics* 1103a14. Strictly, Aristotle does not speak of a parallel between 'ethical and epistemic virtues' but between 'excellence of character'

(*aretê êthikê*) and 'excellence of understanding' (*aretê dianoêtikê*). This need not stop us from appropriating Aristotle's parallel.

43 Hursthouse 2002: 94.

44 Greco 2001.

45 Montmarquet 1987.

46 Chappell 1998, chs. 3, 5–6; Chappell 2001 (a), (c), (d); Chappell 2003.

47 Chappell 1998, ch. 3.

48 'Here and throughout the discussion that follows' (some readers will object) 'you make it sound as if belief were voluntary.' But, I respond, a lot of belief *is* voluntary – though not in the way that action is. See Chappell 1997; also Zagzebski 1996: 58–72.

49 Chappell 2003.

50 In fact, I believe that there are technical reasons why neither maximizing strategy works: for these, see Chappell 2001 (b). Still, we can get *nearer* a maximizing strategy in epistemology than in ethics.

51 Some philosophers of science – e.g. Larry Laudan and Bas van Fraassen – deny that science aims at truth, rather than at some less ambitious objective such as 'empirical adequacy'. No matter. This will just mean that, instead of 'p is true' implying 'p is intrinsically to be believed', 'p is empirically adequate' will imply 'p is intrinsically to be accepted'.

52 Murdoch 1970: 34.

53 Murdoch 1970: 52.

54 Murdoch 1970: 66.

55 Murdoch 1970: 59; 1970: 42.

56 Eliot 1950, Act 1, Scene 3.

57 Wright 2004: 206-7.

Bibliography

Anscombe, Elizabeth. *Intention.* Oxford: Blackwell, 1957.

Anscombe, Elizabeth. 'The first person', in S. Guttenplan (ed), *Mind and Language: Wolfson College Lectures 1974*. Reprinted in D. Rosenthal (ed), *The Nature of Mind* (Oxford UP, 1991).

Anscombe, Elizabeth. 'Causality and determination', in Sosa (ed), *Causation and Conditionals.* Oxford UP, 1975.

Aquinas. *Summa Theologiae.* Many editions; translation available online at www.newadvent.org/summa.

Aristotle. *Nicomachean Ethics, Metaphysics, Topics, de Anima, de Caelo, de Mundo, Posterior Analytics.* Many editions; the Greek–English parallel texts provided in the Loeb Classical Library (Harvard UP) are very useful.

Armstrong, David. *A Materialist Theory of the Mind.* Humanities Press, New York, 1968.

Asimov, Isaac. *The World of Carbon.* London: Macmillan, 1962.

(John) Aubrey's 'Life of Hobbes'. Excerpted in Hobbes 1994.

Augustine. *de Libero Arbitrio* [395–6 AD]. Many editions, e.g. *St Augustine: on free choice of the will,* trans. L. H. Hackstaff and Anna Benjamin. New York: Prentice Hall, 1994.

Ayer, Alfred Jules. *Language, Truth and Logic.* London: Gollancz, 1936.

Ayer, Alfred Jules. *The Problem of Knowledge.* London: Macmillan, 1956.

Bacon, Francis. *Aphorisms.* In Bacon's *Novum Organum,* available online at www.luminarium.org/sevenlit/bacon/baconbib.htm.

Baker, Lynn Rudder. *Persons and Bodies: a constitution view.* Cambridge UP, 2000.

Belloc, Hilaire. *The French Revolution.* London: Hutchinson University Library, 1911.

Bentham, Jeremy. *Introduction to the Principles of Morals and Legislation,* J. H. Burns and H. L. A. Hart (eds). London: Athlone Press, 1970.

Bentham, Jeremy. *Memoirs,* in vol.10 of John Bowring (ed), *Bentham's Works* [1843]. Reprinted London: Thoemmes Press, 1994.

Berkeley, George. *Berkeley: Three Dialogues between Hylas and Philonous*, C. H. Turbayne (ed). New York: Library of Liberal Arts, 1954.

Berkeley, George. *Of the Principles of Human Knowledge*. Many editions. Available online at www.marxists.org/reference/subject/philosophy/works/en/berkeley.htm.

Blackburn, Simon. *Spreading the Word*. Oxford UP, 1984.

Blackburn, Simon. *Essays in Quasi-Realism*. Oxford UP, 1993.

Boghossian, Paul. 'The Rule-Following Considerations', *Mind* 1989, pp.507–49.

Boonin-Vail, David. *Thomas Hobbes and the Science of Moral Virtue*. Cambridge UP, 1994.

Butler, Joseph. *The Analogy of Religion* [1736]. Oxford UP: The World's Classics, 1907.

Butler, Joseph. *Fifteen Sermons preached at the Rolls Chapel*. London: Bell, 1953.

Camus, Albert. *L'Étranger* [1942], trans. Joseph Laredo. London: Penguin Classics, 2000.

Candlish, Stewart. 'Private Language', entry in the online *Stanford Encyclopaedia of Philosophy* (1998), at http://plato.stanford.edu/entries/private-language.

Carlyle, Thomas. *The French Revolution*. London: Dent, 1906.

Cavell, Stanley. *The Claim of Reason*. Oxford UP, 1999.

Chalmers, David. *The Conscious Mind: in search of a fundamental theory*. Oxford UP, 1996.

Chappell, Timothy. *The Plato Reader*. Edinburgh UP, 1996.

Chappell, Timothy. 'Rationally deciding what to believe', *Religious Studies* 1997.

Chappell, Timothy. *Understanding Human Goods*. Edinburgh UP, 1998 (a).

Chappell, Timothy. 'The incompleat projectivist', *Philosophical Quarterly* 1998.

Chappell, Timothy. 'Two distinctions that do make a difference', *Philosophy* 2001 (a).

Chappell, Timothy. 'Option Ranges', *Journal of Applied Philosophy* 2001 (b).

Chappell, Timothy. 'The implications of incommensurability', *Philosophy* 2001 (c).

Chappell, Timothy. 'A way out of Pettit's dilemma', *Philosophical Quarterly* 2001 (d).

Chappell, Timothy. 'Practical rationality for pluralists about the good', *Ethical Theory and Moral Practice* 2003.

Chisholm, Roderick. *Perceiving*. Oxford UP, 1957.

Chisholm, Roderick. *Theory of Knowledge*, 3rd edn. Englewood Cliffs, NJ: Prentice Hall, 1989.

Churchland, Paul. *Scientific Realism and the Plasticity of Mind*. Cambridge UP, 1979.

Churchland, Paul. 'Eliminative Materialism and the Propositional Attitudes', *Journal of Philosophy* 1981. Reprinted in D. Rosenthal (ed), *The Nature of Mind* (Oxford UP, 1991).

Craig, Edward. 'Nozick and the sceptic: the thumbnail version', *Analysis* 1989.

Craig, Edward. *Knowledge and the State of Nature*. Oxford UP, 1990.

Cottingham, John. *Philosophy and the Good Life*. Cambridge UP, 1998.

Dancy, Jonathan. *Contemporary Epistemology*. Oxford: Blackwell, 1985.

Darwin, Charles. *The Descent of Man*. London: John Murray, 1871.

Davidson, Donald. *Essays on Actions and Events*. Oxford UP, 1980.

Davidson, Donald. *Inquiries into Truth and Interpretation*. Oxford UP, 1984.

Dawkins, Richard. 'In defence of selfish genes', *Philosophy* 1981.

Dawkins, Richard. *The Selfish Gene*, 2nd edn. Oxford UP, 1989.

Dennett, Daniel. *Consciousness Explained*. London: Penguin, 1991.

Derrida, Jacques. *Limited Inc.* Baltimore: Johns Hopkins UP, 1977.

Descartes, René. *The Philosophical Writings of Descartes*, trans. John Cottingham, Robert Stoothoff and Dugald Murdoch. Three vols. Cambridge UP, 1984.

Dretske, Fred. 'Epistemic Operators', *Journal of Philosophy* 1970.

Dummett, Michael. 'Truth', *Proceedings of the Aristotelian Society* 1958–9.

Eliot, Thomas Stearns. *Four Quartets*. London: Faber and Faber, 1944.

Eliot, Thomas Stearns. *The Cocktail Party*. London: Faber and Faber, 1950.

Ewin, R. E. *Virtues and Rights*. Boulder, CO: Westview, 1991.

Fodor, Jerry. Article in the *Times Literary Supplement*, 3 July 1992.

Fogelin, Robert. *Walking the Tightrope of Reason: the precarious life of a rational animal*. Oxford UP, 2003.

Fraassen, Bas van. *The Scientific Image*. Oxford UP, 1982.

Frege, Gottlöb. *Begriffsschrift* [1879] and 'On sense and reference' [1892]. In Michael Beaney (ed), *The Frege Reader* (Oxford: Blackwell, 1997).

Freud, Sigmund. *The Ego and the Id* [1923]. London: Hogarth Press, 1947.

Freud, Sigmund. *Beyond the Pleasure Principle* [1920]. London: Hogarth Press, 1955.

Gassendi, Pierre. *The Selected Works of Pierre Gassendi*, ed. and trans. Craig Brush. New York, 1972.

Gaukroger, Stephen. *Descartes: an intellectual biography*. Oxford UP, 1995.

Geach, Peter. *Mental Acts*. London: Routledge, 1957.

Geach, Peter. 'Ascriptivism', *Philosophical Review* 1960.

Geach, Peter. *Reference and Generality*. Cornell UP, 1962.

Gertler, Brie (ed). *Privileged Access*. Burlington, VT: Ashgate, 2003.

Gibbard, Alan. *Wise Choices, Apt Feelings*. Oxford UP, 1990.

Giddens, Anthony. *Modernity and Self-Identity*. London: Polity, 1991.

Glover, Jonathan. *I: The Philosophy and Psychology of Personal Identity*. Harmondsworth: Penguin, 1988.

Goldman, Alvin. 'Discrimination and perceptual knowledge', *Journal of Philosophy* 1976.

Goldman, Alvin. 'In Defense of the Simulation Theory', *Mind and Language* 1992.

Grayling, A. C. 'Scepticism and justification', online at www.acgrayling.com/scepticism/ Scepticismjust.html. No date.

Greco, John. 'Virtue Epistemology', entry in the online *Stanford Encyclopaedia of Philosophy* at http://plato.stanford.edu/entries/ epistemology-virtue.

Greco, J. and Sosa, E. (eds). *The Blackwell Guide to Epistemology*. Oxford: Blackwell, 1999.

Griffin, N. and Routley, R. 'Towards a logic of relative identity', *Logique et Analyse* 1979.

Habermas, Jürgen. *The Theory of Communicative Action*. Beacon Press, 1981.

Hale, Bob. 'Can There Be a Logic of Attitudes?', in J. Haldane and C. Wright (eds), *Reality, Representation, and Projection*. New York: Oxford UP, 1993.

Harrer, Heinrich. *Seven Years in Tibet*. London: Rupert Hart-Davis, 1953.

Heal, Jane. 'Truth', *Proceedings of the Aristotelian Society* 1987–8.

Heidegger, Martin. *Being and Time* [1926], trans. John Macquarrie and Edward Robinson. Oxford: Blackwell, 1962.

Herodotus, *Histories*, trans. Aubrey de Selincourt. London: Penguin Classics, 1996.

Hintikka, J. *Knowledge and Belief.* Ithaca, NY: Cornell UP, 1962.

Hobbes, Thomas. *The Elements of Law* and *Human Nature.* In Molesworth (ed), *The English Works.* London: Bohn 1840.

Hobbes, Thomas. *Leviathan,* Edwin Curley (ed). Indianapolis: Hackett, 1994.

Hollingdale, R. J. *Nietzsche: the man and his philosophy.* Cambridge UP, 2001.

Hollis, Martin. *Models of Man.* Cambridge UP, 1977.

Hookway, Christopher. *Scepticism.* London: Routledge, 1990.

Hopkins, Gerard Manley. *Sermons and Devotional Writings,* C. J. Devlin (ed). Oxford UP, 1959.

Hume, David. *Treatise of Human Nature* [1739–40], E. C. Mossner (ed). London: Penguin Classics, 1969.

Hume, David. *Enquiries concerning Human Understanding and concerning the Principles of Morals,* P. H. Nidditch (ed). Oxford UP, 1974.

Hursthouse, Rosalind. 'Virtue Theory and Abortion', reprinted in Hugh LaFollette (ed), *Ethics in Practice,* 2nd edn (Oxford: Blackwell, 2002).

Jackson, Frank. 'Epiphenomenal qualia', *Philosophical Quarterly* 1982.

Jackson, Frank. 'What Mary didn't know', *Journal of Philosophy* 1986. Reprinted in F. Jackson (ed), *Consciousness* (Dartmouth: Ashgate, 1998).

Jackson, Frank. 'Mind and Illusion', in A. O'Hear (ed), *Minds and Persons* (Cambridge UP, 2003).

James, William. *Principles of Psychology.* Cambridge, MA: Harvard UP, 1890.

Kant, Immanuel. *Critique of Pure Reason,* trans. Norman Kemp Smith. London: Macmillan, 1929.

Kant, Immanuel. *Groundwork of the Metaphysics of Morals,* M. Gregor (ed). Cambridge UP, 1998.

Kavka, Gregory. *Hobbesian Moral and Political Theory.* Princeton UP, 1986.

Kerr, Fergus. *Theology after Wittgenstein.* Oxford: Blackwell, 1986.

Kim, Jaegwon. 'What is "naturalised epistemology"?', in J. Tomberlin (ed), *Philosophical Perspectives 2: Epistemology.* Atascadero, CA: Ridgeview Publishers, 1988.

Kirk, G. S., Raven, J. E. and Schofield, M. *The Presocratic Philosophers.* Cambridge UP, 1983.

Kitcher, P. S. 'In Defense of Intentional Psychology', *Journal of Philosophy* 1984.

Kripke, Saul. *Wittgenstein on Rules and Private Language*. Oxford: Blackwell, 1982.

Lewis, David. 'What experience teaches', in W. Lycan, *Mind and Cognition: a Reader* (Oxford UP, 1990).

Locke, John. *Essay concerning Human Understanding* (1690), P. H. Nidditch (ed). Oxford UP, 1975.

Lodge, David. *Nice Work*. London: Secker and Warburg, 1988.

Loeb, Louis. 'The Cartesian Circle', in J. Cottingham (ed), *The Cambridge Companion to Descartes*. Cambridge UP, 1992.

McCulloch, Gregory. *The Life of the Mind*. London: Routledge, 2003.

McDowell, John. 'Values and Secondary Properties', in T. Honderich (ed), *Value and Objectivity: Essays in Honour of J. L. Mackie* (London: Routledge, 1985).

McDowell, John. *Mind and World*. Cambridge, MA: Harvard UP, 1994.

McDowell, John. *Meaning, Knowledge, and Reality*. Cambridge, MA: Harvard UP 2001.

McGinn, Colin. *The Mysterious Flame: conscious minds in a material world*. New York: Basic Books 1999.

Mackie, J. L. *Ethics: inventing right and wrong*. London: Penguin, 1977.

Mackie, J. L. 'The Law of the Jungle', *Philosophy* 1978.

Malebranche, Nicolas. *The Search after Truth*, trans. Thomas Lennon and Paul Olscamp. Columbus, OH: Ohio State UP, 1980.

Marx, Karl. *Eight Theses on Feuerbach*, in K. Marx, *The German Ideology* (New York International Publishers 1947).

Marx, Karl and Engels, Friedrich. *The Communist Manifesto* [1848]. London: Penguin, 1967.

Marx's and Engels' Works, vol. 4. Berlin: Dietz, 1959–68.

Midgley, Mary. 'Gene-juggling', *Philosophy* 1979.

Mill, John Stuart. *Utilitarianism*, in M. Warnock (ed), *Utilitarianism* (London: Fontana, 1969).

Miller, Alex. *An Introduction To Contemporary Metaethics*. Cambridge: Polity Press, 2003.

Millikan, Ruth. *White Queen Psychology and other essays*. Boston: MIT Press, 1993.

Monk, Ray. *Wittgenstein: the duty of genius*. London: Penguin, 1990.

Montaigne, Michel de. *Complete Essays*, trans. Donald Frame. Stanford UP, 1957.

Montmarquet, James. 'Epistemic Virtue', *Mind* 1987.

Moore, G. E. 'A Proof of the External World', *Proceedings of the British Academy* 1939.

Moore, G. E. *Principia Ethica* [1903], T. Baldwin (ed). Cambridge UP, 1993.

Murdoch, Iris. *The Sovereignty of Good*. London: Routledge, 1970.

Nagel, Thomas. 'What is it like to be a bat?', *Philosophical Review* 1974. Reprinted in Nagel, *Mortal Questions* (Cambridge UP, 1979).

Nemirow, Laurence. Review of Nagel's *Mortal Questions*, *Philosophical Review* 1980.

Newton, Sir Isaac. *Principia Mathematica* [1687]. Online at http://members.tripod.com/~gravitee/.

Nietzsche, Friedrich. *Twilight of the Idols* and *The Antichrist*, trans. R. J. Hollingdale. London: Penguin, 1968.

Nietzsche, Friedrich. *Genealogy of Morals*. Selections in Hollingdale, *A Nietzsche Reader*. London: Penguin, 1977.

Nozick, Robert. *Anarchy, State and Utopia*. Oxford: Blackwell, 1974.

Oderberg, David. *Applied Ethics*. Oxford: Blackwell, 2000.

Olson, Eric. *The Human Animal: personal identity without psychology*. Oxford UP, 1999.

Olson, Eric. 'Comments on McMahan', from a 2002 symposium on Jeff McMahan, *The Ethics of Killing* (Oxford UP, 2002).

Papineau, David. 'Normativity and Judgement', *Aristotelian Society Supplementary Volume* 1999.

Parfit, Derek. *Reasons and Persons*. Oxford UP, 1984.

Percival, Philip. 'Epistemic Consequentialism', *Aristotelian Society Supplementary Volume* 2002.

Perry, John. *The Problem of the Essential Indexical*. Oxford UP, 1993.

Plato. *Apology, Crito, Republic, Theaetetus, Meno*. Many editions; the Greek–English parallel texts provided in the Loeb Classical Library (Harvard UP) are very useful.

Prior, Arthur N. 'Thank Goodness That's Over', in Prior, *Papers in Logic and Ethics* (London: Duckworth, 1976).

Ptolemy. *Almagest*, trans. Gerald Toomer. Princeton UP, 1998.

Putnam, Hilary. *Reason, Truth and History*. Cambridge UP, 1981.

Quine, W. V. 'Epistemology Naturalised', in Quine, *Ontological Relativity and Other Essays* (Columbia UP, 1969).

Rea, Michael. *World Without Design*. Oxford UP, 2002.

Reid, Thomas. *Inquiry into the Human Mind on the Principles of Common Sense* [1764] and *Essays on the Intellectual Powers of Man* [1785]. Both in Reid, *Inquiry and Essays* (Indianapolis: Hackett, 1983).

Ridley, Aaron. *The Origins of Virtue*. London: Viking, 1996.

Robinson, William. 'Epiphenomenalism', entry in the online *Stanford Encyclopaedia of Philosophy* (Spring 2003), at http://plato.stanford.edu/archives/spr2003/entries/epiphenomenalism.

Rodis-Lewis, Geneviève. 'Descartes: development of his philosophy', in J. Cottingham (ed), *The Cambridge Companion to Descartes* (Cambridge UP, 1992).

Rorty, Richard. *Philosophy and the Mirror of Nature*. Princeton UP, 1979.

Rowlands, Mark. *Externalism: putting mind and world back together again*. Chesham: Acumen, 2003.

Royce, Josiah. *Philosophy of Loyalty* [1908]. Vanderbilt UP, 1995.

Ruse, Michael. 'The Significance of Evolution', in P. Singer (ed), *Companion to Ethics* (Oxford: Blackwell, 1991).

Russell, Bertrand. *The Problems of Philosophy*. London: Allen and Unwin, 1912.

Russell, Bertrand. 'On the nature of acquaintance', in R. C. Marsh (ed), *Logic and Knowledge* (London: Allen and Unwin, 1956).

Russell, Bertrand. 'Reply to D. H. Monro', *Philosophy* 1960. Reprinted in Charles Pigden (ed), *Russell on Ethics* (London: Routledge, 1999), pp.165–6.

Russell, Bertrand. *My Philosophical Development*. London: Allen and Unwin, 1959.

Ryle, Gilbert. *The Concept of Mind*. London: Penguin, 1949.

Safranski, Rudiger. *Nietzsche: a philosophical biography*. New York: Norton, 2003.

Sartre, Jean-Paul. *Being and Nothingness*, trans. Hazel Barnes. London: Methuen, 1958.

Schama, Simon. *Citizens: a chronicle of the French Revolution*. New York: Random House, 1989.

Scheffler, Israel. *Science and Subjectivity*. Indianapolis: Bobbs-Merrill, 1967.

Scruton, Roger. *Kant*. Oxford UP, 1982.

Searle, John. 'Minds, Brains, and Programs', *Behavioral and Brain Sciences* 1980. Reprinted in D. Rosenthal (ed), *The Nature of Mind* (Oxford UP, 1991), pp.509–19.

Sidgwick, Henry. *The Methods of Ethics*. London: Macmillan, 1874.

Singer, Peter. *Practical Ethics*. Cambridge UP, 1993.

Skinner, B. F. *Beyond Freedom and Dignity*. New York: Knopf, 1971.

Skorupski, John. *John Stuart Mill*. London: Routledge, 1989.

Smith, Adam. *The Wealth of Nations* [1776]. London: Bantam, 1993.

Sorell, Tom. *Hobbes*. London: Routledge, 1986.

Spencer, Herbert. 'Progress: Its Law and Causes', *The Westminster Review*, April 1857.

Spinoza, Baruch de. *Ethics*, trans. R. Elwes. Available online at www.mtsu.edu/~rbombard/RB/ Spinoza/ethica-front.html.

Strawson, Galen. 'The self', *Journal of Consciousness Studies* 1997.

Strawson, Peter. *Individuals: an essay in descriptive metaphysics*. London: Methuen, 1959.

Strawson, Peter. 'Freedom and Resentment', in G. Watson (ed), *Free Will* (Oxford UP, 1982).

Stroud, Barry. *The Significance of Philosophical Scepticism*. Oxford UP, 1984.

Tait, Katharine. *My Father Bertrand Russell*. New York: Harcourt Brace Jovanovich, 1975.

Taylor, Charles. *Sources of the Self*. Cambridge UP, 1989.

Tolstoy, Leo. *War and Peace* [1869], trans. Rosemary Edmonds. London: Penguin 1957.

Tooley, Michael. *Abortion and Infanticide*. Oxford UP, 1996.

Tuck, Richard. 'Hobbes and Descartes', in G. A. J. Rogers and Alan Ryan (eds), *Perspectives on Thomas Hobbes* (Oxford UP, 1988).

Tuck, Richard. *Hobbes*. Oxford UP, 1989.

Turing, Alan. 'Computing Machinery and Intelligence', *Mind* 1950.

Wachowski, Larry and Andy. Screenplay (1997) of *The Matrix*, available online at www.hundland. com/scripts/TheMatrix_1997.txt.

Watson, J. B. 'Psychology as a Behaviorist Views It', *Psychological Review* 1913.

Weir, Alan. 'Objective content', *Proceedings of the Aristotelian Society* (Supplement), 2003.

Wiggins, David. *Sameness and Substance Renewed*. Cambridge UP, 2001.

Williams, Bernard. *Descartes: the project of pure enquiry*. London: Penguin, 1978.

Williams, Bernard. 'Internal and external reasons', in Williams, *Moral Luck: Philosophical Papers 1973–1980* (Cambridge UP, 1981).

Williams, Bernard. 'The point of view of the universe: Henry Sidgwick and the ambitions of ethics', in Williams, *Making Sense of Humanity and other philosophical papers 1982–1993* (Cambridge UP, 1995).

Williams, Bernard. *Truth and Truthfulness*. Princeton UP, 2002.

Williamson, Timothy. *Knowledge and its Limits*. Oxford UP, 2000.

Wittgenstein, Ludwig. *Tractatus Logico-Philosophicus*. London: Routledge, 1922.

Wittgenstein, Ludwig. *Philosophical Investigations*. Oxford: Blackwell, 1958.

Wittgenstein, Ludwig. *On Certainty*. Oxford: Blackwell, 1969.

Wittgenstein, Ludwig. *Remarks on the Foundations of Mathematics*. Boston: MIT Press, 1983.

Wright, Crispin. 'Scepticism and Dreaming: Imploding the Demon', *Mind* 1991.

Wright, Crispin. 'Truth in Ethics', in B. Hooker (ed), *Truth in Ethics* (Oxford: Blackwell 1996).

Wright, Crispin. 'On Epistemic Entitlement', *Proceedings of the Aristotelian Society* (Supplement), 2004, pp.167–212.

Zagzebski, Linda. *Virtues of the Mind*. Cambridge UP, 1996.

Zangwill, Nick. 'Norms and Mind', *Philosophical Studies* 1998.

Index